American Champions

A History of Business Success
Part I : 1711 - 1890

Arthur G. Sharp

International Information Associates
Yardley

Library of Congress Catalog No. 91- 73333

Sharp, Arthur, G.

American Champions:
A History of Business Success

Part I: 1711-1890

International Information Associates

P.O. Box 773, Morrisville, PA 19067 U.S.A.

Current Printing (last digit):

10 9 8 7 6 5 4 3 2 1

Printed in the United States of America

TABLE OF CONTENTS

ACKNOWLEDGEMENTS
AND THANKS

DEDICATION

To my Mother and Father. Without their encouragement, I would never had seen the value in knowing how to read, write, or research—and this book would not have been written (at least not by me).

SPECIAL THANKS

I thank Rich Bradley for suggesting the idea for this book, and for publishing the volume.

ACKNOWLEDGEMENTS

I could not have compiled the information in this book without a lot of help. So, I would like to offer my thanks to the following individuals and organizations for their help. I would also like to thank the anonymous people in a variety of organizations whose names may be unknown, but whose help is appreciated nonetheless.

Debbie A. Baker
.................Coors

Janis Berry
.................Greater Austin Chamber of Commerce

Janet M. Bley
.................Homestake Mining Company

R. A. Bogan, Jr
.................Louisiana Companies

Denise J. Brown
.................Greater Baton Rouge Chamber of Commerce

David J.Bugea
.................Premier Bank

Michael Davies
.................*Hartford Courant*

Paul & Paulie Drumm
.................Kenyon Corn Meal Company

David Epstein
.................Huntington's Book Store

William F. Fitzpatrick
.................Dexter Corporation

Welcome to the World of Survivors

How does a company outlive its founders? That is a question we are about to answer. We'll do it through the histories of several corporations in this country that have done so. Not only have these organizations outlasted their founders, but, in many cases, their founders' children and grandchildren as well! More important, they show no signs of going out of business in the immediate future. They are survivors—and role models for business operators of the future.

Out of fairness, the companies selected are presented according to their age. For purposes of this book, no one company stands out from the rest. Each has done well in its existence. That they have all lasted as long as they have is indicative of their success. Granted, there are differences among them. For example, their product lines are decidedly different, as are their sizes, company cultures, and philosophies, they operate in different geographical areas...in short, there is nothing to link them together. Nothing, that is, except their longevity, success—and inclusion in this book.

Of course, not every company that boasts of a century or more of business is included here. There are far too many for that. Just to get an idea of how many, look at Chapter 17, which lists only a fraction of the businesses across the United States that qualify for 100 or more candles on their birthday cakes. The list offers proof that longevity in the business world is not uncommon. Why is that?

There are numerous reasons. For example, it is a safe bet that most of the companies listed have been guided by a succession of astute executives. There is a correlation between age and acquired, applied wisdom. Executives who learn *and apply what they learn* cannot help but steer their companies toward success, and it is no secret that well-run companies tend to last for a long while. For such businesses, the first hundred years or so are crucial. Once they get over the century mark, their chances of surviving longer grow better. However, there is no guarantee that surviving a century and beyond will keep a company in business.

There are some factors that are beyond the control of managers, such as mergers, continued industry slumps, and changing societal values. All these have serious impacts on individual businesses, and are often beyond the control of management. Banks continually swallow one another. Construction companies fall victim to recessions, depressions, and just plain slowdowns. Newspapers give way to more accessible forms of media such as television and radio. In such instances, age cannot help a company. There are stories galore that prove that.

Look at what was until recently the nation's oldest bank, First Pennsylvania Bank, for example. The bank traces its beginnings to 1781, when Robert Morris placed before Congress his plan for a national bank to be known as the Bank of North America. Morris was sworn in as the nation's Superintendent of Finance on June 27, 1781. Within a few months, he built the bank's subscription to a respectable level of $70,000. The bank did so well that it took a great deal of business away from its chief rival, the Pennsylvania Bank.

The Bank of North America needed more than the money it took in from former Pennsylvania Bank subscribers to survive, though. It needed a large infusion of cash. Through sheer luck, $470,000 fell into the bank's vaults and practically guaranteed its future.

As the Revolutionary War wound down in 1781, the government sought money to finance the struggle. The Dutch offered a large loan, which the Americans accepted. John Laurens, a Special Minister to the French Court, persuaded the King of France to personally guarantee the $470,000 loan. The King dispatched the money to America on a French frigate, which docked in Boston. Unfortunately, the bank for which the money was intended was in Philadelphia, along with the nation's government! To make matters worse, the British army was camped between the two cities and their navy had Philadelphia blockaded. That presented no problem for Robert Morris!

Morris sent 16 wagons from Philadelphia via a round-about route to fetch the money and return it to his bank. The drivers made the round trip successfully. By November 1781, the money lay in the Bank of North America's vaults. That prompted more and more people to become customers.

Morris took advantage of that stroke of luck to increase the bank's capital. Slowly but surely, the Bank of North America evolved into the nation's oldest bank. Unfortunately, it lost that title on a technicality on January 1, 1991.

As Stephen C. Masters, Vice President of the CoreStates Financial Corporation, based in Philadelphia, reports:

> First Pennsylvania Bank, which traced its heritage (through mergers) to the first federally chartered commercial bank in the United States, was itself acquired by CoreStates Financial Corp on March 5, 1990, and through a consolidation of bank charters, no longer exists as a separate legal entity.

However, he adds, "CoreStates' lead bank, Philadelphia National Bank, was chartered in 1803." So, technically, First Pennsylvania Bank still lives. Its official life ended at the ripe old age of 209, but it continues to exist in spirit. Some older companies simply disappear.

One example of a business that had to give up completely was Connecticut's oldest construction firm, the C. F. Wooding Company. Five generations of the Wooding family steered the company through 124 years of operation. They survived many a crisis, including several wars and the "Great Depression." However, time and one-too-many a crisis caught up with the company late in 1990.

A spokesman for the firm, Terry Wooding, told a *Hartford Courant* reporter that closing the business was "the only intelligent choice." He cited a lack of work and the impending recession as reasons for closing the company. Wooding continued by saying "It's a big decision, and not an easy one, but when you look at the economy's forecast, it was the only decision that could be made." The hard economic times were the biggest factor in Wooden's decision to close down the company.

"If it was going to get better in the foreseeable future," he said, "we obviously would wait it out, but there was nothing telling us we'd see a change for at least two years. The horizons were just too far out there." Indeed, those horizons are there for every company. It just takes some firms a lot longer to reach them than others, and if they cannot get to them at all, they fail. Certainly, it is tough to fold a company after 124 years of existence, but there are times when it has to be done. After all, it is a strong company that makes it to its 100th birthday, and it takes a unique combination of factors to allow a business to survive beyond that. It is those factors that are the focal point of this book.

There are times when circumstances are beyond management's control and it can only hang on and hope for the best. Look at the 1990 saga of the nation's oldest continuously published daily newspaper, the *New York Post*.

On September 15, 1990, employees were busy preparing the paper's last edition. They planned on printing the *Post's* history, including reminiscences of former employees, in the final edition. The paper had run into financial difficulties which management considered almost insurmountable. People simply were not buying a lot of newspapers in 1990. They could get news from television and radio just as easily, and with a lot less effort. They may have purchased every copy of the rumored final edition as mementoes of the *Post's* proud history, but, as things turned out, they did not have to. Instead of the history, the "final edition's" headline read "It Ain't Over Yet."

Fortunately, the paper's labor unions granted owner Peter Kalikow about $19 million in concessions to save the *Post* and their jobs. The decision may have done nothing more than postpone the inevitable. But, after 187 years of publication, that was better than nothing. Certainly, it is not easy to fold a company after almost two centuries of operation. Any company that old is worth fighting for—and the large number of companies that have passed their 100th birthday attests to that.

There are thousands of companies in this country that are over a century old. To include them all in one book would be impossible—at least in one writer's lifetime. In light of the surprising number of companies that do survive for a century or more, weeding out candidates for this book was not easy.

THE SELECTION PROCESS

The companies whose histories appear in this book are as diverse as can be. There are large companies with worldwide reputations, small ones which may not be known outside their communities, some which are conglomerates, a few which operate within very narrow product confines...in short, there is a unique mix of businesses. Regardless of size or product line, they all have glorious histories which are worth recounting.

I would like to offer special thanks to my wife, Betsy, who has grown used to my writing retreats and idiosyncratic lifestyle. She may not like it, but she is used to it, so together we will survive (and it would be nice to do so for 100 years).

Michael H. Fruth
.... Pratt & Lambert

Richard N. Hargraves
.... Laclede Gas Company

A. J. Harris
.... Baton Rouge Lumber Company

John A. Hemma
.... Greater Providence Chamber of Commerce

R. E. Johnson
.... Baton-Rouge Water Company

Paul C. Lasewicz
.... Aetna Insurance

Lee M. Liberman
.... Laclede Gas Company

Terry Loftus
.... Procter & Gamble

Michael E. Magill
.... The Greater Knoxville Chamber of Commerce

Calla Maxey-Trexler
.... South Carolina State Development Board

Twila Merlivan
.... State Publishing Company

Jim Quinn
.... Pierre (SD) Economic Development Corp.

Jeffrey A. Twining
.... Elgin-Butler

Sean Watters
.... Louisville Area Chamber of Commerce

J. Ross Willis
.... Atlanta Gas Light Company

CHAPTER 1

Welcome to the World of Survivors

How does a company outlive its founders? That is a question we are about to answer. We'll do it through the histories of several corporations in this country that have done so. Not only have these organizations outlasted their founders, but, in many cases, their founders' children and grandchildren as well! More important, they show no signs of going out of business in the immediate future. They are survivors—and role models for business operators of the future.

Out of fairness, the companies selected are presented according to their age. For purposes of this book, no one company stands out from the rest. Each has done well in its existence. That they have all lasted as long as they have is indicative of their success. Granted, there are differences among them. For example, their product lines are decidedly different, as are their sizes, company cultures, and philosophies, they operate in different geographical areas...in short, there is nothing to link them together. Nothing, that is, except their longevity, success—and inclusion in this book.

Of course, not every company that boasts of a century or more of business is included here. There are far too many for that. Just to get an idea of how many, look at Chapter 17, which lists only a fraction of the businesses across the United States that qualify for 100 or more candles on their birthday cakes. The list offers proof that longevity in the business world is not uncommon. Why is that?

There are numerous reasons. For example, it is a safe bet that most of the companies listed have been guided by a succession of astute executives. There is a correlation between age and acquired, applied wisdom. Executives who learn *and apply what they learn* cannot help but steer their companies toward success, and it is no secret that well-run companies tend to last for a long while. For such businesses, the first hundred years or so are crucial. Once they get over the century mark, their chances of surviving longer grow better. However, there is no guarantee that surviving a century and beyond will keep a company in business.

There are some factors that are beyond the control of managers, such as mergers, continued industry slumps, and changing societal values. All these have serious impacts on individual businesses, and are often beyond the control of management. Banks continually swallow one another. Construction companies fall victim to recessions, depressions, and just plain slowdowns. Newspapers give way to more accessible forms of media such as television and radio. In such instances, age cannot help a company. There are stories galore that prove that.

You will recognize some of the companies profiled here as some of the oldest, most respected business organizations in the country. Others you may not recognize at all. That should not be surprising. Certainly, not every company has an easily recognizable name or product that is familiar to everyone. Look, for example, at the Dexter Corporation.

Dexter, headquartered in Windsor Locks, Connecticut, has struggled with an image problem for years. As soon as some people hear the company's name, they automatically associate it with shoes. Their misconception has nothing to do with the quality of Dexter's products or geographical location. Rather, it has to do with what Dexter produces and to whom it sells. Dexter makes things like tea bags and sausage wrappers. It is also involved heavily in space-related technology. But how many people walk into a store to buy an empty tea bag, sausage wrapper, or space ship? Obviously, very few. Other businesses, though, purchase great quantities of these products from Dexter. So, Dexter continues to produce—as it has for well over 200 years!

On the other hand, there are companies like Procter & Gamble. The vast majority of consumers in the country, and probably the world, can identify this company name. Here's a company that has been in business since 1837, and which continues to grow. One of the reasons for this growth is the company's diversity and the public's recognition of its products and reliability.

Virtually every home in America has at least one of P & G's products in it somewhere. The company's product lines include such diverse items as Ivory® Soap (perhaps its most recognizable product), Pringle® Potato Chips, and Citrus Hill® Orange Juice. Television viewers think often of Procter & Gamble, the sponsor of the first soap operas. So, Procter & Gamble has no problem with brand recognition—or with longevity.

Many of the other companies in this book fall somewhere in between Dexter and Procter & Gamble. Some, e.g., the *Hartford Courant*, Atlanta Gas Light, and the Louisiana Companies, are local in nature. Others, like Coors, may operate globally but deal in product lines that are not generally considered glamorous or essential by consumers. (As you shall see, Coors produces much more than beer!)

All have overcome problems in innovative ways. Each has had its share of "Hall of Fame" CEOs, responded well to changes in the marketplace and environment, and gained customers' trust and confidence. Some of the companies are well known. Others are not. Regardless of how well known they are, they have all made their mark on the corporate world and have been selected based on their success.

WE DID NOT PLAN TO GROW THIS OLD, BUT NOW THAT WE HAVE, WE LIKE IT

Like most entrepreneurs, the founders of the businesses included in this book did not start with any plans to endure for hundreds of years. They recognized the indisputable fact that life is ephemeral and that they, too, were mortal. To be sure, few people start businesses with the idea of maintaining them beyond their own lifetimes. After all, no entrepreneur can gaze into a crystal ball and predict the future of a given enterprise. Predictions do not have as much influence on a business' staying power as do factors like hard work, determination, and luck.

Surely, few beginning entrepreneurs note in their business plans that "We will still be in business 150 years from today." Rather, most of them start operations with more immediate concerns: supporting themselves and their families and possibly passing the business on to their descendents. Often, they succeed in reaching these goals—and establish a thriving enterprise in the bargain. Such a company is the Elgin-Butler Brick Company, located in Austin, Texas (see Chapter 11). Occasionally, the business passes out of family hands but is perpetuated nonetheless. There exists no better example of such a company than what is currently known as Huntington's Book Store in Hartford, Connecticut (see Chapter 5).

Businesses such as Huntington's prove beyond the shadow of a doubt that company founders do not always set out to establish companies that will last forever. They survive nonetheless because they provide a valuable service to a community, which simply will not let them go out of business. Thus, they pass from owner to owner in perpetuity seemingly in defiance of owners' wishes.

Let's face it: most owners of start-up businesses are too concerned with immediate survival to worry about where the company will be in 100 years. Often, they view the future as a by-product of the present. They reason that if a company cannot survive the present, there is no sense worrying about the future, whether it be tomorrow, ten years, or a century or two from now.

A century or two from now? A timeframe like that is irrelevant to most business owners, especially those just starting. Yet, as the following chapters prove, some companies do survive that long—and even longer. There is no magical trick to doing so. Their survival hinges on a unique combination of factors that come together to keep them in business. Managers can control some of these factors. Others occur naturally. Just what factors are controllable and which are not is the subject of this book—and explain why the companies profiled herein are the role models for today's entrepreneurs to follow. The basic reason is simple: **THEY ARE CHAMPIONS!**

CHAPTER 2

1711

Kenyon Corn Meal Company

ALMOST 300 YEARS OF GRINDING IT OUT

There exists in Usquepaugh, Rhode Island, a mill which historical records date back to at least 1711. The mill has had a succession of owners and name changes since its founding. It has even changed sites once or twice, although a mill cannot move too far from its source of power, which, in this case, was water for the first two centuries of its existence. Through all these vicissitudes, the Usquepaugh mill has ground out meal for almost three centuries. The mill has never been more productive than it is today.

11

Whether the 1711 founding date is accurate or not is a matter of conjecture. For that matter, how accurate are the historical records of any company? Dating individual companies' "birthdays" is quite often a matter of choice. Some companies date their "birthdays" from the day they opened their doors; others use their date of incorporation. In truth, incorporation can occur years after the company actually begins operations. For example, an individual can start a business in 1991, take on a partner in 2004 and change the name of the company, then incorporate in 2020. Choosing the actual "birthday" in such a case is optional. Such is the case with the Kenyon Corn Meal Company.

Usquepaugh (spelled Usquepaug on the official Rhode Island Tourism Division/Department of Economic Development's Visitor's Map) was originally called Cottrells, after Gershem Cottrell was deeded land in 1693. Rowland Robinson purchased land from Cottrell in 1708, after which the name of the settlement changed to Robinsons. A mill was mentioned in the deed. Robinson bought more land and a dwelling house in 1711. William Robinson sold three tracts of land, a house, and mills to Peleg Mumford in 1713 and nearly 300 acres more to him in 1739. Not surprisingly, the name changed again to Mumford's Mills.

In 1744, Mumford deeded land, house, and a grist mill to Jerah Mumford. It was not until 1820 that the Kenyon name became associated with Usquepaugh. Throughout these dealings, a grist mill continued to operate in the community.

The post office christened Usquepaugh officially in 1836 when it established a branch in the community. It was another fifty years before the name Kenyon became associated with the grist mill. The company has operated under its present name since 1886.

Paul Drumm, Jr., the current owner of the business, is sure the mill actually dates back to the 1600s. Although he has not uncovered solid evidence to substantiate his belief, he hopes to some day. Drumm is an avid historian who enjoys tracing his company's roots, especially in light of its continuity and contemporary success. The Kenyon mill demonstrates beautifully the relationship between history and continuity—and it has plenty of both. So, no matter which date is the real "birthday," one thing is certain: the Kenyon Corn Meal Company is one of the nation's oldest companies, and it shows no signs of going out of business any time soon.

Drumm is the latest in a series of mill owners. Each has made significant contributions to the operation; Drumm plans to continue the innovations they pioneered.

CHRONOLOGY OF OWNERS OF KENYON'S GRIST MILL

- ☐ 1840s—Cornelius Sweetland (sometime in the 1840s; the exact date is unknown)
- ☐ 1886—John Tarbox, who built the present mill, John C. James, John Woodmansee, Stillman Barber
- ☐ 1906—Charles M. Hanson
- ☐ 1909—Charles D. Kenyon, whose name the mill now bears, was the first to package the corn meal
- ☐ 1938—Archibald B. Kenyon, who ran the mill after his father's death
- ☐ 1954—William Sykes

- ☐ 1956—Joseph Crocker
- ☐ 1957—Gordon Pennoyer
- ☐ 1959—Albert E. Powell, who established the concession business at fairs and events
- ☐ 1962—John A. Mulligan, Sr.
- ☐ 1971—Paul Drumm, Jr., who established the mill store and the gift food business

Two important names missing from the list are Ed and Charley Walmsley, who never owned the company, but served as millers through most of the 20th century. They established a record for longevity that is practically unrivaled in business history. Ed, Charley's father, worked as a miller for about 50 years. Charley exceeded that record; he worked as the miller for *66 years!* As history shows, it is safe to say that they perpetuated the existence of Kenyon Corn Meal Company.

SMALLER THAN A ONE-HORSE TOWN

Kenyon Corn Meal Company is as unique as is the name of the town in which it is the primary employer. (The company employs six people, which is an indication of the size of the town!) Usquepaugh (which is actually a part of both Richmond and South Kingstown) is possibly a misspelled version of "usquebaugh," a Scottish whiskey. How the community's name derived is something historians can debate forever. What is important is that the town does exist—and is synonymous with the name Kenyon.

As indicated previously, historical records prove the existence of a grist mill in the town. For the most part, the mill operated on a barter system and provided local residents with a place to process their corn.

About the only other industry in town was a woolen mill which fire destroyed in 1870. The owners, Daniel Rodman and James Spaulding, rebuilt it bigger and better, but not well enough to resist more fires. Fire damaged the mill in 1883, and another blaze destroyed it again on May 24, 1884. The owners did not rebuild it. Consequently, the people who worked there drifted away from Usquepaugh, leaving the grist mill as the only industry in the town. That has not changed in over 100 years.

THIS HISTORY MAY SOUND CORNY, BUT...

The earliest listed owners had no intentions of placing the mill on the map. Sweetland, Tarbox, and Hanson simply ground the corn brought in by local farmers. Charles D. Kenyon was actually the first proprietor to envision the expansion of the mill for commercial purposes.

Kenyon purchased the plant from Hanson in 1909. He envisioned producing enough johnny cake meal to stock the shelves of all the grocery stores in South County. He wasted no time implementing his plans.

Before we go any farther here, let's define a couple of terms. First, there is no such entity as South County, Rhode Island. It's actually a collection of several towns that compose a mythical county which includes most of the state's prime tourist attractions. According to the official Rhode Island travel map mentioned earlier, "Johnny Cake", originally "Journey Cake," is a unique and delicious Rhode Island food specialty. It is served in many of the state's restaurants, often with native sausage.

The map also reveals that "The most authentic description of making Rhode Island jonnycakes is found in *The Jonnycake Papers,* by T. R. Hazard:

> ...an old-fashioned jonnycake made of white Rhode Island corn meal, carefully and slowly ground with Rhode Island fine-grained granite mill-stones, and baked and conscientiously tended before the glowing coals of a quick green hardwood fire, on a red oak barrel head supported by flat-iron.

It is also described technically as a bread made of oatmeal or wheat flour or a kind of corn bread baked on a griddle. In truth, people have been arguing about the real definition of Johnny Cake for years, especially in Rhode Island. The argument is so intense there is a Society for the Propagation of the Jonnycake Tradition in Rhode Island. (The account of the argument below is simplified, to say the least. To discuss the merits of the Johnny Cake vs. jonnycake argument would require a book of its own.)

There are two spellings of Johnny Cake in Rhode Island. The other is jonnycake, which many Rhode Islanders consider their tastiest claim to fame. The battle over which is the correct spelling has even caused fistfights in the state legislature. Generally, jonnycakes can be made only with Indian white-cap flint corn, a rare—and limited—local strain. Johnny Cakes mean that some of the ingredients derive from out-of-state sources. Whichever definition applies, the controversy helps Kenyon Corn Meal's sales, as people continue to clamor for the company's products. But now back to our story.

Kenyon took over the mill in the spring of 1909. That gave him just enough time to visit local farmers and encourage them to grow the right kind of corn, i.e., Indian white-cap flint. They responded with alacrity. Luckily, the growing season was good. As a result, the farmers supplied plenty of corn.

Kenyon began at once to mill the corn, which he supplied to regional grocers in 25 and 50 pound sacks under the brand name Kenyon's Johnny Cake Meal. The product grew in popularity at once. It became so popular, in fact, that Kenyon installed a new turbine water wheel and another set of grist stones. Even that was not enough. He procured yet another set of wheels from an abandoned mill in nearby Narragansett. And still the plant grew.

Kenyon installed a type of mill which ground all the corn unsuitable for commercial meal into cattle feed. This meal became an instant success among local farmers. Not one to sit back and reap profits from only one product line, Kenyon branched out into making cider, too. That business, like the others, took off. Unfortunately, the strain of producing enough apples for the cider press wore out the local orchards, so the cider business fell by the wayside after a few years.

The next addition to the business was Charles Kenyon's son, Archie. After Archie graduated from college, he joined his father—and wasted no time making suggestions. Archie felt that it would be easier for users of the company's meal to use 3 or 6 pound packages, rather than the larger sacks. His father agreed. The smaller packages grew in favor.

As sales grew, Kenyon's sales territory expanded. The company began shipping products via truck and train to supplant the horse-drawn wagon that Archie used to transport the meal. By the late 1920s and early 1930s, the company's sales territory included the entire state of Rhode Island, and parts of Connecticut and Massachusetts. Archie attributed this expansion in part to World War I.

Rationing inhibited civilians' purchases of certain products during the war. In order to buy a bag of wheat flour, a person had to buy the equivalent in some other cereal. So many people chose corn meal as the equivalent that Rhode Island Johnny Cake mix became very popular. This was fine with the Kenyons—and their sales.

Not surprisingly, the "Great Depression" had an adverse impact on the Kenyons' business. Archie found full-time work in Providence in order to supplement his income. After his father died in 1938, Archie struggled to juggle the duties of his full-time position and the operation of the grist mill. He managed to handle both until 1954, when he had to choose one or the other. Archie decided to sell the mill to William Sykes in 1954. That ended 45 years of ownership by the same family, but the break was temporary.

FROM CONSISTENCY TO INCONSISTENCY AND BACK

There was a succession of owners over the next five years. About the only things that remained constant were the millers. The Walmsleys remained no matter who owned the business. Then, Mr. and Mrs. Albert E. Powell bought the place in 1959—and returned it to the Kenyon family, since Mrs. Powell was Charles D. Kenyon's grandniece. The Powells made major changes at once.

They developed several new, attractively packaged mixes, e.g., brown bread, corn muffin, clam cake, and pancake. They also introduced Johnny Cake meal made out of the more plentiful white dent corn. This innovation dispelled the myth that authentic Johnny Cake mix could be made only from Indian white-cap flint. More important, it allowed the mill to produce even more corn meal.

The most significant innovation the Powells introduced was the establishment of a concession business at fairs and events, particularly the Springfield (Massachusetts) Fair. The misnamed fair, which is now called the Eastern States Exposition, features exhibits from the six New England states. Each state has a pavilion shaped like its state capitol building. There, the Powells introduced thousands of people to Rhode Island Johnny Cakes made of Kenyon's Corn Meal. The cakes became immensely popular.

George Haupt, who helped Mr. Powell put up the first booth in the Rhode Island building on the fair grounds in 1960, reported that he fried 4,000 cakes the first year and 6,000 the next. That began a tradition that is still carried on today. More than a tradition, it is a revenue bonanza for the company.

Paul Drumm reveals that the Exposition accounts for one-third of the company's annual revenues! His booth is so attractive that some people have asked him to relocate the mill intact to the fair grounds! Another group has offered to pay Drumm for dismantling the mill board by board and reassembling it anywhere he chooses in Massachusetts. Drumm, who has an intense allegiance to his native state of Rhode Island and a deep appreciation for the role of history in business, has declined both offers.

The Powells sold the mill in 1962 to John A. Mulligan, Sr. He, in turn, sold it to Drumm, who proved to be as innovative in his approach to business as were his predecessors.

IT'S HARD TO BEAT THIS DRUMM

Drumm knew next to nothing about the milling business when he took over. He had worked as a computer repairman for IBM and MAI for several years until a back injury put an end to that career. He and his wife searched for a self-owned business in which he could utilize his skills. Once he learned the mill was available, he jumped at the opportunity to purchase it. The Drumms remortgaged their house and everything else they owned. They paid off all these debts in twelve years.

Drumm's first task was to learn everything he could about the milling business. The Walmsleys came in handy in that respect. Between the two Walmsleys, Drumm could access over 100 years of milling history. This was something that he admits he needed badly. He devoted the first year to learning as much as he could about the business, promising that there would be no changes in the operation for six months and no major changes for a year. Once he started making changes, though, the company's reputation grew considerably. One of the first steps Drumm undertook, once the year-long moratorium ended, was to expand the product line considerably. Gradually he added to the limited number of products the preceding owners had featured and initiated a mail order business featuring different gift packages. Today, Kenyon offers:

- 10 different stoneground meals and flours

- 7 old-fashioned mixes made with Kenyon's flours
- 13 "New England Delicacies," e.g., clam cake/chowder dinner, Indian pudding, corn, cranberry, and red pepper relish, and apple, blueberry, and cranberry pancake syrups
- 17 preserves and jellies under the "Queen's River" label

The products are available in a variety of retail outlets and by mail order. Drumm looks for even more expansion. "Even though we are milling 60-100 tons of grain per year, which sometimes requires a seven-day work week, we are operating at only ten percent of capacity," he says. "As the demand for our product continues to increase, we should have no problem meeting it—as long as we can get the materials to mill."

Today, Drumm is searching far and wide for the quality corn and grains which go into Kenyon's products. Local farmers can no longer provide even a fraction of the corn he uses, so Drumm purchases raw products from as far away as Maryland. "But," he promises, "as long as there is a demand for our products, we will find the *quality* material to produce them."

Quality is an important ingredient in any of Kenyon's products. "We will not provide our customers with inferior products," Drumm vows. "That would not only be unethical, but it would run contrary to the mill's history." Then, with a laugh, he adds that "We sell more history than product anyway."

History is important to Drumm. After all, any company that has been in business as long as Kenyon must be aware of its roots. Kenyon is luckier than most. The company's succession of owners had the Walmsleys to carry on the mill trade much the same as it was done back in the 1700s—and to relate the history of the business and the town. Consequently, the owners have maintained their sense of history and tradition, both of which are packed into every product the company sells. Drumm's concern with history is reflected in the greeting he and his staff give visitors to the mill. The company operates a gift store across the street from the mill. When visitors stop in, the Drumms enjoy striking up conversations with them concerning the history of Rhode Island, milling procedures, or any other relevant topic from which they might learn something—and that includes just about anything. The Kenyon staff is always eager to add to the company's lore and to learn something that might help it improve its products. This is an excellent way for the company to enhance its image and improve its products, and it's a lesson from which any business can benefit.

Drumm is not only concerned with history, but with customer loyalty. His son Paul III says that it is not unusual for Paul Sr. to spend an entire weekend tracking down a problem brought to his attention by a customer.

"Dad does not like problems of any type," he says, "especially those that affect customers. He will talk to people for hours in order to track a complaint, and he does not rest until that complaint is resolved." The senior Drumm's attention to resolving problems and satisfying customers is admirable, but, as he observes, "it is nothing more than any good company executive will do to retain a customer base and assure quality."

In that respect, Kenyon Corn Meal is on an equal footing with its larger competitors like Pillsbury and General Mills. Of course, companies like those two have considerably more modern resources to fall back on when they look into their problems.

The Kenyon Corn Meal Company makes meal today much the same as millers did 300 years ago. Whereas commercial millers pulverize their grains in modern machines and include several chemical processes, traditional companies like Kenyon grind their products. Basically, the grain is dumped into a hopper and then fed through a chute, or boot, which shakes as the grindstone turns. The boot guides the kernels into an opening in the top stone.

The boot at Kenyon is literally that. As the Drumms suggest laughingly, it is their concession to innovation. It is actually the top part of a firefighter's boot which serves admirably as a guide. The kernels are ground between the top and bottom stones. The resulting flour works its way to the outside of the stones, where it is swept into a chute connected to a collection container. There is a slight difference in Kenyon's milling procedure.

Kenyon uses stones made of Rhode Island granite, rather than the traditional sandstone, which is much softer. The Rhode Island stones produce a finer, more consistent meal than other types. It is the difference in the grinding procedures that makes Kenyon's product more palatable than its competitors, and which leads to the company's marketing success.

"I have had fun building this business," Drumm admits. "Part of the fun has been working closely with [his son] Paulie, who will be running this operation someday. I know that when I leave the company in his hands, it will be well taken care of. But I am not ready to leave just yet."

Indeed, Drumm has many more things to accomplish before he retires. For example, he wants to build a separate packing plant to relieve the overcrowding extant in the facility today. As mentioned previously, he wants to increase production, and expand his product line even more. Today, the company is shipping 200 cases of meal products per week, compared to only 50 when Drumm took over in 1971. The increase is significant, but is not yet at the level Drumm would like to see it.

"We may be growing slowly," Drumm says, "but at least we are growing. Whereas some companies may judge their success in terms of millions of dollars in profits, we look at ours a bit differently." He certainly does.

"We measure our success according to our ability to keep operating," emphasizes the senior Drumm. If that is how success is measured, then the Kenyon Corn Meal Company is a resounding success. After all, it has been in existence in one form or another for almost three centuries. The ability to operate that long sets the Kenyon Corn Meal Company apart from a lot of other enterprises that have come and gone over the years—and sets the standards for the rest of the companies profiled in this book to follow.

CHAPTER 3

1764

The Hartford Courant

CURRENT THEN, "COURANT" NOW

October 29 is a date that will live forever in the minds of business historians—and readers of the *Hartford Courant.* (The name *Courant* was common for English-language newspapers in the 18th century. Oddly enough, the name stems from the Dutch word for newspaper.) On October 29, 1929, there occurred the never-to-be-forgotten stock market crash. One hundred sixty five years earlier, on that same date, the first issue of the *Courant*, America's oldest newspaper in continuous circulation, appeared.

The opening paragraphs of that inaugural edition, which was known then as the *Connecticut Courant,* are as true today as they were then:

> Of all the Arts which have been introduc'd amongst Mankind, for the civilizing Human-Nature, and rendering Life agreeable and happy, none appear of greater Advantage than that of Printing: for hereby the greatest Genius's of all Ages, and Nations, live and speak for the Benefit of future Generations—

> Was it not for the Press, we should be left almost intirely (sic) ignorant of all those noble Sentiments which the Antients (sic again) were endow'd with.

> By this Art, Men are brought acquainted with each other, though never so remote, as to Age or Situation; it lays open to View the Manners, Genius and Policy of all Nations and Countries and faithfully transmits them to Posterity. But not to insist upon the Usefulness of this Art in general, which must be obvious to every One, whose Thoughts are the least extensive.

The Benefit of a Weekly Paper, must in particular have its Advantages, as it is the Channel which conveys the History of the present Times to every Part of the World.

The page also carried a pledge that the paper would carry only news that could be verified, along with as many items as possible of local interest. Finally, the *Courant* announced a publishing schedule contingent on readers' acceptance of the paper.

The *Connecticut Courant*,(a Specimen of which, the Public are now presented with) will, on due Encouragement, be continued every Monday, beginning on Monday, the 19th of November, next: which encouragement we hope to deserve, by a constant Endeavor to render this Paper useful, and entertaining, not only as a channel for News, but assisting to all Those who may have occasion to make use of it as an Advertiser.

Obviously, readers encouraged the *Courant* to continue printing, as it is still going—and growing—strong today, 227 years later.

OLDER THAN THE NATION, AND GROWING OLDER BY THE MOMENT

Thomas Green was 29 years old when he decided that Hartford needed a newspaper. His was by no means the first in the state. James Parker, the 18th century's equivalent to Rudolph Murdoch, had established the *Connecticut Gazette* at New Haven in 1755. Parker, a partner of Benjamin Franklin, also operated the New York *Weekly Post Boy*, aka *Gazette*, and the *Constitutional Courant* at Woodbridge, New Jersey. Green decided, however, that Hartford needed its own newspaper. He certainly chose an appropriate time to establish it.

Newspapers were growing in importance in New England in the latter half of the 18th century. According to historian Jackson Turner Main, "They had great educational value, printing not only laws and political information but a variety of economic, literary, and scientific matter." In fact, they were among the most significant teaching tools of the time, especially for the tradesmen. As one newspaper editor said, Only by reading newspapers would the "lower and poorer sort of people" obtain useful knowledge. Green agreed. His timing was impeccable.

THE *COURANT* IS A REVOLUTIONARY IDEA—AND SO IS THE WAR AGAINST ENGLAND

It did not take the *Courant* long to establish its views regarding American independence. Early in 1765, Britain's First Lord of the Treasury prepared to introduce a Stamp Act, which called for taxes on newspapers, almanacs, legal documents, playing

The Courant: 1776 & 1781

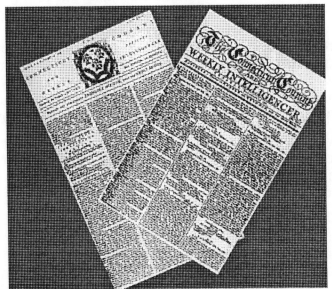

Courtesy of The Hartford Courant, Hartford, CT

cards, and dice, all of which had to bear a stamp signifying that the tax was paid. Green took exception to the proposed tax and published his views regarding it in the *Courant*. By doing so, he established a precedent which subsequent editors have followed over the years, i.e., using their newspaper to express their views candidly, concisely, clearly and accurately.

Connecticut's economy at the time was in a downturn. The state's citizens had no money to pay additional taxes on anything. The March 11, 1765, issue of the *Courant* described the situation as "melancholy; foreign trade embarrassed; our private debts many, and the cries of the needy continually increasing." Green was even more to the point in his May 20 issue, when he wrote succinctly "THERE IS NO MONEY." Green simply did not pull any punches. Of course, Green was no more eager to have the British march into his office and shut down his paper than he was to pay taxes. Consequently, he voluntarily stopped printing for a month in 1765 to avoid complying with the Stamp Act. He resumed after that and continued publishing for another five years. No doubt the British were relieved when he sold the paper in 1770 to his assistant, Ebenezer Watson. Unfortunately for them, the new owner was every bit as outspoken as Green!

Watson took over at a trying time in the country's history, just when grumblings against British rule were becoming a cry for independence. He took the side of the "rebels."

There has never been a time in the history of the United States when opinion has been so divided over an issue as it was in the 1770s. Watson did his bit to stir up the colonists. Of course, not everyone agreed with the *Courant's* opinions then, any more than they do now, but Watson, as his successors have done since, tried to print opposite viewpoints. In so doing, t h e *Courant* has retained a loyal following and amassed a record for longevity unmatched by any other newspaper in the United States. It has done this in spite of the fact that Hartford is located midway between Boston and New York City, which has forced the *Courant* to compete with venerable papers such as the *New York Times* and the *Boston Globe*. Such competition was not around during the Revolutionary War, though, and that worked to the *Courant's* benefit.

The *Courant* had the largest circulation of any newspaper in the colonies during the war. Its circulation grew from about 700 to 8,000 during the period. The increase probably had to do with the fact that the *Courant* was an outspoken backer of the Americans' cause. The editor made no bones about whose side the paper was on when he printed these accusatory words after the Battle of Lexington.

> AMERICANS! Forever bear in mind the BATTLE of LEXINGTON:—where British troops, unmolested and unprovoked, wantonly, and in a most unhuman manner fired upon and killed a number of our countrymen, then robbed them of their provisions, ransacked, plundered and burnt their houses! Nor could the tears of defenceless (sic) women, some of whom were in the pains of childbirth, the cries of helpless babes, nor the prayer of old age, confined to beds of sickness, appease their thirst for blood!—or divert them from the DESIGN of MURDER and ROBBERY!

There was no doubt that the *Courant* was anti-British, and it paid for its sentiments.

On January 27, 1778, the *Courant's* paper mill burned down mysteriously at a time when paper was in short supply to begin with. It was so hard to get, in fact, that Watson had been unable to publish in January 1776 because there was none available. Thus, the fire proved particularly disastrous.

Since the sophisticated arson investigation techniques available to today's fire marshals were not extant, no one could pinpoint the exact cause of the blaze. The most likely suspects were people loyal to the king, but who actually did it was secondary to getting the paper printed. Fortunately, the Connecticut legislature came to the *Courant's* rescue. It authorized a lottery to raise 1,500 pounds (about $5,000) to construct a new mill. In the meantime, the *Courant* printed a few issues on wrapping paper. No doubt, the British wished that a plague would strike the paper's office. Unfortunately, it had already.

A few months before the mill burned, on September 22, 1777, the *Courant* announced that Ebenezer Watson died of smallpox at the age of 33. The paper stayed in the family hands, though. He left it to his 27-year-old wife, Hannah, who became one of the first women publishers in the country. Regardless of who owned it, the paper continued to grow, both in circulation and innovation, war or no war.

First, in 1780, advertisements disappeared from their traditional place on the front page. Next, in 1783, the *Courant* printed Noah Webster's "Blue-Backed Speller," which was the first time it appeared in print. Years later, the *Courant's* owners, Hudson & Goodwin, made large profits from Webster's *Speller*. Then, in 1787, the paper printed the proposed new Constitution in full as a news item. More than that, it substantiated its support for the Constitution by printing several articles on the need for a stronger union of the states. The *Courant* also printed unanswered letters written by advocates of the document. As usual, the paper made crystal clear its support on an issue, a habit which did not always work in its favor.

WELL, WE CAN'T ATTACK THE BRITISH ANYMORE, SO LET'S ATTACK THE PRESIDENT

In the early 1800s, many of the growing number of newspapers in the country became partisan in nature. (By 1800, there were more than 150 newspapers in the United States. Ten years later, that figure had doubled!) The *Courant* was no exception. Never afraid to tackle what it perceived as a controversial issue head on, it singled out President Thomas Jefferson for particular abuse.

The *Courant* accused Jefferson of being a godless slave owner, a tool of France, and an enemy of the Constitution. The final straw occurred in 1806 when the paper ran a story implying that the administration had sent 60 tons of silver to France as a bribe. As far as Jefferson was concerned, this was too much to ignore. His administration indicted the *Courant* for criminal libel. The case got as high as the U.S. Supreme Court, which ruled in the *Courant's* favor in 1812. The decision convinced the editors more than ever that the press was a powerful tool, so they decided to improve the quality of their presses.

In 1816, the *Courant* took advantage of the sophisticated technology of the time to acquire a new press that printed two pages simultaneously. This was a major step forward for the paper, which needed to get ahead of its Hartford rivals. Twenty years later, the paper made another bold move when it became a daily newspaper published Monday through Saturday. It maintained the weekly edition, though, for those who preferred their news on a less frequent basis. The two editions gave the *Courant* a large presence in the city and more leverage to battle its ten competitors in the struggle for circulation supremacy. The editors and owners simply refused to shy away from the competition, regardless of what they had to do to beat it—even if they had to become the *National Enquirer* of their time.

**THE *COURANT* MAKES THE *NATIONAL ENQUIRER*
LOOK AS HARMLESS AS A CHURCH BULLETIN**

For the most part, little of importance happened in
Hartford's newspaper industry during the first part of
the 19th century. The United States was busying itself
growing, and newspapers did little but report what
was going on. For a while at the middle of the century,
though, the *Courant*, through publishers Thomas Day
and Theodore W. Dwight, became a vehicle to espouse
bigoted and radical views.

The Courant: 1815, 1878 and 1898

Courtesy of The Hartford Courant, Hartford, CT

Dwight was a champion of native-born Americans.
At one point, the *Courant* referred to the Irish section
of Hartford as "Pigville" and accused Catholics of
wanting to eliminate the Protestant Bible from public
schools. Day was even more outspoken!

Day printed numerous articles poking suspicion at the Catholic Church, immigrants of all nationalities, and Negroes. For example, he wrote in one editorial that "The Caucasian variety is intrinsically a better breed, of better brain, better moral traits, better capacity every way, than the Negro, or the Mongolian, or the Malay, or the Red American." Previous publishers had taken gentle pokes at minorities before, but never as blatantly as this.

Back in the December 1, 1775, issue, Watson had written about slaveowners who sold their slaves not for inhumane reasons, but simply because their behavior exasperated the owners. Watson suggested that a particular slave had been sold because of "Too great fondness for a particular Negro wench in his old neighborhood." A few months later, in the April 5, 1776, issue, he castigated the British for using slaves to try to convince the colonists that their struggle for independence was futile.

The British had attempted to incite the slaves to revolt and kill their masters. Watson was not about to let his readers forget this British infamy. In a series of 36 items entitled "Remember," which he addressed to the American people through his newspaper, he wrote, "Remember the bribing of Negro slaves to assassinate their masters." In neither case had he written anything derogatory about the slaves, and no ensuing editor or publisher did, either. Consequently, Day became an exception, but he became more discreet as the Civil War approached. The War gave the *Courant* a chance to restore its editorial integrity and support the abolition of slavery. It did both.

That the *Courant* enjoyed a reputation for integrity and candidness in Hartford was not questioned. Many of the paper's employees were invited to sit as directors of major companies in the city because of their integrity. For example, John L. Boswell, the paper's owner and publisher from September 1836 to July 1854, when he died of a viral infection, was a Director of the newly formed Aetna Insurance Company (See Chapter 7). He was one of the people who motivated the company's founder to invest his money in this new enterprise.

Boswell had accused Hartford's financial leaders in an editorial of being too conservative. As he put it, "Hartford's capitalists are asleep on their moneybags." He suggested that the city suffered from the lethargy consuming the very people who were supposed to be its business leaders. Unfortunately, as the history of Aetna shows, he did not live to see how the company's management made him eat those words. Boswell died just as the nation entered the most critical phase of its history up to that point. Besides, many people of the period thought the newspapers were as lethargic as the business leaders. The advent of the Civil War changed that.

It wasn't until the presidential campaign of 1860 that the *Courant* got into the cause of slavery and the possibility of war wholeheartedly. The editors looked forward to the chance. After all, the *Courant* could claim one thing that none of its competitors could: it had already reported firsthand on one major war (the Revolution) and a minor one (the War of 1812). As 1860 neared, it appeared that it would have a chance to follow a third. But, the *Courant* felt that perhaps one man could help the nation avert that war. It therefore backed Abraham Lincoln.

HONEST ABE MADE A HIT WITH HARTFORD—AND THE *COURANT*

Abraham Lincoln was not the first presidential candidate to visit Hartford, nor was he the last, but he may have caused more excitement than any of those who came before or after him.

Lincoln's appearance in Hartford on March 5, 1860, came at a time when the United States was split over the slavery issue. Feelings between pro-slavery (connected with the Democrats) and anti-slavery (associated with the Republicans) supporters were heated. Both major parties campaigned vigorously to sway voters to their side of the issue.

Neither party was against slavery completely. The Democrats advocated the spread of slavery into the western territories. The Republicans, on the other hand, wanted to restrict slavery to the South, to "wash the hands of the nation of all contamination with its guilt."

Lincoln was running for president as a member of a party that was only six years old. He not only had to come face to face with a highly controversial topic, but he had to persuade people that the relatively new party was the best equipped to handle it. This is where the *Courant* could be helpful.

The paper's editors were aware that if a war occurred their only contribution would be to print the news and sway people to follow their consciences in supporting the Union government. In Connecticut, the production of the supplies needed to carry out the war would be done by manufacturers equipped for the task. The many insurance companies based in the state would provide coverage for the men who fought the battles. What else could the *Courant* do but try to convince the public that Lincoln was the best man to preserve the Union? It did the job well.

Connecticut's Republicans jammed the Hartford City Hall well before Lincoln was scheduled to speak. He did not disappoint them, delivering a speech filled with humorous allusions to the quaint slavery viewpoints of his Democratic rivals.

He told them of a gentleman seated in front of him on a railroad car in New Haven who had a large cyst on his neck. "That wen [a cyst containing sebaceous matter] represents slavery," Lincoln told the crowd. "It bears the same relation to that man that slavery does to the country. That wen is a great evil; the man that bears it will say so. But he does not care to cut it out. He bleeds to death if he does, directly. If he does not cut it out, he shortens his life materially."

He summed up his speech with bombastic oratory: "Let us not be slandered from our duties or intimidated from preserving our dignity and our rights from any menace, but let us have faith that Right, Eternal Right, makes might, and we understand our duty, so do it."

The crowd burst into a frenzy. The Hartford Cornet Band struck up a lively tune and led a procession to the mayor's home, where Lincoln planned to spend the night. His speech impressed the *Courant's* editors, who wrote:

> The speech of Mr. Lincoln at the City Hall last night was the most convincing and clearest speech we

> ever heard made....There could not
> have been even a ten-year-old boy in
> that crowd who did not leave that
> room satisfied that Mr. Lincoln was
> right and had argued his points
> man-fashion.

Lincoln and the *Courant* combined succeeded in urging the people of Hartford to do their duty to their country, an accomplishment that no local newspaper or other presidential visitor to Hartford had done better before—or has done since.

The *Courant* had a great impact on the outcome of the 1860 election. It backed Lincoln enthusiastically, and when he won the race, the paper printed a headline proclaiming "VICTORY! VICTORY! WE'VE GOT 'EM!" That was the most exuberance the normally staid paper had shown in its 96-year existence. Even when many people in the North grew disillusioned towards the end of the war, and were urging Lincoln to stop the fighting, the *Courant* maintained its support for Lincoln. Despite the fact that Connecticut's Republican party was dangerously close to breaking with Lincoln over the conduct of the war, the *Courant* stuck to its principles. In fact, it was the only influential Republican newspaper in the state that did!

Overall, the *Courant* was subdued in its coverage during most of the war. Even when the *Courant* announced in its April 10, 1865, issue that Lee had surrendered, it wrote simply "A Word to the Union Men of Hartford: THE REBELLION IS ENDED." It was time for the *Courant* to become a little rebellious on its own.

EAST IS EAST, AND WEST IS WEST—AND NEVER THE TWAIN SHALL MEET

The United States entered a new era, "The Gilded Age," after the Civil War ended. The label was not attached to it until two men with Hartford connections, Mark Twain and Charles Dudley Warner, wrote a novel of that name which was published in 1873 (or 1874, depending on which expert you rely on). The book satirized the corrupt politics, coarse manners of the *nouveau riche*, and the get-rich-quick schemes so common among businessmen that marked the period, which lasted roughly between 1865 and the 1880s. The era also brought about a dramatic change in journalistic philosophy.

Rather than presenting clone-type column after column of dull, unimaginative news, editors opted to spice up their writing by giving heavy doses of stories on crime and personalities. To do so, they relied heavily on interviews, an innovative technique at the time. The *Courant* chose not to be innovative.

Of course, the *Courant* was not unalterably opposed to personal interviews. In fact, it had carried the first personal interview published in a Hartford newspaper. That occurred after a May 1853 train wreck in Norwalk, Connecticut. The train plunged through an open drawbridge. Fifty people died in the tragedy. One of the survivors, Dr. Gurdon W. Russell, was riding in a car which split in half. The forward part fell into the river. Russell, fortunately, was sitting a few feet behind that section.

He immediately began rescuing and treating the people who were injured. Russell gave an in-depth interview to the *Courant* recounting the disaster. So, though the editors may not have been fond of the interview technique, they had a nose for news, and would take advantage of any medium to see that it was presented quickly and accurately. It did not, however, stop them from speaking out against the "New Journalism."

The editors wrote that the new approach was "Ungentlemanly Journalism" marked by the "vile invention of interviewing." They preferred their conservative presentation style that would later earn the paper the nickname "The Old Lady of State Street." Maybe the name was appropriate at the time, especially since many of its local competitors were much more flamboyant in their style. Those papers may have been flamboyant, but they were not as durable as the *Courant*, which has, to date, outlasted over 40 competitors in Hartford!

The *Courant* took seriously its obligation to present the news in as unbiased a fashion as possible (excluding editorials, of course). It also devoted extensive space to the arts in Hartford as part of its plan to print as diverse a range of news as possible. The fact that the city was a haven for the literary giants of the time heightened its coverage of the arts. To this end, it appointed Charles Dudley Warner, who was a co-owner, editor, and president of the *Courant* from 1867-1900, as its literary editor.

Warner gave up his law practice in Chicago to move to Hartford and assume a job as a newspaper editor. He took up residence in a house on Nook Farm. There, in 1871, he published a whimsical book based on his experiences as an amateur gardener. The book,

My Summer in a Garden, became an instant hit. At the same time, a visiting author named Samuel L. Clemens, better known as Mark Twain, became a hit with Warner. The two struck up a fast friendship.

Twain was in Hartford to finish the proof of his first book, *Innocents Abroad*. Publication was not a sure thing. In fact, the president of the publishing firm did not want to produce the book! Eventually, the firm did publish *Innocents Abroad*, which quickly became the second-best seller of the time. The first was *Uncle Tom's Cabin*, written by Harriet Beecher Stowe. By co-incidence, Stowe owned a home at Nook Farm.

Stowe had a long love affair with the Nook Farm area. Having lived there throughout most of her teen-age years with her sister, Catherine, she decided to build a house in a grove by the Park River. As a young girl, she dreamed of owning her own home in Hartford, but never had the financial means until *Uncle Tom's Cabin* became popular. Even that did not occur over-night.

Stowe's story appeared first in 1851 in a Washington DC-based magazine, the *National Era*. She earned $300 for the work. The story served as a catalyst for fame and fortune. It was not until 1863 that she built her house in Hartford. Her presence no doubt influenced other writers, Clemens among them, to live at Nook Farm.

Clemens, flushed with success and enamored by Hartford, built a house on the river bluff on Farmington Avenue. The front of his quaint house faced Warner's home. There was a well-beaten path between the two houses, since the two were not only friends, but co-authors. Twain really enjoyed his life in Hartford.

He wrote in a November 1, 1876, letter to J. H. Burrough, of Cape Girardeau, Missouri, "I live in the freest corner of the country. There are no social disabilities between me and my democratic personal friends. We break the bread and eat the salt of hospitality freely together and never dream of such a thing as offering impertinent interference in each other's political opinions..." Twain was so happy he tried to buy into the *Courant.* The offer flattered the publishers; they considered it carefully. Finally, for unknown reasons, they turned him down.

Both sides recognized the refusal as a business decision, though, and there were no hard feelings. The *Courant* printed a very warm tribute to Twain on the front page of its April 22, 1910, edition the day after his death. Despite the loss of a chance to be associated closely with the nation's most popular author, the *Courant* continued to flourish.

In 1880, the *Courant* moved into a new building on State Street in Hartford. This was a prelude to upgrading the paper's printing technology. Thirteen years later, the *Courant* installed its first typesetting machines, which ended the era of handset type. Next, in 1896, the *Courant* changed its weekly edition to a "tri-weekly" for country readers who did not wish to take the daily paper.

There occurred another significant milestone for the paper in 1897, when it printed its first editorial cartoon. Certainly, this was a sign that the *Courant* was maturing, but under its own terms and according to its own philosophy. That it was also incorporating the latest innovations and technology available to the newspaper industry whenever it could reflected the publishers' prudent and optimistic management style. As the 1800s drew to a close, the *Courant* was poised to meet the challenges of the 20th century.

WELCOME TO THE 20TH CENTURY

Now that they had a fairly new office complex and publishing plant complete with modern presses, the editors decided to expand their areas of publication, their circulation—and their techniques. One of the paper's initial steps to convert to "state-of-the-art" technology was to publish the paper's first spot news photograph. The *Courant's* managing editor captured a photo of President Theodore Roosevelt hopping off a train in Hartford and printed it in the August 22, 1902, edition. Recognizing the dual historic importance of the event, he assigned an engraver to work throughout the night to surprise readers with the photograph the next morning. The advance of photographic and printing techniques made the photo's publication possible. The *Courant* was quick to respond to another technological revolution—the development of the automobile.

In 1904, the *Courant* published its first automotive section, which included correct dress styles for women riders. There was brief respite from change until 1913, when the paper introduced its first Sunday edition. One year later, it dropped the tri-weekly. Shortly thereafter, the paper's staid approach to presenting the news did a 180-degree turn. The "Old Lady of State Street" took on the appearance of one of today's racier tabloids.

A young managing editor, Emile Gauvreau, who was in his early 20s, decided to change the *Courant's* traditional approach to presenting the news. Under his guidance, the paper focused heavily on crime, sex, and photographs. That era lasted for four years, after which the publishers invited Gauvreau to take his talents elsewhere. He moved to the *New York Evening Graphic* and boosted its circulation to 500,000 with a sensational style that earned the paper the nickname "The New York Evening Porno-Graphic." After Gauvreau's departure, the *Courant* reverted to its conservative approach to the news. One event of note that occurred during the Gauvreau era was the *Courant's* expansion into another media: radio. The paper began operating a radio station, WDAK, in 1922. Perhaps the highlight of its existence was a classic *faux pas* that occurred when then vice president Calvin Coolidge delivered a speech on the station only to discover later that the station was off the air at the time!

In 1928, the *Courant* realized another first, at least in its history. It hired Mary Goodrich, Connecticut's first aviatrix, as the paper's first female reporter. That did not make the paper any more liberal in its approach to the news. With the onset of the "Great Depression," it could not afford to change anyway. Like most of the country, it could not afford much of anything.

WE'LL GIVE YOU FOOD FOR THOUGHT—AND HOW TO BUY FOOD FOR $9 A WEEK

The *Courant* struggled through the depression along with the general population. It did as much as it could to hold the line on subscription prices and ease its readers' financial burdens. For example, it ran a series of articles on "How to Feed Four on $9 a Week" and "Last Minute Market Basket News." It applied the hints in the article to running itself on a limited budget. The paper held the line on costs at 3 cents per daily copy and 10 cents for the Sunday edition. (It was not until 1938 that the price of a daily paper went up to 4 cents.) Together, the *Courant* and its readers survived those trying years, only to be faced with a few more as World War II broke out.

As usual, the *Courant* did best what it had done during wartime since 1776. It simply reported the news and exhorted readers to perform their patriotic duty to aid in the war effort. It also outgrew its State Street headquarters. In 1950, the *Courant* moved to a newer, more spacious facility on Broad Street. The move was necessitated in part by the paper's discovery of the suburbs as a good place to sell papers and the concomitant steady increase in the number of subscribers. Between 1946 and 1964, the paper's 200th birthday, for example, circulation more than doubled, from 52,000 to 130,000. The paper had expanded to 13 news bureaus and more than 100 correspondents calling in local news. The *Courant* had become a regional paper, instead of a local—and that spelled the end of its primary competition.

THE *COURANT'S* GOOD LUCK IS A BAD SIGN FOR THE *TIMES*

For years the *Courant* had competed closely with its cross-town rival *Hartford Times*. During most of the years in which they struggled to gain the upper hand from one another, the *Times* was the circulation winner. Finally, in 1965, one paper became dominant. The *Courant* overtook the *Times* in daily circulation. In 1976, the *Times* went out of business, leaving the

Courant as the only daily newspaper in Hartford. That was good news for the *Courant,* but it also made it extremely attractive to outside buyers.

ANOTHER SIGN OF THE TIMES IS MIRRORED IN THE PURCHASE OF THE *COURANT*

1979 was both a sad milestone and an optimistic harbinger of the future for the *Courant.* That was when 215 years of local ownership ended for the nation's oldest continuously published newspaper. The Los Angeles-based Times Mirror Company paid $215

The Courant: 1963, 1969, 1971 and 1991

Courtesy of The Hartford Courant, Hartford, CT

million for the *Courant.* That caused a lot of local people to wonder whether the paper would survive. Indeed, after the first few years under Times Mirror ownership, even that company's executives had to wonder the same thing.

Times Mirror management changed the *Courant's* historical emphasis on local news to a wide area focus. The paper was replete with regional stories, feature writing, and investigative projects. This did not set well with local activists, who were not shy about making their feelings known.

WE'D RATHER THE *COURANT* NOT HANG AROUND UNDER ITS CURRENT FORMAT—AND WE'LL HANG THE EDITOR TO LET MANAGEMENT KNOW THAT

The activists charged that Times Mirror had abandoned the city. They demonstrated outside the *Courant's* Broad Street headquarters and hung Editor Mark Murphy in effigy. The protests had some effect.

The Hartford Courant, Hartford, CT

Courtesy of The Hartford Courant, Hartford, CT

Murphy left the *Courant.* New editor and publisher Michael J. Davies replaced him and began to make major changes.

Although Davies' arrival was beneficial to the *Courant,* it did not mean the end of the paper's problems. Several suburban dailies took advantage of its troubles in the early 1980s to increase their own subscription numbers. One of the paper's reporters, Andrew Krieg, left his job and wrote a book published in 1987, *Spiked,* which accused Davies and the Times-Mirror organization of deceiving readers in pursuit of a Pulitzer Prize. (To date, the *Courant* never has won this coveted prize.) Despite the attacks, the *Courant* flourished under Davies' guidance.

Davies returned to a local emphasis and restored circulation gradually. (Davies has since moved to Baltimore to become publisher of the *Baltimore Sun.* Two men replaced him: Raymond A. Jansen became publisher and Michael E. Waller assumed the editor's position.) It is not surprising that management paid heed to the public's dissatisfaction with the direction in which the paper was going. After all, as Davies said, part of the reason the *Courant* has gotten to be the country's oldest surviving newspaper is its responsiveness to readers' changing needs. Can management do any less?

Davies placed special emphasis on service to customers. He kept in constant touch with readers through frequent columns and explained what was going on at the paper. Significantly, he did not shy away from admitting that the paper makes mistakes from time to time.

IF WE SEE $1 MILLION BUCKS GO DOWN THE DRAIN, WE'LL FIX THE DRAIN

A classic case of a system gone wrong occurred during 1985. The *Courant* spent $1 million for a computerized circulation system in an effort to take advantage of technological advances to improve its service. As luck would have it, the system, which Davies described as "perhaps the biggest and most sophisticated in the country," was plagued by the inevitable "bugs" inherent to computerized systems. This caused a minor, temporary loss of circulation visible only to the *Courant* management.

Bugs in the system prompted a lot of subscribers to complain to the paper about the poor service they were getting. While the circulation and data processing departments worked feverishly to exterminate the bugs, the number of subscribers declined. Davies explained in the most available medium handy—his paper—what the problems were. The staff managed to correct the automated system and get it to do what it was designed to do. Finally, it had the desired effect. Circulation rates increased to an all-time high 226,000 daily and 300,000+ Sunday subscribers. That was due to service and management's willingness to admit to a mistake and correct it as quickly as possible.

The automated circulation system was just one of the *Courant's* innovations. Others included the introduction of "Northeast," the paper's magazine supplement, in 1982, and state-of-the-art presses in 1986. Management drew national attention to the paper in 1989 by introducing Fax Paper, a one-page news summary published every afternoon to give business executives a sneak peak at tomorrow's news. The *Courant* did not concentrate exclusively on its internal affairs, though. The paper became more involved than ever in local service to the community.

The *Courant* has a proud history of being an active participant in community affairs. Certainly, any company that is not a good "corporate citizen," especially in today's social environment, is doomed to fail. The *Courant's* management had no desire to suffer such a fate.

Historically, the paper helped bring about the creation of a city parks system in Hartford in the 1890s. In the 1940s, it pressed for a reform of the city's government. The new management pledged to continue such involvement.

In 1986, the Times Mirror Company and the *Courant* provided a major leadership grant for the Hartford Courant Center for the Arts, which provides rehearsal and administrative space for the region's leading performing arts organizations. It continued sponsorship of Camp Courant, a free summer day camp for inner-city youths that the paper has sponsored for 80 years. All of this has not gone unnoticed, nor has the quality of the paper itself.

In 1986, the *Courant's* peers voted it the best Sunday paper in New England. That's not quite a Pulitzer Prize, but it's close. There's no telling when the Pulitzer will come, but management is not content with sitting back and waiting for it. Under Times-Mirror ownership, the *Courant* continues to expand and improve.

Consider these statistics. Since 1980, the *Courant's* news staff has increased from 200 to about 350. Its total workforce doubled from about 815 to 1,600. The paper has spent more than $72 million to

51

add new press capacity. Weekday circulation has increased from 215,000 to 228,000. Sunday circulation has jumped from 287,000 to approximately 315,000. There is no doubt that the *Courant* is still growing even after 227 years!

Before he left, Davies stated that "I think the *Courant* has become a trend setter. If you look around the country and say, 'What are the half-dozen newspapers which are innovative, which are on the move?' I think the *Courant* would be among them." Current events lend credibility to that!

The paper has just finished a major expansion project at its Broad Street headquarters and launched a major program of zoned news and advertising. The goal of these moves, Davies explained, is "to secure the *Courant's* future into the next century." If the first 227 years are any indicator of the continued success of the *Courant*, that future is secured, which is no doubt good news for the people in its circulation area.

Chapter 4

1767

Dexter Manufacturing

A COMPANY THAT HAS SUCCESS IN THE BAG

There are few companies in this country that are over 200 years old. One of these, the Dexter Company, based in Windsor Locks, Connecticut, holds a unique record for longevity.

Dexter, founded in 1767, is the oldest manufacturer in continuous existence in the state. It is also the oldest to have the same family ownership, now in the 7th generation. What is particularly interesting is that Dexter has continued success in the bag. After all, it has a virtual monopoly on a product that few other companies make: tea bag paper.

53

To be sure, this Windsor Locks, Connecticut-based company makes more than tea bag paper. In fact, it is a diversified corporation that manufactures a variety of products in six markets: aerospace, automotive, electronics, food packaging, industrial assembly and finishing, and medical. Obviously, Dexter has changed considerably since it opened its doors in 1767 as a clothier. One thing has not: the company's ability to adapt to new markets and fill niches with specialty products. It is this trait more than any other that has been the key to Dexter's success—and which promises to guarantee its future.

DEXTER HAS MORE FIRSTS THAN GEORGE WASHINGTON

George Washington, who was around to buy some of Dexter's products, was reputed to be first in war, first in peace, and first in the hearts of his countrymen. Dexter must have been first in everything else.

Dexter manufactured the first packaged sheets of toilet paper, which was sold initially with a wire loop so it could be hung on a convenient nail or hook. The paper came in two grades: Star Mills™ and Congress Mills™. The latter was the lower priced of the two, as well as the harsher. The company abandoned these products in the 1930s (the history of Procter & Gamble in Chapter 6 may help explain why).

In 1910, Dexter manufactured the first condenser or capacitor paper in the United States. (A capacitor is a device consisting of two or more conducting plates separated from one another by an insulating material and used for storing an electrical charge.) It was designed for use in manufacturing the dry type of condensers or capacitors. The paper was widely accepted until after World War II, when its use declined.

Dexter also introduced the first catalog cover paper. Three cover papers, Princess®, Unique®, and Levant®, were well known throughout the world. Another company first was the so-called electrolytic absorbent capacitor paper. It was even a company first that brought Dexter into the atomic age.

Dexter's technical developments in the late 1950s and early 1960s with micro glass fiber papers led to a request for the company to manufacture a special paper based on this technology. The sales engineer assigned to the project reported that this paper, if it successfully fulfilled all specifications, would be used in all ocean going vessels to the extent of several pounds of paper per ship! That was a lot of paper, and Dexter proved equal to the challenge.

The company developed the paper, called Dexiglas®, and then learned that there was a "small" change in the original market research report. The material would be used only on all atomic powered ocean going vessels. This reduced the projected sales considerably, but the effort was not a total loss. Dexiglas became an integral part of the nation's atomic submarines and was used by various industries. Dexiglas may not have been one of the company's most glamorous firsts, but it was a first nonetheless. It was neither the company's first first nor its last first. It was just one of many firsts in a list that goes on and on. None of them, however, can top a first recorded by Charles H. Dexter.

THIS COMPANY REALLY KNOWS HOW TO FLOAT A LOAN

Every company has apocryphal stories in its history that allegedly illustrates why it has been successful. Dexter has one, too. In Dexter's case, though, the story happens to be true and *does* epitomize the ethical foundation upon which the company is built.

Until December of 1989, all the chief executive officers of the Dexter Corporation were members of the founding family and very active business operators. The first Dexters ran the village grist, saw, and fulling mills. In a linear fashion, each succeeding generation built on the accomplishments of its predecessors. Each new generation invested the business acumen it acquired into strengthening the company—and individual family members' characters. Not surprisingly, then, each succeeding CEO was at least as morally upright as his predecessor. Charles H. Dexter, who became CEO in 1855, typified their integrity and, by extension, the corporation's.

Charles was an active business operator who loved to tinker in the basement of his father's gristmill. He was like a budding scientist with a chemistry set. One of his diversions was to experiment with making paper wrapper from Manila rope in the basement of his father's gristmill. That led to the formation of a partnership in 1847 with his brother-in-law, Edwin Douglas, an engineer who had come to Windsor Locks to superintend the construction of the Enfield Canal. Later, Dexter headed the Connecticut River Company, which provided waterpower for the town and looked after navigation above Hartford, which was (and still is) about eleven miles south.

The Connecticut River is prone to heavy flooding in the spring. It ran particularly high in 1854. The water ran so high that year that land communication with Hartford had been cut off. On May 1, Dexter suddenly remembered he had a note maturing at a Hartford bank. He was not about to let a little water stop him from making that payment.

Dexter chartered a small steamboat to take him downriver. There were few navigational aids available to help the captain steer a course. So, instead of taking the traditional route downstream, he sailed his vessel right up State Street in Hartford, which connected with the river, and moored alongside a drugstore on Front Street. Dexter disembarked, entered the bank, and paid his note on time. Perhaps few other people would have gone to the extremes this man did, but members of the Dexter family always have. The company's history is proof of that.

A COMPANY THAT DRESSES FOR SUCCESS

Dexter traces its roots to Seth Dexter I. Dexter was 22 years old when he established a clothier works in what was then known as Pine Meadows. (Its name changed to Windsor Locks in 1854.) Based on his family's history, it was inevitable that he would open a business of some kind.

The Dexters were an entrepreneurial lot. Thomas Dexter, the first member of the family to arrive in America (he reached the colonies in either 1629 or 1630), was hardly off the boat before he had established profitable business enterprises. His son, William, and his grandson, Benjamin, continued the family's entrepreneurial efforts well into the middle of the 18th century. Benjamin's son, Seth I, who was born in Rochester, Massachusetts, in 1745, merely carried on tradition when he opened his business. Not surprisingly, his son, Seth II, who was also a clothier, joined him eventually in the family business.

The Dexter Company introduced the art of cloth dressing to Pine Meadows. The family members had gained considerable experience in the industry back in Massachusetts. More important, they trained numerous young men in the art of cloth dressing. As America expanded westward, many of the Dexter "graduates" set up businesses in new places. Dexter's influence had quite an impact on the clothing business in the United States. While his influence expanded westward, Seth Dexter I diversified in Pine Meadows.

Seth acquired the interests of a local saw mill in partnership with Jabez Haskell. In 1784, they built a grist mill just below the saw mill. Both fell victim to progress, though. Lumbering diminished in importance in Connecticut, as did grain farming. Dexter and Haskell did not look at the declines in these industries as setbacks. Rather, applying true entrepreneurial spirit, they viewed them as opportunities.

They continued the saw mill operation, which never did turn much of a profit, and turned the grist mill into a feed mill and store. (According to one local historian, the saw mill was operating as late as 1875. Dexter was processing spruce logs and turning them into paper pulp.) Eventually, when neither business was no longer viable (this was in 1928, a long time after Seth and Jabez died), the company razed the mills and established a parking lot!

Seth Dexter I died in 1797 at the age of 52. He left the company in good hands, though. His son, Seth II, took over.

SETH II BECOMES THE SALT OF THE EARTH—AND A SALT VENDOR BESIDES

Seth II was reportedly the richest man in Pine Meadows in 1797. He was worth the princely sum (for the time) of $8,000. He had no intention of squandering his wealth or running the business into the ground. In fact, he branched out a bit. He expanded into the importation of Turk Island salt, which was brought directly by boat to the company warehouse. One of his most important contributions to the family business, though, was his son Charles Haskell Dexter.

C. H. Dexter was born in Pine Meadows in 1810. He inherited the Dexter family's business acumen and tinkering. It was C. H. more than anyone who established the company's commitment to research and development. This commitment, in turn, has helped the Dexter Corporation plan for the future through carefully controlled growth plans. C. H. spent a great deal of his time in the basement of the old Haskell and Dexter grist mill trying to make wrapping paper from Manila rope and "jute manila" from old saltpeter bags from powder mills in nearby Hazardville. His experiments paid off. Young Dexter made a wrapping paper from Manila rope that was so thick "it took a man of some pull to tear it." He did not restrict his tinkering to making paper. He is reputed to be the first person to use lime in the stock he created, which had the effect of killing any germs in the fibres. Obviously, C. H. Dexter was a talented man. Unfortunately, he did not apply his findings commercially at once.

It was not until 1836 that Dexter began to manufacture paper for sale. Even then, it made only 200 pounds a day. It was from that 200 pounds a day of manila wrappers that the company grew steadily into a specialty producer of absorbent and filter papers, including almost all of the porous tea bag papers in the world. A lack of room and power limited production severely, so in 1840 Dexter moved the paper-making equipment into a frame building on the east bank of the Windsor Locks Canal. This move led to a gradual increase in output, but the company was still strapped for space.

In 1847, Dexter built a new mill under the name C. H. Dexter and Company in order to keep up with the demand for its paper products, which were considered among the best available in the industry. More important from a business standpoint, the business turned a considerable profit. C. H. took advantage of his skills to provide the company with more power.

There existed in Windsor Locks (nee Pine Meadows) a power company called the Connecticut River Company, which was an albatross around its shareholders' necks. C. H. became the company's president in 1855; within 14 years, he turned the company into a profitable business. The company became so successful that several new industries moved into Windsor Locks to take advantage of the power created by the Connecticut River Company. That was a boon for the community. However, Dexter's death on August 20, 1869, offset the boon a bit.

Local historian Henry Stiles described C. H. Dexter as one of the most influential people that Windsor Locks had ever known. This was fine praise indeed, since the preceding generations had been extremely civic minded too. As Stiles wrote, "he was of quick and clear apprehension, systematic in business. Hopeful and earnest in all he undertook, responding freely and gladly to calls for help, whether in money or personal services." The community and the business would miss him, but, as his predecessors had done, he left them both in good hands.

C. H. DEXTER IS LAID TO REST, BUT HE LEAVES A SON AND A COFFIN BEHIND

Two years before he died, C. H. took his son Edwin D. and his two sons-in-law, B. R. Allen and Herbert R. Coffin, into the business. He reorganized the company as C. H. Dexter and Sons. Allen left the business quickly. Edwin and Herbert carried on admirably after C. H.'s death.

Coffin, who was born in Boston in 1840, moved with his father to Windsor Locks in 1862. They started a wool scouring business under the name of H. R. Coffin and Company. Five years later, they sold the company. From that point on, Coffin devoted almost all his time to the papermaking business. He did spend some time as president of the Connecticut River Company and a director of the Medlicott Company, which manufactured knit goods.

Coffin and Edwin Dexter took immediate steps to expand the business. They enlarged the paper mill considerably and added a new paper machine and other supplementary equipment. Theirs was an auspicious start—but it soon turned into disaster.

On December 17, 1873, a serious fire almost destroyed the Dexter complex. The company incurred a loss of $80,000, of which insurance covered only $50,000. That did not deter Coffin and Dexter. They ordered the construction of a new mill and leased two more, the Albro and Bennett Mill in Windsor Locks and the Franklin Mill in nearby Suffield, to continue production in the interim.

Once again, Dexter's owners turned a disaster into an opportunity. Not only did they rebuild the plant at considerable expense, but they constructed one described by Stiles as one of the "most complete mills in the country, filled with the latest and best machinery, running entirely on specialties, colored manila, and other novelties of only the finer grades, and with a capacity of five tons a day." The new, up-to-date, brick structure opened in 1875. Dexter pioneered the production of paper pulp from polar wood by the soda process, using lumber floated down the Connecticut River. But, technology caught up with them quickly. After only six years, the soda process became passe and Dexter was ready to expand yet again.

In 1881, Coffin and Dexter built a substantial addition to the mill and added more modern equipment, including one machine that manufactured high-grade white paper and colored French tissue. This marked Dexter's departure into specialties—and set a standard for the future.

Six years later, they added more equipment to increase production. Edwin D. Dexter did not live to see that expansion, however. He died at Saratoga, New York, in 1886. H. R. Coffin assumed full ownership of the property and the business. He continued the company's ambitious expansion program.

For fifteen years after Edwin Dexter's death, Coffin made extensive improvements and extended the company's lines and sales. Then, he died in 1901. His sons, Arthur D. and Herbert R. Coffin II, took over and operated the company as a partnership.

H. R. Coffin's death shocked the residents of Windsor Locks. One person in particular made sure that on the day of his funeral no work took place. The gatetender at the head of the canal on whose banks the Dexter plant stood prevented any water from entering the canal that day. Such was the respect accorded the Dexter family in Windsor Locks.

Herbert R. Coffin's sons were determined to direct the company to greater heights. Arthur was a throwback to W. H. Dexter in that he liked to experiment. In his case, he worked with long-fiber papers. Eventually, Dexter incorporated, Arthur became the company's president, and Herbert became Vice President. The company really came of age under their leadership.

DEXTER LOOKS GOOD ON PAPER—AND PAPER MAKES DEXTER LOOK GOOD

One of their first moves was to acquire the Franklin Mill which they had leased after the 1873 fire and used ever since. The company made significant modifications to the equipment housed in the mill with the purpose of making the highest quality light-weight papers. Subsequently, the Connecticut River Company, which was planning greater power developments that would flood the Suffield mill site, purchased the facility on December 22, 1913. Dexter continued to make paper in the mill for a time. The company did start to dismantle the equipment to move it to Windsor Locks. Strangely enough, a fire destroyed the structure in 1914. It was an ironic end to a building that had been so valuable to the company as a fire replacement.

The Franklin mill aside, Dexter continued to expand the Windsor Locks plant. It added a new boiler plant, production buildings, facilities and equipment, and a new administration building. The next major step was the purchase of the American Writing Paper Company in Manchester, Connecticut, about fifteen miles from Windsor Locks, in 1929. There, Dexter employees conducted extensive experiments and successfully developed long fiber papers. When 1935 rolled around, long fiber paper was a commercial reality and a part of Dexter's line. At that point, the company no longer had a need for the American Writing Paper building. It sold the structure and moved production of the paper to Windsor Locks.

STEEPING TEABAGS AND STEEP PROFITS

The introduction of porous teabags may not carry the same import in some people's minds as the inventions of electricity, radio, lasers, or other significant innovations. At Dexter, however, its impact was tremendous.

David Linwood Coffin, until recently the company Chairman, suggested in 1967 that the introduction of long fiber porous teabags "represents the technical foundation of our present operation to a very large degree." For that reason, the event deserves prominent space in any history of Dexter.

The man who discovered the process of making the paper was not a Dexter. He was Fay Osborne, an M.I.T. graduate who joined the company on October 16, 1922. Osborne, who had a Bachelor of Science degree in Chemical Engineering, had a lifetime fascination with the paper-making process. As a youth in Sunapee, New Hampshire, he spent countless hours at a local plant watching pulp being turned into paper. So, when Dexter offered him employment after he graduated from M. I. T., Osborne accepted readily.

As Osborne recalls, Arthur Coffin was "ahead of his time and saw the advantage of technology." Even though this was the 20th century, not many industry leaders grasped the importance of research in producing innovative products. More often than not, it was the leaders who did that guaranteed themselves long-term success. In 1922, however, technical people in the paper industry were rare. Thus, by hiring Osborne, Dexter received a decided advantage in the development of new products.

Coincidentally, Arthur Coffin's son Dexter had just graduated from Yale. Arthur set up a laboratory beater (a machine which produces paper) that held five pounds of fiber for the young men's convenience. As research facilities go, it was certainly nothing elaborate.

The room in which the beater was contained measured about 10 feet by 10 feet. It contained a small desk, a chair (both of which had been constructed in the plant Carpenter Shop), and the beater. It may not have been much, but, as Osborne said, "I would not have been more thrilled if it had cost a million dollars." Coffin gave Osborne free rein to order equipment. In a short while, Osborne filled the room with the test tubes, beakers, graduate cylinders, chemicals, and other materials needed to conduct quantitative and qualitative analyses. Coffin, ever the pragmatist, suggested to Osborne that he learn the paper-making process from the ground up before he became too deeply involved in his experiments. Osborne followed the suggestion and combined the two activities at a mill hand's salary of only $17.33 a week, which was

$4.67 less than his weekly room and board! Fortunately, his wife got a job as a telephone operator in Hartford to make up the difference. Despite his low pay, Osborne plunged into his work.

Osborne spent the next five years seeking new ways to improve Dexter's paper products or make technological breakthroughs. He had three major advantages at the company. Two had to do with Dexter: he could tap the experience and knowledge of the old-line papermakers employed by Dexter, and utilize the state-of-the art machinery available in the plant. The third was a personal characteristic, and one which separates successful entrepreneurs from those whose efforts more often than not go to waste. That is patience.

Osborne quickly picked up on the cut-throat nature of competition in the papermaking business. During his first five years with Dexter, the company manufactured many special high grade papers it had developed over the years. Among them were high-grade toilet paper (Dexter produced the first packaged sheets of toilet paper), very thin electric condensor tissue, colored wrapping tissue, and wire insulation. As quickly as Dexter placed these products on the market, competitors copied them and cut into its sales. As Osborne remembers, "Competition was so keen and ruthless during this time that our management kept pushing for new products and especially something that could be patented."

There was no doubt that Osborne could do that. He did receive one U.S. patent on anti-tarnish tissue paper during his first five years with the company. Osborne was not a man to rest on his laurels, though. He knew that better things lay ahead for him and the company (which were, in his eyes, one and the same). Osborne applied himself to discover those better things.

ALL THIS FOR A TEABAG?

In 1926, Osborne came across a box of cigars with each cigar wrapped in a very unusual tissue. The long, strong, flexible tissue piqued his curiosity due to its soft, strong, gossamer feel. He did some detailed research into the origin and make-up of the material and discovered that it was made in Japan from a native fiber through what was known as the "hand-made" process. This excited Osborne, but it perplexed him at the same time.

In the "hand-made" process, each small sheet is formed on a handsheet mold, one sheet at a time, instead of being made on a continuous web as on a paper machine. While this results in a sturdy product, it means only a few pounds of tissue can be made in a day by an individual worker. Consequently, the tissue would be very expensive where labor was high—as it was in the United States.

Osborne realized that Dexter would be interested in a product of this type. Further research had shown him that such a product could be used in many applications. He had discovered a similar product, also made in Japan by the "hand-made" process, that was used to make stencils. More important, this type of tissue was used extensively throughout the world. He believed that if these tissues could be made on a paper machine in a continuous web Dexter would have a new, revolutionary product at a reasonable cost—a true competitive edge. Osborne decided to dedicate his efforts in that direction. The company supported him wholeheartedly.

Dexter's management recognized that the combination of the company's practical paper making knowledge and Osborne's technical expertise was extremely valuable. Consequently, it provided him with a new laboratory that contained eight times the floor space of the old one. The lab was part of a new addition to the company's mill. Osborne practically moved into his laboratory.

He wrote, "So with a brand new laboratory and a brand new conception of longer fibered papers, I was more enthused than ever in my work, or I should say my pleasure." He added that there was a catch. "My wife began to wonder if I had married her or the Dexter mill. However, she took it in stride as she knew I was happy even with the long hours." This type of dedication is hard to find in many companies today, but it certainly paid off for Osborne—and Dexter.

Osborne studied the Japanese tissues in detail and arrived at some important basic conclusions regarding fiber length, width, characteristics, and uniformity. Thus began a long period of trial and error as Osborne tried to convert the hand-made process to machines.

Between 1926 and 1928, he analyzed the tissues. He concluded that he would have to find a unique fiber and develop a special process to duplicate the Japanese material. He spent a good part of these two years getting all the available commercial fibers and subjecting them to various digestions. This process discouraged him considerably, since each fiber seemed to lack one or more of the required qualifications, e.g., they had to have the proper length and width, and be rigid, cylindrical, and non-entangling in water. He tried wood, jute, palm, sisal, cotton, pineapple...in short, practically every fiber known to the industry. All had one shortcoming or another. Osborne refused to give up.

There was one sample he tried that held a bit of promise. That was a commercially produced wood pulp called "Super-Sulfite." He isolated the fibers in the product that held the characteristics he wanted. They turned out to be red-stained fibers known as musa textilis, or wild banana, better known as manila hemp. This hemp is grown in the Philippines and used for making rope. This discovery set Osborne off in a flurry of unsuccessful experiments designed to process the fibers into a suitable product.

During 1929 and 1930, Osborne spent a lot of time trying to find out how he could get long fibers of Super-Sulfite dispersed in water without having them entangle when cast upon the wire screen of the handsheet mold. He found a way, but it required the use of 100 times more water as the company used to make their regular slurries (a thin, watery mixture of a fine, insoluble material, as clay cement, soil, etc.) That was an obstacle to making the porous tissue Osborne had in mind—but it was hardly insurmountable.

In 1931, Osborne moved out of the laboratory and into the plant. He obtained a bale of Manila hemp from the Philippines and tried several chemical "cooks" that would dissolve the bond between the individual fibers, without weakening the total fiber package or changing its shape. After several attempts, he found the right combination. All that was left to do was to transfer the process from the handsheet stage to a paper machine that could make a continuous roll. It was not an easy task.

Osborne knew at the outset of this stage that he would have to have long fibers, a lot of water, the right machine—and a new angle on the problem. The fibers and water were the least of Osborne's problems. He had a new angle in theory, but none of the company's regular machines could handle the slurry of the pulp Osborne used. That meant that Dexter would have to build a new one of its own design.

OSBORNE HAS A PREGNANT IDEA—AND IS ABOUT TO GIVE BIRTH

Osborne had a theory that the slurry from which the tissue would be made had to make contact with a wire screen traveling uphill at a rather steep angle. This, he thought, might stop the fibers from rolling into bunches that would result in a poor formation. In order to prove his theory, the company would have to develop an inclined moving wire screen. There was no such machine in house, and it would take years to have one built. If it is true that necessity is indeed the mother of invention, Osborne was about to give birth with the help of the mill's mechanics. Together, they worked with Osborne and constructed a machine that met his specifications. It was back to the drawing board—and the laboratory—for Osborne.

Osborne decided to build the machine in his laboratory. After several months of work, the mechanics completed Osborne's machine, which was 20 feet in length with a pitch of 20 degrees on the wire screen. (It is interesting to note that the machine would not even have fit into Osborne's old laboratory!) Within the first ten minutes of its operation, Osborne realized that he had what he wanted. It had taken seven years to reach this point, but he "was sure now that it was possible to produce this new type product in a continuous web." Osborne and Dexter were about to make their mark on the world—and assure that the company would find a unique niche in which to operate.

As so often happens in the business world, luck stepped in and played its role. Osborne had been conducting his research at a time when Dexter was a bit strapped financially. It was the time of the "Great Depression." The Manchester plant Dexter had purchased in 1929 had been idled for lack of orders of carbonizing papers. There was a small paper machine there that seemed ideal for Osborne's experiments. Dexter's executives decided this would be ideal for his purposes, as it would not have any impact on the company's production in Windsor Locks. They gave Osborne their blessing.

Dexter had no drafting department at the time, so Osborne gave Chester Reed and his mechanics a rough sketch of the way he wanted the machine converted. It took considerable time and $15,000 (which Osborne estimated would have cost $15 million in 1975) to complete the job, but complete it they did. After the first trial run, Osborne had to wonder if the time and effort were not wasted.

The first experiments failed. The fibers did not form a sheet on the wire as they had on Osborne's experimental machine. As Osborne described the day, "They just rolled into bunches without going up the wire. It looked like a complete failure. This was probably the low point of my whole business career." Osborne would not quit, though. He simply applied some thought to the problem—and came up with the solution in a very short time.

Osborne traced the problem to the fact that the wire screen had been inactive so long it picked up a waxy coating that prevented water from flowing freely through it. They (Osborne was always careful to attribute part of his success to anyone who helped him) shut off the slurry, scoured the wire screen with acid, steamed it with a high pressure steam hose for about two hours, and then turned the machine back on. SUCCESS!

The slurry formed a sheet on the wire screen and went up the wire with no rolling back, just as it had done on the laboratory machine. There were still a couple of minor problems to iron out, but basically Osborne was pleased. As he said, "I was sure at this point that we were on the road to where we wanted to go."

THE POROUS PAPER BECOMES A COMMERCIAL SUCCESS

By the winter of 1934, Osborne was ready for limited commercial runs ranging from 100-400 pounds of the paper. He decided to use a mixture of super-sulfite pulp and Manila hemp. The paper looked peculiar and had unusual characteristics, but it was a viable product, and that was all Osborne wanted.

Osborne personally visited International Silver Company in Meriden, Connecticut, to sell his new paper. The company ordered several hundred pounds of the new paper in which to wrap some very high grade silverware. The product pleased International Silver, which submitted *immediate* repeat orders. Not only did this enhance Dexter's revenues at a time when business needed a boost, but it gave the company a chance to gain experience in producing the new paper.

Buoyed by his initial success, Osborne visited Cornell Dubilier in New York City. It, too, ordered several hundred pounds of the paper to use in winding its electrolytic condensers. Like International Silver, Cornell Dubilier submitted repeat orders in rapidly increasing quantities. Quickly, the experimental machine became a production machine—and it was running full time on the daytime shift. Unfortunately, the Manchester plant was less than ideal for full-scale production of the paper.

The winter of 1934 was unusually cold. As the plant had been closed for some time prior to Osborne's takeover, the heating system had deteriorated to the point where it shut down. Luckily, Osborne did have live steam to dry the paper, but that was about the extent of the heat in the building. As Osborne recalls, "We had a couple pails of water which we kept warm with a live steam hose and when our hands got cold, which was very often, we would immerse them in these pails of water." Warming hands was about all the experience some of the mill workers had!

Dexter did not want to interrupt its main production lines in Windsor Locks, so the people they assigned to Manchester were inexperienced. Osborne had a carpenter fire the boiler and start the steam engine used for power. His instructions were "to start the fire, shovel on the coal, and keep water in the boiler." Osborne became a machine tender, even though he had no experience. One of his laboratory assistants fed the beater, which processed the pulp into paper. It was certainly a watered-down crew. Nevertheless, it beat the water system in the plant.

Due to the plant's age, and the fact that Dexter did not plan to use it for long, the water filter system had become unusable. It was so bad that small fish would occasionally come up on the wire screen along with the fibers! Workers had to pick dirt, leaves, paper scraps, and many other forms of trash off the wire by hand. Life was pretty difficult for Osborne and his crew, particularly because they worked up to 14 1/2 hours a day.

They would leave Windsor Locks at 5:30 a.m., drive to Manchester, build the fire in the steam boiler, furnish the beater, and get the stock into the paper machine about 9 a.m. (if they were lucky). They would generally complete their production about 7 p.m., get back to Windsor Locks around 8 p.m., eat quickly, and go to bed. That did not seem to bother Osborne, nor did it dampen his enthusiasm towards his employer. He expressed his loyalty by saying, "These were long days but well worth it as we were sure we had a good thing going for Dexter." That good thing would not last forever.

OSBORNE'S DEPRESSION IS DUE TO THE COUNTRY'S DEPRESSION

Osborne applied for two patents based on his successful work with the new paper. One was on the process; the other was on the article. Using foresight, Osborne applied for patents in a number of foreign countries, including England, as well.

Osborne continued to experiment with the paper. By 1935, he had in place the process and equipment to produce paper using 100 percent Manila hemp. The next step was to move the process to Windsor Locks.

Dexter decided to convert one of its machines at Windsor Locks to produce the new paper. Working conditions were a lot better there and the product was more uniform and a lot cleaner. This was important, because word was getting around that Dexter had some new products that customers had already purchased and found to their liking. Every order gave Dexter more experience in producing larger and better quantities of the paper. Soon, the one converted machine could no longer handle the workload.

Osborne received good news in 1936. His U. S. patents on long fiber paper had been granted, which meant that the foreign patents probably would be too. Then, the Depression struck.

Business problems were besetting Dexter. Orders on regular grades of paper had fallen to such a low that the company was lucky to be operating three days a week. Dexter had trouble meeting its payroll, in fact. Many times Dexter had to borrow money to pay its employees. All the company's officers cut their salaries to the point where they could just survive. Even this was not enough.

Dexter's bankers called a meeting at which they announced the company could only receive their help for two months more. After that, they said, the company would be out of business. The managers had come too far with the company to let that happen. That's where the patents came in handy. At the bankers' meeting, Osborne had asked the bank president whether he felt that the patents could be used to extend the loans further. He said no. Hopefully, he was a better banker than a judge of the worth of patents.

ENGLAND STARTS ANOTHER REVOLUTION—AND THIS TIME BOTH SIDES WIN

The Crompton Paper Company in England heard about Dexter's new long fiber papers and expressed an interest in the English patent. In response, Dexter Coffin and the company's patent attorney, Ted Lindsey, visited England to talk with Crompton officials about selling the patents. Their mission was a success! They sold the patents for between $80,000 and $100,000. This re-established Dexter's credit at the bank and kept the mill running. The company began at once to push the new long fiber line. The money also helped offset the results of another disaster.

The devastating Hurricane of 1938 blew through Windsor Locks—and almost blew it away. Flooding connected with the storm covered the main floors of the mill and power house with six feet of water. This ended production for several weeks and necessitated a very expensive clean-up, which was funded in part by the Crompton money. Dexter bounced back nicely from its adversities, though. The next flood to hit the company was one of new products.

THIS IS ONE FLOOD THAT NO ONE WANTS TO STOP

Actually, the flood began as a trickle in 1937 when Dexter began developing and selling papers for uses that it had never sold before. Among them were greeting cards, vacuum bags, lens tissues, model airplanes, diapers, coffee filters, and teabags. Customers clamored for Dexter's paper products, and the company was happy to oblige.

Osborne worked personally with many vendors to develop new products. He worked closely with the Chicago-based Visking Corporation to develop a new meat casing to replace the traditional animal gut. The companies entered a joint venture to develop such a meat casing. Their initial efforts met with nothing but failure. That was something that did not faze Osborne. After numerous tries, Dexter and Visking finally produced a paper that could be used to enclose meat. From there, it was a simple step to making teabags.

In 1938, when Osborne turned his attention to teabags, very few people used individual bags. The preferred medium was cotton gauze. Not only was it expensive, but the tea generally tasted like cotton. One way to eliminate this problem was to use expensive grades of tea, which would not break up into tiny particles and settle on the bottom of the cup. This put tea out of a lot of people's price range. The cotton gauze bags were also very difficult to stitch.

As soon as they heard about Dexter's new paper, many tea manufacturers approached the company to see if it could be used to make teabags. Osborne investigated the matter. His finding was simple: it could. Osborne produced several sample rolls of teabags for them. They allowed for an improved taste, fewer tea leaves in water, easier packaging—and they were much more economical besides. The tea manufacturers switched to Dexter's teabags almost overnight! That marked a milestone for Dexter. In fact, over fifty years later, teabags still play an important role in Dexter's business!

IF THE PLANT EXPANDS ANYMORE, WE'LL HAVE TO BUILD A NEW TOWN

The demand for products soon outstripped the company's manufacturing capacity. Dexter had to purchase two used machines from other companies to meet the demand. (It could not afford new ones, since the effects of the Depression continued to limit revenues.) That gave the company a total of six paper-producing machines. Three made an old type of short fibered paper; the others made the new long fiber products. By 1940, Osborne's long fiber products began pushing out the old ones completely.

By the time World War II started, all six machines were producing long fiber paper and the company was back on solid financial footing. The most significant factor in its increased business lay in the fact that in its production of long fiber paper Dexter dominated a virtually non-competitive field. The onset of the war brought with it a new threat, however.

Since Osborne had made the decision to produce the new paper from 100 percent Manila hemp, the war could disrupt supplies of the raw material. Dexter circumvented this problem by stockpiling all the hemp it could. By mid-summer 1941 every available warehouse in the Windsor Locks area contained Manila hemp. Dexter's management was pleased—until the government informed them they could neither buy any more hemp nor use what they had on hand, since it was all earmarked for military use. That touched off a sudden search for a substitute. Who better to find it than Fay Osborne?

THERE'S NO SUBSTITUTE FOR EXPERIENCE—OR MANILA HEMP

Osborne began with natural fibers. He could not find one that worked as well as Manila hemp. As he said in 1941, "I just about concluded that there just was not a fiber in the world that would do our job." As usual, that did not stop him from looking. He kept up the search to no avail. Just how correct he was became evident in 1975, when he reiterated his statement. "Now, 34 years later, I still am of the same opinion." However, the search did not include manmade fibers.

Osborne obtained some rayon from the American Viscose Corporation. He worked with rayon because it was the cheapest of the manmade fibers. Even they did not work well in making paper. Osborne did use small percentages of rayon in some of his paper grades. The value in the experiments did not come through until after the war. Dexter's technicians learned a great deal about synthetics while searching for a Manila hemp substitute. They applied what they learned after the war ended. It made Dexter one of the first paper manufacturers in the country to use synthetics in making paper. As history has shown, being among the first was not new for Dexter then—and it is not now.

Another substitute that Dexter used was old rope. After all, most of it was made from Manila hemp in the first place. All Dexter had to do was extract the oil from the material, which constituted about 20 percent of the rope. The company would send bales weighing as much as 600 pounds to dry cleaners to have the oil removed. The process was not 100 percent effective,

since the cleaning could not remove all the dirt in the old rope. The resulting paper was of a lesser grade than Dexter liked to produce, but it was war time, so customers were happy to get any paper they could.

Dexter had just about reached the end of its rope literally when the war ended. Ironically, just before that time, Dexter did find a suitable alternative to Manila hemp in Costa Rica. Osborne felt that it would have been a satisfactory substitute, but once the war ended, the supply of genuine Manila hemp resumed. The company returned to its normal operations—and a "new, improved" teabag.

PUTTING THE HEAT ON A NEW TEABAG

During the war, tea makers asked Dexter to develop a new teabag which could be sealed by a heat-seal rather than stitching. Osborne began his search for such a product in 1943. As usual, it took a lot of trial and error, but he succeeded. The first effort was only a partial solution. It involved spraying a chemical on one side of the paper via spray guns and drying it before it penetrated all the way through. That did not work. First, the spray guns clogged incessantly. Worse, some of the solvent remained in the bag and altered the taste of the tea. That did not suit tea makers or tea drinkers to the proverbial "tee." The next attempt in 1944 was more successful.

Osborne learned about a product called VINYON®️ fiber, which was produced by the American Viscose Corporation in continuous filaments. He ordered enough for a trial run.

Osborne conducted a few experiments that only other scientists would understand and came up with a viable teabag that could be heatsealed. Dexter applied for a patent on the method in 1944; the company received it three years later. This marked a major step forward in the production of teabags.

About the time Dexter received the patent, Osborne and his staff found another method that was more suitable to the new process. This involved a resin made by the American Cyanamid Corporation. The use of the resin eliminated a separate treating process applied after the paper was made. The new process was more economical, which is always welcome news to any manufacturer. It was especially pleasing to Dexter at this point in its existence.

Between 1947 and 1952, Dexter concentrated on restoring the quality in its products that had been affected by World War II. It also developed more new products such as glass fiber webs, interliners for clothing, hospital products, and automobile oil filter media. Naturally, the company needed more machinery to meet production demands. This time, it invested in new, rather than used, machines.

Dexter purchased two new, faster, wider machines capable of increasing production dramatically. As history shows, installing new machines was a classic case of the tail chasing the dog. No sooner did the new machinery come on line than Osborne discovered new ways of making material that required the latest technology to produce. He became involved in making better use of manmade fibers. Once again, he received a patent that would be helpful to Dexter in the years ahead.

In 1949, Osborne was granted a patent for synthetic fiber paper. Patent in hand, he continued the search for the ultimate manmade fiber. A new teabag crisis interrupted his quest.

THE GREAT HEATSEAL TEABAG CRISIS OF 1954

While the world recovered from the effects of the Korean Conflict, Dexter had a battle of its own. Tea manufacturers never stopped pestering Osborne to come up with a better product. They cited in particular a slight aftertaste that melamine resin, the product that gave teabags their wet strength, left in drinkers' mouths. This prompted Dexter to switch from melamine resin to aminoplast. Allegedly, it provided ample wet strength without the aftertaste. Osborne sent a few samples of the new product to tea makers, all of whom changed over to the new process. By June of 1954, they were sorry they did.

DEXTER IS LEFT HOLDING THE BAG

Complaints started rolling into Dexter from manufacturers and consumers that teabags were falling apart in their tea cups. This puzzled Osborne, because tests had not indicated any problem with the aminoplast. The new teabags had been on the market since the previous December. Osborne could not understand what happened between then and June. Suddenly, the cause dawned on him! It was the humidity.

A "crash investigation," as Osborne described it, showed that aminoplast was very sensitive to high humidity. Having learned that, Osborne switched back immediately to melamine resin. That hardly resolved

the problem, though. Dexter still had a large inventory of the aminoplast teabags at its mill and in the tea makers' warehouses—and millions of teabags on store shelves.

Here was a big test of consumer faith in Dexter's products. Ordinarily, most people could not identify who makes teabags. They don't even care as long as the tea tastes good. In 1954, they learned.

Newspapers picked up on the "teabag crisis." It was the most publicity tea had received since the famous party in Boston back in 1773, when Dexter was only six years old! One editorial in particular bore the headline, "Vot's da matter mit da teabags." (That's a headline no newspaper could get away with today!) As Osborne reacted in a classic understatement, "This is one editorial we could have done without."

It was a foregone conclusion that Dexter would sustain a tremendous financial loss from scrapping thousands of pounds of the aminoplast teabag paper. Its major concern, however, was how the situation would affect the company's relationship with tea makers and the public. Based on the trust that customers had developed in the company over the years, Dexter had nothing to worry about.

Every tea maker recalled all the defective bags it could isolate, tore the tea out, and scrapped the paper. This caused the tea manufacturers to lose money, too. Not surprisingly, they could not recall all the affected teabags, so customers continued to complain. Nonetheless, the tea makers were very cooperative and their relationships with Dexter did not change. Dexter weathered the great teabag crisis—and continued to grow. It had to do so without Fay Osborne, though: he retired in 1960 after 38 years of valuable service. Osborne ended his career at Dexter as a Vice President & Technical Director and director of the corporation. He may not have been a Dexter or a Coffin, but he will certainly rank as one of the most important figures who ever contributed to the company's success.

OSBORNE MAY HAVE WORKED IN MYSTERIOUS WAYS, BUT HE DID NOT WORK ALONE

Not all the activity at Dexter during the Osborne era centered around him. Dexter D. Coffin, Sr., who took over the company presidency in 1936, worked tirelessly to expand the company.

Many of his accomplishments have been detailed in the preceding pages, since he and Osborne worked closely together. There were some changes, though, that were not connected to Dexter's long fiber paper business.

One of Dexter's boldest moves took place in the mid 1950s, when the company decided for the first time to accelerate its growth through diversification and acquisition. In 1958, it acquired the assets of Standard Insulation Company, of East Rutherford, New Jersey, which produced laminates, pre-impregnated products, and closure materials. A few years later, Dexter concluded that this business did not fit its long-range plans, so the company divested itself of the operation. This marked a move to a policy of acquiring geographical specialty formulators of industrial finishes—and a spate of activity.

Dexter's introduction to the specialty chemical business came on July 1, 1961, when it acquired a chemical coatings company based in Rocky Hill, Connecticut. Next, it purchased the Lacquer Products Company Division, of Cleveland, Ohio, on May 1,

1962. A year and a half later, on November 1, 1963, Dexter acquired what was then its largest addition, Midland Industrial Finishes Company Division, Waukegan, Illinois. The new purchases led to two divisions: C. H. Dexter and Sons, manufacturers of industrial papers and webs, and the acquisitions, which formed a product finishes and adhesives group. These moves began a trend toward acquisition, divestment, and growth that characterized the 1970s and 80s, and continues today.

In recent, years, Dexter has restructured its operations in an attempt to drop weak performers and develop its strengths. For example, it sold its carbon fiber business in 1989, even though it has a huge growth potential. Company president K. Grahame Walker, the first non-family member to become CEO of the company (he assumed his post in April, 1989), explained that "We got out of carbon fiber because it will take a lot longer for these materials to be used extensively in aerospace." He added that "We saw this as a game for companies with very deep pockets." Nonetheless, Dexter remained in the lucrative aerospace market with a structural glue that binds composite material together. Obviously, company management picks and chooses its spots wisely.

In July 1990, Dexter purchased a sealants business from CIBA Geigy Corporation. A month later, it signed a letter of intent to buy Moore Plastics of Cleveland, Ohio, a privately held maker of sealants used primarily in the automotive industry. The latter purchase represents an extension of Dexter's business in engineered adhesives, coatings, and sealants. The company expects the two acquisitions to complement one another. More important, they signal Dexter's commitment to expansion. As further proof, Dexter has even taken a page out of professional sports general managers' books and pulled a trade!

On August 21, 1990, Dexter announced it had exchanged its Mogul Water Management Systems-Europe operations for W. R. Grace's mold release business in Heidelberg, West Germany. Under the agreement, Dexter would receive some cash and an unspecified capital gain. Such trades may not be common in the business world, but companies seeking to improve their positions in certain industries will complete them if they are beneficial. Dexter's management has always had a keen insight into what's good for the company, so the fact that it should engage in uncommon practices should not come as a surprise to anyone. That is in keeping with Dexter's business philosophy of aiming at high profits by choosing markets with high growth potential.

A perfect example of the company's approach to profitability is its technology that coats the inside of extremely thin modern two-piece tin cans. The technology is superior because it covers 100 percent of the cans, whereas competitors' spotting process may be inconsistent. In order to sell this process, Dexter will invest in building coating operations near plants that make tin cans. As Walker explained, "We follow our customers where they set up plants to make tin cans."

Projects like that may boggle some people's minds, but not those of Dexter's faithful "fans" and shareholders. The people who are familiar with Dexter's history are well aware that management has traditionally made wise business decisions. Otherwise, the company would not have existed in the same place for well over 200 years—as it might just well do for another 200 or more.

The people of Windsor Locks have grown used to Dexter's presence. Apparently, the company has grown used to being there. In the late 1960s, management reaffirmed its commitment to Windsor Locks and growth by breaking ground for the largest single expansion in the company's history. The company installed yet another state-of-the-art paper machine, its fourth such addition since 1955, and constructed a large finished goods warehouse. Management also made it clear that it was not tied exclusively to one location.

Concurrent with the Windsor Locks expansion, Dexter started construction of new technical and expanded warehouse facilities at the Midland Industrial Finishes Company in Waukegan. At the same time, ground breaking took place in Hayward, California, for a product finishes and adhesives plant to be called Dexter-Midland Company. That was about as far west as Dexter could go. The next step was international expansion. That came soon enough.

Dexter opened a wholly-owned sales subsidiary in Brussels to market its products. Today, it operates about 50 properties in the United States and foreign countries, including West Germany, the United Kingdom, France, and Singapore. There is more European expansion in the future. Walker believes that European unification is a major opportunity for Dexter. As he observes, "Unification drives our opportunity, and if Dexter is not positioned for it, we won't take part in the growth." It is Walker's job to make sure the company is positioned correctly. That is why he is preparing for the 21st century now—and why Dexter continues to grow even though it has been in business well over 200 years. That is an enviable record. Why has the company been so successful?

IT MAY BE AN OLD COMPANY, BUT ITS EXECUTIVES ARE YOUNG

David L. Coffin has studied the history of the Dexter Corporation in minute detail. He attributes its success to two primary factors: heavy emphasis and dependence on research and development and young leadership. The latter is a bit surprising to students of business, and, as will be seen in ensuing chapters, runs contrary to what most successful companies have done. More often than not, businesses prefer to cultivate their CEOs over long periods of time. Yet, when David L. Coffin took over the company from his father in 1958, he was only 32 years old. That may sound young, but he was the third oldest man to assume the company's presidency!

Seth Dexter I, founded the company at age 22. His son, Seth II, took over at age 20. Charles H. Dexter became president at age 31. Then came the Coffins.

Herbert R. was only 29 when he assumed the presidency. Arthur D. was 33, and Dexter D. Coffin, Sr., was 38. These seven men averaged 29 years of age upon becoming president. That may not be the ideal age for CEOs in many companies, but it has worked for The Dexter Corporation—and no doubt it will continue to do so. There may be some changes, as Walker says "Dexter in the 1990s will be less about history and more about survival." Based on the company's past performance, it will no doubt survive, write more history—and continue to hold success in the bag.

Chapter 5

1835

Huntington's Book Store

THEY'LL BE HERE A LONG TIME: YOU CAN MAKE BOOK ON THAT

Huntington's is purportedly the oldest continually operating bookstore in the United States. Whether or not that is true is a matter of semantics. Cokesbury's, a bookstore in Cincinnati, has been in business since 1820. However, it opened as a "bookroom," rather than a bookstore.

Cokesbury's was a part of the Methodist printing house (currently known as the United Methodist Publishing House, based in Nashville, Tennessee) founded in Philadelphia in 1789. Folks in Cincinnati would drop into Cokesbury's to peruse the publications there. If they saw something they wished to purchase, they could. So, technically, although the proprietors called the shop a "bookroom," it was a retail store. And, 170 years or so later, it still is! Whether it is older than Huntington's is a moot point. Both stores have rich—and long—pasts. Semantics aside, they both deserve credit for surviving as long as they have, regardless of which is oldest.

The irony with Huntington's is that the store is no longer owned by anyone named Huntington. In fact, it was 125 years old before it assumed that name! The store has operated under a succession of owners over the years, but is has been a Hartford landmark no matter what its official name has been at any given time.

Names aside, Huntington's has been in business under some moniker since 1835, and promises to continue operating as long as there are books to be sold. It has been a virtual "hand me down" operation over the years, passing from the hands of one dedicated owner to another. For the most part, the owners had no connection other than their love for books and the literary world in general. Their love has kept Huntington's going for more than 150 years—and is the major reason it has survived.

Huntington's opened for business in 1835 as Packard & Brown. Caleb Packard, who had come to Hartford from Bridgewater, Massachusetts, in 1817, and Flavius Brown, a transplant from nearby Hebron, Connecticut, purchased the H. F. Sumner Company, which had been established in 1830. Packard and Brown bought the business "for the sale and publication of books." Local residents described the store as a dark and tiny hole in the wall, lighted evenings until nine o'clock or later by whale oil lamps. However it was illuminated, it sparked the light of knowledge in Hartford, which has not been extinguished in the city to this day.

Packard and Brown did not remain in business very long. Packard retired from the book business in 1838. Brown joined forces with Edward W. Parsons, who arrived in Hartford via Amherst, Massachusetts and Troy, New York. Their store, Brown & Parsons, remained in business until 1852.

Brown and Parsons added a new wrinkle to the store's services. They published several books of regional interest or by local authors. Consequently, Hartford's literary notables began patronizing the store almost exclusively. They spent so much time there it almost became their regular meeting place! Their presence attracted national and international authors, which further increased the store's image and sales.

Charles Dickens visited Hartford in 1842. Dickens' visit sparked a huge increase in the sale of two of his books, *Pickwick* and *Oliver Twist*. Brown and Parsons were astute enough to capitalize on the sales. They advertised that they "have always on hand a large assortment of School, Classical, Theological, Medical, Law and Miscellaneous Books." Their innovative sales technique paid off. Business grew so much that the owners expanded their operation by purchasing a competitor, the John Paine firm. Their business continued to grow.

Brown and Parsons had a flair for drawing attention to their store. In 1846 they moved to Main and Asylum Streets in downtown Hartford to capitalize on the central location. They also added the first show windows in town. Business remained brisk, but not enough to suit Edward Parsons. He retired from the book business in 1852 and left Brown to run the store himself until 1858.

Brown acquired a new partner, William H. Gross, in 1858. Gross had thorough training in the book business. He had served an apprenticeship with the William J. Hammersley bookstore in Hartford, followed by several years with the A. S. Barnes publishing house in New York. His expertise, combined with Brown's experience, led to unprecedented success.

Brown and Gross carried a variety of books for Hartford's ever-growing population. They concentrated on classics and books by local authors, but customers could find almost anything they wanted at the store. During the Civil War, for example, they sold large numbers of infantry and cavalry tactics books to Union soldiers. During the war, late in 1864, Brown and Gross hired a 12-year-old assistant, Leverett Belknap, as a handyman. His tasks included opening the store at seven a.m. every day, pulling up the shutters, removing cloths from the counters, sweeping the floors, washing the windows, and locking the shop every night at nine. He must have liked his job, for he stuck around a long time. In 1891, 27 years after he joined the firm, he became George F. Warfield's partner in the store's ownership.

The store served many purposes during the tenures of Brown and Gross. It was a waiting room for trolley passengers, a ticket office for theater and sporting events, and a meeting place for famous persons. Abraham Lincoln dropped in to the store on March 6, 1860, where he met Gideon Welles, a resident of nearby Glastonbury. They talked for a long while about national politics. Welles must have impressed Lincoln. After he became president, Lincoln appointed Welles to his cabinet as Secretary of the Navy.

Mark Twain was a frequent visitor to the store. He bought books such as August Rodney Macdonough's translation of *The Lovers of Provence, Aucassin and Nicolette,* Craig Knox' *The Little Folks' History of England,* and Sidney Lanier's edition of *The Boy's King Arthur,* in addition to several reference books. Twain developed a close working relationship with Gross and Brown. That relationship received a serious blow when Flavius Brown died in February of 1880. Gross purchased Brown's share of the business and associated himself with Leverett Belknap as a partner. They retained the name of Brown and Gross until 1891, when Gross died. Belknap then changed the name of the store to Belknap & Warfield to honor his new partner, George F. Warfield.

Warfield had worked for Gross and Brown since 1884. He became a partner in 1890, so the addition of his name to the store's marquee did not come as a surprise to anyone. Belknap and Warfield continued to run the business as had their predecessors—successfully.

History repeated itself in 1903. Belknap hired a 13-year-old boy, Israel Witkower, a native of Vienna, Austria, as an assistant. Seven years later, Belknap retired from the bookstore after 46 years in the business. As usual, there was someone to carry on the business.

Warfield purchased Belknap's portion of the business and carried on under his own name until 1929. He did take on a new partner in 1920, though: young

Witkower. And who became the new owner after War-field's resignation effective January 1, 1929? Israel Witkower.

One of Witkower's first moves was to declare that there would be "no changes in management, policy or personnel, the same clerks and the same business policies being maintained." Witkower did make some major changes, though. He added a circulating li-brary, a greeting card department, an Old Book Bar-gain Basement, and a mart for old and rare books. He instituted many of these new moves to help the store survive the "Great Depression," which it did.

Over the years, the name of the store changed, but its role as a meeting place for local citizens and na-tional and international luminaries did not. Celebri-ties continued to visit and local people continued to patronize the store. Witkower built the business to new heights during his 31 years as owner. He had had enough by 1960, though, so he retired after what amounted to a lifetime with the bookstore. Witkower sold the store to Trumbull Huntington, whose name it still bears. In doing so, he set a precedent.

Trumbull Huntington had no previous connection with the bookstore. Historically, each succeeding owner had practically grown up in and around the place. That was not the case with Huntington. How-ever, this proved to be nothing more than a brief dis-ruption in the chain.

One of Huntington's first employees was Isaac Ep-stein, who began working at the store in 1960. Eight-een years later, Epstein bought the place! He in turn introduced his son David to the business. David is now operating the store, which continues in business as Huntington's.

David Epstein says he has no plans to change the name of the store. "People have known the business as Huntington's for 30 years," he explains. "The store has an excellent reputation for service, commitment to local writers, and the promotion of literature in general. I see no reason to change it."

Young Epstein's analysis of the store's reputation in the community capsulizes its history. The store has served Hartford well for over a century and a half, and promises to do so for a long time to come. Civilization may have changed since the store first opened its doors back in 1835, but Huntington's reputation for service has not. It is this reputation that has kept the store's doors open, and as long as there are books to be published and authors to write them, Huntington's will most likely keep them that way.

Chapter 6

OHIO

●Cincinnati

1837

Procter & Gamble

A PROCTER TAKES A GAMBLE—AND A SUCCESS IS BORN

Cincinnati, facetiously called "Porkopolis," was a rapidly growing, thriving river city in the early 1800s. Industries such as shipbuilders, breweries, and packing houses dominated the local economy. Since the packing houses drew most of the attention, people began calling the community "Porkopolis." The name became synonymous with Cincinnati—as did the names William Procter and James Gamble.

Procter and Gamble signed a partnership agreement on October 31, 1837. No doubt neither of these serious-minded, stolid businessmen assigned any significance to the fact that it was Halloween Day. (That's not surprising. Halloween was not a major event back in the early 1800s.) To them, masks, costumes, and disguises would have been totally inappropriate for businessmen. In their minds, October 31 was simply a business day on which they formed a company. They had no idea of how that company would grow, but there is no disguising the business impact Procter & Gamble has had as a successful corporate entity—and as a model for other businesses to follow.

To be sure, Procter and Gamble were not strangers to one another. In fact, they were brothers-in-law with similar goals, talents, and foresight. They had been working together long before their partnership became official. The documents they signed on October 31 were merely technicalities in the partners' minds. They were men of action who did not wait for the formality of signing papers to make their company a reality. They took the pigs they would rely on so heavily by the snouts and got right down to business.

For example, in anticipation of the legalities of forming the business, Gamble contacted a chemist in Philadelphia to seek the latest information on soap and candlemaking. Together, Procter and Gamble purchased for $1,000 on June 22, 1837 a tract of land adjoining the Miami-Erie Canal. There can be no doubt that they shared a belief in a successful future for their company. As history and Barney Krieger have proved, their optimism was warranted.

WHO IN THE HELL WAS BARNEY KRIEGER?

Perhaps the name Barney Krieger has no importance in Cincinnati business circles today. Maybe it didn't in 1837, either. Yet, in a way, Barney Krieger and the thousands of his little known counterparts who have worked at P&G over the years epitomize the company's success.

Barney Krieger was P&G's first employee. He worked for the company 47 years. In so doing, he set a precedent for longevity that has lasted to this day and explains in part why the company has survived so long.

Procter and Gamble believed fully that the success of their business was inextricably entwined with their employees. This theme has been constant throughout the company's history. As former company president Richard Deupree said:

> If you leave us our money, our buildings, and our brands, but take away our people, the company will fail. But if you take away our money, our buildings, and our brands, but leave us all our people, we can rebuild the whole thing in a decade.

That statement summed up Procter & Gamble's philosophy regarding the value of people—and the primary reason for their phenomenal success as a corporation as well. Surely neither Procter nor Gamble guessed in 1837 that the company they started would become one of the world's largest corporations. These two men merely saw a business niche they could fill. The rest is history.

HOW TO SUCCEED BY SOFT SOAPING THE PUBLIC

There were 18 soap and candle makers in Cincinnati in 1837. That did not faze Procter or Gamble. They believed there was room for one more, especially one that could produce superior products. Based on their belief, the two scraped together $7,192.24 to open number 19. Getting the money was by no means easy. Neither partner had a lot of personal assets and the country in general was flirting with bankruptcy. Their personal lack of funds and the poor timing of the incorporation (the country was imbedded deeply in the "Panic of 1837" at the time) did not scare Procter and Gamble any more than did the number of competitors. They confronted the odds, took a chance—and won.

P&G began slowly. The company derived the bulk of its income at first from candles. Soapmaking and other products took on secondary importance in the company's early years.

An add in the June 29, 1838, *Cincinnati Gazette* announced:

Oils for lamps and machinery. A fine article of clarified Pig's Foot Oil, equal to sperm, at a low price and in quantities to suit buyers. Neat's Foot oil ditto. Also No. 1 & 2 soap. Palm and shaving ditto. For sale by Procter & Gamble Co., east side Main Street 3rd door off 6th Street.

Ironically, there was no mention of candles, the product on which the company based its business!

Procter had learned the trade of candle making early in his life. As he discovered, there was more to the art than dipping a wick into tallow a couple of times and calling the finished product a candle. The partners felt that some of their competitors did just that, but Procter and Gamble were too concerned with quality to take any shortcuts. Both men had too much integrity to sell products that were less than perfect. Their goal was to produce perfect candles at a reasonable price.

That there was a need for quality locally made candles was evident to Procter and Gamble. If there wasn't, they wondered, why would merchants be importing candles into Cincinnati when there were 19 candlemakers in town?

Procter and Gamble set out to produce quality candles that would satisfy the local people's needs. It did not take them long to fill the niche. The quality candles they produced, combined with their sideline products, not all of which they manufactured themselves, led to modest profits in the company's first decade. (The company did sell candles made by other firms.) By 1848, P&G reported an annual profit of $26,000. More important, at least in the founders' eyes, they earned a reputation for honesty and integrity.

One newspaperman of the time said they were so well respected that "Suppliers of fats and oils could take a signed order from Procter & Gamble and pass it along in lieu of cash." That spoke well of their business ethics and explained why they and their products were so well respected.

THERE IS NO DOUBT THAT P&G IS A STAR PRODUCER

There is no better example of how quickly P&G earned respect than by tracing the history of its logo. One morning in 1851 Procter observed a wharfhand painting crude black crosses on each box in a shipment of candles being shipped from Cincinnati. He could not figure out why this was being done. Being an inquisitive and practical businessman, he asked the young man what he was doing.

The worker explained that many people working on the wharves and boats could not read. Consequently, they could not distinguish between boxes of candles and boxes of soap. So wharfhands marked the boxes with symbols to differentiate between the various products. Procter accepted the explanation with no qualms about the markings on the boxes. What he did not know was that the design was the forerunner of the company's famous logo.

Wharfhands continually modified the black crosses. They changed the crosses to stars and then circled the stars. Then came a cluster of stars within a circle and a quarter-moon drawn roughly like a human profile. Procter and Gamble approved the sophisticated design, which was then painted on all the company's candle shipping boxes. At some point they decided that the man in the moon was superfluous. So, they eliminated it, which they soon regretted.

A jobber in New Orleans rejected an entire shipment of candles because the box did not have the full design. He thought the candles were imitations, which he knew customers would not buy. The jobber wrote that "We want P&G's Star brand candles and no other. They're the only brand we can sell." Procter and Gamble quickly reinstated the man in the moon. William Procter even suggested an enhancement.

Procter decided that the cluster of stars should number thirteen to match those on the first flag of the United States. That led to further modifications and the logo that distinguishes the company today. Procter and Gamble learned a valuable lesson from the incident. Customers *do* pay attention to quality and will be loyal to the manufacturers who produce superior products. That was a lesson that company executives have never forgotten—and probably never will.

IT'S TIME TO MAKE A MOVE

P&G quickly outgrew its original headquarters. By the mid-1850s, the founders saw the need for a larger facility to accommodate the company's growth. Their foresight back in 1837 paid off.

P&G built on the land the two founders had purchased that year. The new factory was a one-story, 32-foot wide, 65-foot long building. That seemed adequate then. The building contained two soap kettles, each of which could turn out 1,000 pounds of soap per week. P&G now had two buildings, one a factory, the other an office. This led to a different type of relationship between Procter and Gamble.

Gamble, who was largely responsible for production, seldom visited the original office. On the other hand, Procter specialized in sales and finances. The two seldom crossed one another's path. They did meet every Saturday night at Procter's house to discuss the business, at which time they made some major decisions. One of these decisions was to have a profound impact on the company's future.

CANDLES BECOME P&G'S STAR PRODUCT

The partners decided in the mid-1850s to concentrate on their own products and drop all wholesale activities. They focused on the production of Star™ candles instead of Adamantines™. (Both were generic types. Stars were made from the stearic acid of lard, whereas Adamantines were manufactured from the stearic acid of tallow.) Procter and Gamble did not have the money to produce both kinds, so they decided to go with Stars, since hog fats, from which the raw materials emanated, were readily available in Cincinnati. An added advantage was the fact that oleic acid (also known as "red oil"), a by-product of the Star candlemaking process, could be used to make better laundry soaps than were then available. The decision paid off handsomely. P&G began producing two new soaps that used red oil as a base. Consumers accepted them overwhelmingly. As a result, soapmaking took on added importance at P&G. The firm put more time and effort into improving its soaps than they had ever envisioned. By 1859, P&G had sales exceeding $1 million annually. Procter and Gamble were pleased, but they had doubts about whether sales would continue to grow. There was a war coming, and they were unsure of how it would affect their firm.

PROCTER AND GAMBLE DON'T JUST SIT ON THEIR SOAPBOXES

The partners knew war was inevitable. The prospects worried them. One of the primary ingredients of their soap, rosin, could be obtained only from Southern sources. They asked one another what that would mean to Northern soapmakers.

Simply put, their soapmaking business would suffer dramatically without rosin. They initiated another of their shared strongpoints: contingency planning.

They sent Procter's oldest son, and new partner, 26-year-old William Alexander, on a rosin buying trip to New Orleans in 1860. Along with him went his cousin, 24-year-old James Norris Gamble, a recent chemistry graduate from the University of Maryland. The two may have been young, but they possessed a keen sense of business. Consequently, neither man lost sight of the urgency of the trip.

The two men proceeded at once to the company's principal rosin buyer and found a vast reserve available for $1 a barrel. They wasted no time in ordering a whole boatload to be shipped immediately! That was the largest single purchase of rosin that any company in Cincinnati had ever made! It was so large, in fact, that it took every available wagon in Cincinnati to unload the cargo and haul it to a vacant lot next to the factory. P&G's competitors laughed. One even remarked upon watching the parade of wagons go by that "There goes P&G's funeral." That turned out to be as erroneous as some people's prediction that the war would be over in three months. The war lasted four years—and so did P&G's rosin supply!

105

WAR MAY BE DIRTY—BUT AT LEAST THE UNION SOLDIERS CAN STAY CLEAN

During the war, rosin prices shot up as high as $15 per barrel, when it was available, which wasn't often. Procter & Gamble was virtually the only soap manufacturer in the country that had enough rosin to make soap for the Union armies. And make soap they did! P&G hired 300 new workers, began night shifts, extended the work week to six days, bought more soapmaking kettles, and acquired new buildings to accommodate the increased production. The overworked employees turned out box after box of soap and candles, not one of which ever failed to pass the inspections of the government's demanding quality control inspectors. While other companies produced shoddy material of all types, P&G simply refused to compromise its reputation for integrity or honesty, or to let the presence of Confederate soldiers delay production.

At one point during the war, Confederate troops threatened Cincinnati. Local officials clamped martial law on the city—except for Procter & Gamble. P&G was the only industry in town to continue operations. Certainly, this did nothing to harm its reputation, nor did the fact that Union soldiers were becoming more and more familiar with the company's name.

If there was one thing that the Civil War did for P&G, it was to make the company's name a household product in Northern homes. Soldiers who unloaded the company's products did not throw away the packing boxes. Rather, they used them as tables, chairs, bureaus...anything a resourceful soldier can devise. The soldiers passed the word about P&G and the quality of its products to the folks back home, and when they returned from the war, they asked for the company's products themselves. As luck would have it (and luck has a lot to do with whether or not a company becomes a success), the war proved beneficial to P&G in more ways than one.

Despite the large purchase of rosin before the war, the company found its supply perilously close to being depleted by early 1865. As usual, the owners were not sitting back and waiting for the day when they could not make any more soap. Rather, they searched diligently for a rosin substitute. Unfortunately, their search was not productive. Luckily, the war ended before the rosin supply ran out completely, but the quest for a rosin substitute continued.

THE WAR BETWEEN THE STATES ENDS—BUT THE WAR FOR NEW CUSTOMERS JUST BEGINS

The end of the war brought a new problem to Northern manufacturers: how would they treat Southern customers. The war left Southerners in dire financial straits. Most brokers in the South could not buy from P&G unless the company extended them long-term credit. William Procter did not see any problem with that. As usual, he was willing to take a risk and look to the future with a great deal of business acumen. He decided to extend the long-term credit his Southern customers needed. "But," he said, "only if each individual decision is based on an evaluation of character rather than assets. Cash balances may vary from year to year, but a reputation for integrity is constant." His attitude earned the respect of many Southerners—and their long-term business besides. The Southern business simply added to the company's post-war success. P&G's growth did not come without problems, though.

WITH RISK COMES OPPORTUNITY

The years immediately following the war were profitable for P&G. In 1867, the company showed capital assets of $800,000 and growing profits. However, another Wall Street panic, this one in 1869, put a crimp in the company's inventories and profits. The return to profitability was a long time in coming. For example, in the first four months of 1879 the company had profits of $34,000. They dropped to $3,000 in the next two, and then dropped into the red for the rest of the year. Profits may not have been strong, but the company's total business volume increased steadily. So did the direction of its production.

Soapmaking took on added importance in P&G's operations. By the mid-1870s, it accounted for 25 percent of the company's sales. Refined kitchen lard, lard oil, and candles accounted for the rest, but the percentages indicated that there was an imminent change in the balance. In 1878, one of the most important events in the company's history occurred to precipitate that change.

PIANO PLAYERS "TICKLE THE IVORY;" P&G'S IVORY TICKLES AMERICA'S FANCY

James Norris Gamble spent a lot of time in the laboratory searching for a soap formula that would give P&G a prominent place in the soapmaking industry. There were approximately 300 soap manufacturers in the country in the 1870s. None had a product that was head and shoulders above the rest. Gamble changed that.

He announced in 1878 that he had developed a white soap formula that would revolutionize the industry. All the partners agreed. They had one problem with the product: its name.

Virtually every soap manufacturer had a white soap, which is what they labeled it. P&G wanted to avoid that generic name. Unfortunately, it could not come up with one that caught their fancy. Then, in a peculiar stroke of luck that helps separate successful companies from their unsuccessful competitors, the company's sales manager, Harley Procter, came up with the name while listening to a church sermon. On a Sunday early in 1879, a minister reading from the psalms said, "All thy garments smell of myrhh and aloes and cassia, out of the ivory palaces whereby they have made thee glad." The word "ivory" stuck in Harley's mind—and with the company as well. Ivory® Soap, the first product most people identify with Procter and Gamble, was born. So was a new tradition: copious advertising.

At the time Ivory was introduced, P&G had an advertising budget of about $1,500 per year. Harley Procter wanted to increase that considerably. Ivory gave him the opportunity to push the partners for more advertising dollars. Once again, luck, in the form of an accident, helped him achieve his goal.

**EVEN IF P&G COULD NOT FLOAT A LOAN, IT HAD A
SOAP THAT COULD FLOAT ALONE**

The ingredients that formed Ivory Soap were mixed
by machines called crutchers. The machine's arms
revolved in the soap mixture until the operator decided
by sight, smell, and taste that it was thick enough to
be poured into soap frames. One day early in 1879 an
operator went to lunch without turning off the machine. When he returned, he was appalled to see that
the mixture had become a frothy, puffed-up mess that
overflowed the vat. Being a conscientious man, he
summoned his supervisor. The two men decided that
although the mixture's appearance had changed, its
composition had not. So, they poured it into the
frames and forgot about the incident.

Soon the company began receiving requests for the
soap that floats. That puzzled officials, since they
were unaware of any floating soap that P&G made.
Then, someone recalled the accident in the mixing
room. Researchers repeated the "accident." Lo and
behold, they found that the resulting soap did float!
To publicize the soap's unique characteristic, the partners increased Harley's advertising budget to $11,000
in 1882. That began a trend toward heavy advertising
that has been a staple of P&G's operations ever since.
(For example, the company's advertising budget in
1988 was $1,506,900,000.) But, in true P&G fashion,
they were not content to rest on its laurels. P&G has
always believed that any product can be improved.
Such was the case with Ivory.

First, Harley Procter applied a process that he had
patented to add to the soap's uniqueness. P&G
notched the laundry-sized bars so consumers could

snap them in half and use the separate pieces for different purposes. Then, the company packaged the bars in a black and white checkerboard wrapper that featured the moon and stars trademark. Finally, P&G paid independent chemists to analyze the soap's purity. They discovered that Ivory was 99.44 percent free of foreign and unnecessary substances. Harley Procter advertised that fact to the public. Soon, "99.44%" became a household term across the country—and Ivory became the nation's preferred soap. That was good news for P&G. The bad news was that the soap's success contributed to the overtaxation of the company's production facilities. Once again fate stepped in.

FIRED WITH ENTHUSIASM—AND BURNED BY FIRE

The company partners were at odds about building a new plant. They expected that the cost of doing so would be exorbitant. Then, on a bitter cold January 7, 1884, fire broke out in the company's complex.

Quickly, the flames consumed the lard oil building factory, spread to the candle works, and invaded the oil storage area. William A. Procter watched the flames from the Queen City Club where he was eating lunch. He saw more than fire, though. Procter saw what would happen if the company's oil supply disappeared. Acting on the spur of the moment, he hailed a cab, dashed off to the nearest Western Union office, and sent telegrams to buyers in key cities instructing them to buy "all available red oil." He recognized that if suppliers heard about the fire first, they would jack up the prices for the oil. That never happened, of-course. Procter's swift actions averted a crisis and helped the company right itself quickly after the fire. In fact, the company emerged from the episode stronger than when it went in!

IS CINCINNATI BIG ENOUGH TO HOLD PROCTER & GAMBLE?

The fire settled the argument over whether P&G should build a new plant. The question became one of "where, rather than "if." While the partners debated, one of the founders, William Procter died. Procter, 83 years of age, passed away in his sleep on April 4, 1884. Everyone connected with the company—and numerous others who were not—mourned his death. Procter himself may have died, but the company he founded lived on!

P&G secured a $1 million loan from the Mercantile Bank of New York to construct its new facility in Cincinnati. On March 23, 1885, the surviving founder, James Gamble, broke ground for the new factory site, to be called Ivorydale.

Ivorydale was as big as some towns. It contained over 20 separate structures connected by an underground network of steam mains and water pipes. There was also a railroad spur linking the facility to the nearby main line. Trees separated the buildings from the street and flower beds meshed with well-manicured lawns. This was no ordinary industrial complex! It was a showpiece designed to make the facility a nice place to work. The only son of company founder William Procter was determined to keep it that way.

COOPERS MAKE BARRELS—BUT THIS COOPER DOESN'T WANT TO KEEP THE COMPANY'S EMPLOYEES OVER ONE

William Cooper Procter (Cooper, as he preferred to be called), left Princeton University in 1883, his senior year, to join the company. Ironically, his arrival coincided closely with the end of Barney Krieger's 47-year-long career. Krieger may have established a trend for longevity at P&G. Young Procter made it his business to continue Krieger's precedent.

The youth learned the business from the ground up, performing every menial task he could and earning the praise of the company's employees. He seemed to identify more with the workers than with management. This affinity worked to everyone's advantage.

Cooper initiated a series of changes aimed at improving the employees' working conditions. The first change came in 1885 when P&G implemented a five-and-a-half day work week. Previously, the employees' work week consisted of Monday through Saturday, 6:30 a.m. to 6 p.m., with time off for lunch. Cooper worked those same hours and learned just how grueling the schedule was. He pushed for half a day off on Saturday. The company agreed with his proposal and set a new precedent in the history of management-employee relations.

His next innovation was the institution of a profit-sharing plan. He experimented with it in several forms over the years before the company finally settled on a plan that satisfied everybody. After all, he may have sympathized with the workers and their lack of benefits, but he was a businessman at heart. He was fully cognizant of the fact that he could not simply give away the store.

As Cooper wrote in his business diary, "Any worthwhile change in the conduct of a business must first and last have the element of lessening the cost." He tied the profit-sharing plan to increased activity. In April 1887, the partners announced the company's first attempt at profit sharing. The plan did not work as well as they had hoped, but it marked another radical step forward in management-employee relations, which has become a company hallmark over the years.

IF CHANGE IS WORTH A FEW CENTS, THEN P&G IS WORTH A FORTUNE

Cooper seemed hell bent on changing P&G completely around. He did not alienate anyone even though he proposed one radical idea after another. He was so well appreciated that the partners admitted him to their ranks in October 1887, the month of the company's 50th anniversary. One of the things he pushed for was to convert P&G to a public corporation. Once again, his idea prevailed. On July 17, 1890, the company held its first stockholders meeting in Jersey City, New Jersey. P&G entered its new era in good shape.

P&G had its new state-of-the-art Ivorydale facility and sales were booming. P&G's two flagship brands, Ivory and a new laundry soap, Lenox®, which was particularly effective in hard-water areas, accounted for the lion's share of the company's revenues. P&G had introduced Lenox knowing full well that it would cut into sales of its older soaps, but that suited them just fine. Management recognized that it was smart business practice to do whatever it took to satisfy customers' preferences. They were astute enough to recognize that it would take more than two products to do that. So, they vowed to develop more products at as low a cost as possible to meet consumers' needs. Consequently, the company created a new laboratory in 1890 devoted exclusively to the development of new products. The 1890s marked a new emphasis on research at P&G. Unfortunately, James Procter was not around to see the results.

On April 29, 1891, the second of the original founders died at his home. His death marked the end of an era in Cincinnati, but the company entered a new one which would have made him and William Procter proud.

The 1890s were good years for P&G. Despite another major recession, the company's profits increased significantly. In 1894, President William A. Procter announced that "The company has no floating debt whatever, all bills being paid in cash." He also reported that the "result...is strong evidence of...how slightly the demand for [our] products has been affected by the general business depression." To be sure, not every year was a record year for P&G, but the company entered the 20th century poised to become one of the nation's strongest corporations.

Consider these figures. P&G's profits exceeded $1 million in 1987 and $1,522,000 in 1904. Dividends increased from $8 a share in 1890 to $20 per share by 1900. In 1901, the directors declared a special dividend of $50 per common share, provided the money was used as part payment for new shares at $100 per share. In 1905, the company's stock was selling at

$390 a share! Managers, employees, stockholders, and analysts looked forward to even better years ahead. The company did not disappoint them.

P&G MAY NOT BE CREATING FRANKENSTEINS IN THE LAB—BUT SOME OF THE NEW PRODUCTS BECOME MONSTERS

Gradually, P&G deviated slowly from its original product line. Candlemaking faded into history, even though the company did sell 10,000 pounds of candles in 1909 to the Isthmian Canal Commission, which used them during the construction of the Panama Canal. For all intents and purposes, though, the light faded from the candlemaking business as P&G concentrated on soap-related products. That line of business was expanding so rapidly that the existing production facilities could not manufacture enough.

P&G expanded the Ivorydale facility to meet increasing production demands. Even though the new kettles yielded 165,000 pounds of soap at each boiling, that was not enough to keep pace with nationwide sales. Thus, the company expanded into Kansas City and Staten Island. It added new products such as White™ Naptha (1902) and Star™ Naptha, a yellow-powdered soap (1903). By 1920, White Naptha became the largest selling brand of soap in the world. Star began to outsell Lenox! That gave management pause to wonder.

Star represented a new approach to business for P&G. Rather than developing it, the company purchased Schultz Soap Company of Zanesville, Ohio, the company that made Star, for $425,000. P&G simply added Naptha to the soap—and a new way of doing business to its history. Schultz may have been P&G's

116

first acquisition, but it certainly was not its last. Acquisitions gave P&G's management food for thought, which led them to thinking about food as a product line.

FAT PROFITS LEAD TO FAT-FREE FOODS

P&G's management had been looking at expansion into different product lines for quite some time around the turn of the century. The company had begun substituting cottonseed oil for refined kitchen lard in soap products. In order to assure a steady supply of the oil, P&G organized a subsidiary in the 1890s, the Buckeye Cotton Oil Company, which owned a single plant located in Greenwood, Mississippi. Over the next decade, Buckeye bought 3 more cottonseed crushing mills and built 5 others. P&G had an ample supply of cottonseed oil for the moment. However, the introduction of a new salad oil threatened that supply.

P&G researchers had been working secretly on a new oil-based food product for a long time in the early 1900s. Finally, they developed a salad oil they felt could be marketed. Management could not agree on whether the company should expand into non-soap related product lines. Some of them suggested that the company's salad oil had not been tested sufficiently. One member, James N. Gamble, said that the company should not offer any products to consumers without learning everything there was to know about it first. That had been P&G's philosophy since 1837. He maintained that there was no sense in changing it now. Management compromised. The company sold its new salad oil only to institutions, but management had their eye on a larger customer—the American public.

P&G quickly refined the product through a series of technological advancements and timely acquisitions. E. C. Keyser, a German chemical engineer, developed a hydrogenation process in which he turned liquid cottonseed oil into a solid. The company reached an agreement with Keyser which gave them the United States rights to the process. In typical P&G fashion, management moved quickly to capitalize on the agreement. P&G started building a new hydrogenation plant at Ivorydale in 1908. It was ready by February, 1909. The next step in the process can be attributed to sheer luck, which always seemed to be on P&G's side.

A Macon, Georgia, businessman, Wallace E. Mc-Caw, offered to sell P&G his manufacturing company. His principal product was Flake White—a shortening! New company president Cooper Procter (he assumed office on April 6, 1907) recommended that P&G buy the business for $1.4 million. The company consummated the deal on January 2, 1909. P&G had all the elements in place to refine and release a new, soft, all-vegetable shortening to the American public. The company named that product Crisco®. By 1912, it became a staple in America's kitchens, and launched P&G into a leadership position in the food industry.

WHILE P&G FIGHTS THE BATTLE FOR PRODUCT SUPREMACY, THE COUNTRY FIGHTS A WAR FOR DEMOCRACY

The years leading up to World War I were profitable for P&G. In 1913, for example, the company's common stock sold for between $555 and $570 per share. That same year, P&G declared the first of twelve consecutive stock dividends of 4 percent. To top it off, stockholders received a new share free for each 25 they held. The financial news was good; it was so good, in fact, that P&G looked into strengthening its international operations! P&G had been exporting soap into Canada for years. Lever Brothers, the company's chief rival, was moving to consolidate several companies in that country in order to gain a dominant position there. P&G decided that the best way to counteract Lever's move was to build a plant in Canada. Such a move, it figured, would give the company an exemption from Canadian import duties and provide access to the country's lower labor costs. As usual, management acted expeditiously. P&G opened its first international plant in Hamilton, Ontario, in 1915. Production concentrated on Ivory and Crisco. Within two years, the company wished it had more plants!

The United States declared war on Germany on April 6, 1917. The move had an immediate impact on P&G, as well as its competitors.

Since the war effort required prodigious amounts of materials to be shipped overseas, there was a question as to where P&G would get the raw materials it needed to continue manufacturing operations. Management remembered their history. They had faced a similar problem prior to the Civil War. Management solved that one by purchasing vast quantities of rosin. If it worked, then, they figured, it would work again.

In anticipation of a long war, P&G purchased a year's worth of raw material, enough to keep all of its plants up and running. The company had enough material to maintain production. Unfortunately, some of its employees were reluctant to work.

In one of the rare times that labor unrest disrupted P&G's operations, workers shut down the Kansas City plant in September, 1917. Cooper Procter, who had never forgotten his commitment to the company's employees, rushed to Kansas City. The local plant manager showed him an extensive list of workers' demands. The workers insisted on compulsory union membership and that the union be given the power to approve all promotions, merit pay, or discharges. They also wanted the elimination of insurance, pension, sick-benefit funds, and profit sharing.

Cooper, who prided himself on his ability to deal effectively with employees at all levels, could not believe that the workers really wanted all this. He personally entertained a committee of workers to find out what they *really* wanted. His perception was correct. The workers would be willing to drop their other demands if they could get an 8-hour workday.

This did not bother Cooper. He had been mulling an 8-hour day for some time. He was hesitant to implement one during the war, though. He explained that to the committee. As he told them:

> Our nation is at war, and we all have a wartime duty to do our utmost to keep production as high as possible. Therefore I ask you to agree to continue to work 10 or 11 hours a day until the war is over. In turn, the company will pay you time-and-a-half for all time over eight hours. After the war, we will institute an 8-hour day. You have my word on that.

120

Cooper's word was as good as gold as far as the workers were concerned. They reopened the plant and there was no further trouble. As things turned out, everyone benefited from the episode, which demonstrated the close management-employee relationship that has played such an integral part in the company's success.

After the war, Cooper Procter established employees' conference committees to effect two-way communications between management and the workers. By way of explaining the importance of this move, he said:

> The chief problem of big business today (remember, this was 1918) is to shape its policies so that each worker, whether in the office or factory, will feel he is a vital part of his company with a personal responsibility for its success and a chance to share in that success. To bring this about, the employing company must take its people into its confidence. They should know why they are doing things, the relation of their work to other departments, and, as far as practicable, to the business as a whole.

With these words, Procter capsulized the essence of effective management-employee relations and summarized the reason why the company has lasted for over 150 years!

True to his word, Procter also implemented the 8-hour workday in the company's plants. He told the employees that the company intended to eliminate overtime pay simultaneously. He emphasized to them that this meant less take-home pay for them unless the company increased their wages. He asked the Ivorydale Employee Conference Plan team to discuss this proposition and get back to him. They did. Much to no one's surprise, they opted for the 8-hour day—but they refused to tell Procter what P&G should pay them!

The committee members said:

> We want the 8-hour day, but it is our unanimous decision that we don't want to say what you shall pay us. You know as well as we that the cost of living has gone up, and you will take this into account. *You have always treated us right and we know you are going to keep on doing it.* (The italics are the author's.)

What better words are there to highlight the smooth employee-employer relationship that P&G enjoyed?

The committee's trust paid off. P&G instituted a new wage scale under which workers received, on the average, the same pay for 8 hours they had been receiving for 10. With that out of the way, P&G could concentrate on post-war business.

THE WAR IS OVER—BUT P&G'S BATTLE HAS JUST BEGUN

Nothing untoward happened to P&G during the war. It was business as usual. The aftermath, however, was not.

P&G's main competitors, Lever Brothers and Colgate, introduced new products that put a serious dent in the company's sales. To compound matters, wholesalers across the country were demanding deep discounts from manufacturers. Management opted to bypass the wholesalers and sell directly to store owners. That seemed like a reasonable solution, especially as far as it concerned Cooper Procter. Why? Because direct selling could eliminate the problem of frequent layoffs, and anything that prevented unnecessary disruptions in workers' lives made Procter happy.

Wholesalers' buying practices indirectly affected production workers' schedules. They tended to watch the commodity markets closely. If the costs of raw materials started to spiral—or even if it looked like they would—wholesalers made heavy purchases of goods that would be affected. They wouldn't make any more purchases until their warehouses were empty. This meant that factories could be idled until that day came. Needless to say, that had an adverse effect on everyone involved.

In 1919, for example, personnel turnover during slack periods rose as high as 11 percent per month. Some employees were laid off and chose not to return when production picked up again. The combination of losing employees and training replacements drained the company's finances. Cooper Procter reasoned that by selling directly to store owners, P&G could control its production rates. After careful consideration and serious controversy among management people, P&G initiated its direct selling program in September, 1919.

The technique did not set well with wholesalers, or retailers, but it delighted competitors, who thought that P&G was slicing its own throat. However, P&G, the trendsetter in direct selling, weathered the storm—and proved the skeptics wrong! By 1923, the program was on solid footing. It was so solid, in fact, that P&G was able to guarantee employees in the Ivorydale, Kansas City, and Port Ivory (Staten Island) plants 48 weeks of work per year! That made industry history. As General Manager Richard Deupree said, "We like to try the impractical and impossible and prove it to be both practical and possible—if it's the right thing to do in the first place." The direct selling plan was definitely the right thing to do at the time, and its implementation set the stage for even greater success for P&G.

WASHING MACHINES HELP P&G CLEAN UP

The "Roaring '20s" were good years for P&G. The roar management was most interested in was that made by technologically advanced washing machines and electric generators. These new machines presaged a new era for people doing household chores—and for P&G as well.

Basically, P&G had stood still as far as introducing new products in the first two decades of the 20th century. For example, the company had not introduced a new soap since 1902. Then, in 1919, it brought out Ivory® Flakes, a light-duty soap intended for washing dishes and hand laundering silk and wool fabrics.

124

Critics labeled it an old product in a new form. P&G did not dispute that. Management was simply positioning itself for the future.

Experts predicted a surge in the production of automatic washing machines in the 1920s. The dramatic increase in the availability of electricity meant that hand washers would become passe quickly. P&G's management believed that would come to pass. In 1921, they introduced Chipso®, which a 1926 advertisement described as "the most amazing success in the history of household soap." Perhaps not even management believed that. They knew that a better soap flake was already being developed.

In 1929, P&G began selling Oxydol®, a granular type soap which was an improvement over its predecessors such as Selox. The company had purchased Oxydol in 1927 from the William Waltke Company of St. Louis in another of its well-timed acquisitions. (Another of the company's products was Lava®, which has long been one of P&G's best selling soaps.) A few weeks later, P&G purchased another St. Louis soap manufacturer, Globe Soap. In this case, the Procter & Gamble did not care about the company's products. P&G simply wanted the production facilities to position themselves for what they foresaw as a burgeoning business to come in the 1930s. Two other acquisitions helped the company in this regard. P&G bought a New York manufacturer simply to acquire Duz® and the James M. Kirk Company of Chicago, one of its most aggressive competitors. There was no doubt that P&G was intent on capturing a major part of the soap-making market.

The key to the Waltke acquisition was Oxydol. Its early success was limited, but the product did precipitate the switch from soap flakes to granules. From that standpoint, it was one of P&G's most important products.

Another product of the 1920s that the company relied on heavily to increase its share of the market was Camay®. Ironically, it became a serious competitor for Ivory. The competition did not upset P&G management, though. They were very willing to match one company product against another. Such competition was good for the company—and its customers as well.

Providing consumers with the products they wanted was important to P&G. Just how important was demonstrated in 1923 when the company launched the industry's first economic research department.

Ostensibly, the department was supposed to keep track of fluctuations in the commodity markets. However, the department head, Dr. Paul Smelser, was more interested in performing market research. The results of his research gave management an accurate picture of consumers' desires—and the chance to become the industry pacesetter in the manufacture of products their customers wanted, rather than what the company thought they wanted. As former company president Edward G. Harness once said, "The successful company is the one which is the first to identify emerging consumer needs and offer product improvements which satisfy those needs. The successful marketer spots a new trend early and then leads it." Certainly, that summed up P&G's approach to consumer needs—a philosophy upon which the company was founded and to which it still adheres today.

IF THE '20S WERE GOOD, THE '30S WERE BETTER

P&G had survived the 1920s in great shape. Management looked at the next decade as a pivotal one for the company. They did not disappoint themselves, their employees, or their stockholders. The only people they disappointed were their competitors, who realized more than ever that competing against P&G was a Herculean—and seemingly impossible, at times—task.

The 1930s began on an optimistic note. Sales in 1930, for example, amounted to $200 million, ten times those of 1907. Of course, the Great Depression affected the company's sales during the decade. At one point, P&G reduced all employees's wages and salaries by 10 percent. Gross sales in 1933 dropped 28 percent from the previous year. Deupree had to issue orders to "save every pin and paper clip." Conscientious employees did far more than that! They saved the company and propelled it toward a future that featured more and more success.

The first major moves in the 30's involved changes in leadership. Cooper Procter stepped up to become the company's first chairman. Richard Redwood Deupree succeeded him as president—and succeed he did!

If there is any decade that can be pointed to as the most critical in P&G's history, it is the 1930s. First, the company began selling an entire new product which resulted from the cottonseed crushing process that was being conducted in its 14 Buckeye mills. Company scientists had learned how to convert the cotton lintners from the process into sheets of pulp.

127

This in turn was sold for use in products like rayon, photographic film, and plastics. The process was so successful that P&G built a $1 million plant in Memphis to manufacture the pulp. Memphis was just one of the cities feeling P&G's presence. Not all of these cities were in the United States.

P&G had been eyeing expansion outside the United States for quite some time. England was its location of choice. When the opportunity presented itself, P&G jumped at the chance. As soon as anyone could say "Union Jack," P&G had purchased the financially ailing Thomas Hedley & Co., Ltd. soapmaking firm, which was located in Newcastle upon Tyne. That got P&G's foot in the European door. Back home, Deupree was exploring yet more uncharted territory: advertising.

IF THERE IS ANYONE WHO HAS NEVER HEARD OF P&G, YOU WILL NOW

1933 was a hallmark year for P&G. That year marked the beginning of a trend that would lead to huge increases in the company's sales. For example, shipments of Ivory Soap nearly doubled between 1933 and 1939. Crisco's shipments almost tripled! Whereas in 1933 P&G's soap brands had accounted for only 36 percent of its total shipments, they rose to 60 percent by 1939. Why? Deupree had discovered the magic of radio advertising.

If the names Procter and Gamble were not household names by the mid 1930s, they certainly were after. The company used a series of radio programs to keep its products in the public's eye. P&G sponsored radio programs like "Vic and Sade," "Pepper Young's Family," and "The Guiding Light." These programs gave birth to the name "soap opera." More important, the company's use of network radio set an advertsing trend that would send the company's profits—and reputation—soaring as its 100th anniversary approached.

100 YEARS OLD—AND WHAT A BIRTHDAY PRESENT

P&G's 1934 net earnings totaled $14.4 million, a 33 percent increase over the previous year. Then, there was another 33 percent increase in 1935. By 1937, P&G's 100th birthday, the company had net earnings of $26.8 million on $230 million in sales. These figures were the direct result of P&G's involvement in heavy advertsing. The company was on a roll. P&G flooded the market with its products; consumers rushed to buy them. Then a flood of a different kind caused a large problem, and showed just how important the employer-employee relationship can be.

In January of 1937, the Ohio River overflowed its banks and inundated the Ivorydale complex. Tropical rains fell day after day to exacerbate the flooding. Workers toiled for hours stacking sandbags around the water-soaked buildings to no avail. When it became obvious that their work was futile, they retreated to the buildings' interiors to move equipment and products to the upper levels. They formed bucket brigades to transfer boxes by hand to the upper reaches of the buildings. All regular work was suspended, but, in tribute to employee loyalty, practically every worker who could reach the plant did so to help with the salvage operation. (Ironically, Richard Deupree was one of the few who could not reach the plant! All the roads leading directly to it were underwater. So, he moved to the top of a hill overlooking the complex and directed the operation from there.)

Eventually, the river, which had at one point risen 80 feet above its normal level, receded and the crisis passed. Other than dampening the workers' spirits, the flood had little lasting impact on P&G. It is no wonder, then, that historian Edward Hungerford once wrote, "a concern may make money for itself and still maintain a labor relationship that is clean-cut, generous, and fair; that it may retain the full regard of its workers as well as its own self-respect." That idea was nothing new in 1937—and it has not changed since.

NEW PLANTS HERE AND THERE AND EVERYWHERE

Another measure of the company's growth in the 1930s was the constant expansion. P&G acquired the Cotton Oil Refining Company (Portsmouth, Virginia, 1931), Sabates, S.A. (Havana, Cuba, 1931), Hewitt Soap Company (Dayton, Ohio, 1933), and the Philippine Manufacturing Company (Manila, 1935). The company also constructed two more plants of its own in Baltimore (1930) and Long Beach, California (1931). The company was also planning a new building in Ivorydale which would eventually place P&G in the forefront of product research and technology.

THE FIRST HUNDRED YEARS ARE ALWAYS THE BEST—BUT THE NEXT 100 MAY EVEN BE BETTER

The company's first 100 years had been good ones. The story of its growth is practically unparalleled in American business history. Richard Deupree summed up the company's success in a speech marking the close of P&G's first century—and presaging the beginning of its next.

According to Deupree, the company's success was attributed to the facts that it had:

- placed foremost in its efforts the building of a strong organization
- concentrated on the uniform production of goods of high quality
- maintained at all times the highest efficiency in its manufacturing plants
- recognized the importance and value of research in its sales, manufacturing, and advertising departments, as well as in its personnel

What Deupree did not say was that P&G had gone beyond recognition of the value of research. It had converted what it learned into a copious advertising program that made P&G a household word and increased sales dramatically. Research was important to P&G. In fact, Deupree suggested that his company had a slightly different interpretation of the word, when he said:

> In referring to *research*, I realize that the word has been so generally used that its significance may not be entirely clear. With us, research means an extensive study of all the problems which are involved in this business, both of the present and as

they may be anticipated for the future. Research has more than paid for itself.

That was an understatement! Research had not only paid for itself, but it had placed P&G in a position where it was poised to dominate the soapmaking industry in its second century of business. The emphasis on research would also have a significant impact on the company's production of food products. Obviously, P&G had no intention of resting on its laurels—and it did not!

OKAY, SO WE RESEARCH A LOT, BUT JUST HOW DOES IT PAY OFF?

P&G's research in the 1930s resulted in several new and "improved" old products. Among the most significant new products was Dreft®, the first synthetic detergent for all-around household use, Drene® liquid shampoo, and Sweetex®, a bulk shortening that allowed commercial bakeries to make sweeter products. The company also refined Crisco. This in itself was of extreme importance to P&G and demonstrates how quickly and efficiently the company responds to competition.

Ever since being introduced to consumers in 1911, Crisco had been the leading all-purpose home vegetable shortening. Then, in January, 1936, Lever introduced Spry®, a contender to the throne. Spry was an excellent product and a marketing threat to Crisco. However, its appearance did not catch P&G by surprise. Company researchers had been trying for several years to improve Crisco. Although there had been some debate over changing it drastically, since it was a winner already, management decided that they could not take Spry's appearance lightly. So, researchers stepped up their pace and found a way to combine the best features of Crisco and Sweetex. They called the resulting product Sure-Mix Crisco, which gave new meaning to the words "new and improved."

P&G's Engineering Division also got into the act. They designed a new container that kept the product fresher longer and added a clever key-type lid to make it easier to open. Crisco quickly regained its position as a leader. The episode demonstrated that P&G did not take its competition lightly. It also proved the importance of research. As one company researcher noted, "It isn't enough to invent a new product. Through constant improvement we must manage every existing brand so that it can flourish year after year in an ever-changing, intensely competitive marketplace." Certainly, the company that follows this advice is one that is bound to be successful, as P&G has proved time and time again.

WAR AGAIN—AND P&G IS READY

In retrospect, the 1930s were good years for P&G. The company set a new record for profits with the 1937 net earnings of $26.8 million. Net earnings for fiscal 1938-39 jumped to $25.3 million! On the labor front, the company's guaranteed employment plan was 15 years old and still working well. The company achieved another milestone in 1936 when it pioneered a one-week vacation "with pay" plan for its plant workers. P&G even found a new advertsing medium: television!

In the summer of 1939, the Brooklyn Dodgers and Cincinnati Reds played the first major league baseball games ever televised. Fittingly, Procter and Gamble sponsored the telecast in which "Red" Barber read Ivory soap commercials between innings. The pioneering instinct at P&G evidenced itself once again. The company was always on the lookout for new ways to promote its products, and new buildings in which to make them. Three new plants were being built in Quincy, Massachusetts, London, England, and Surabaja, Java (now Indonesia). The company was primed for expansion—and for World War II.

For the most part, wartime rationing restricted P&G's growth. Much of the company's research and production went into the war effort. There were not enough workers to help the company grow anyway. At the height of the war, 30 percent of the workforce was serving in the armed forces of the United States, Canada, and England. The company's biggest contribution to the war effort involved the operation of munitions plants in Wolf Creek, Tennessee, and Aberdeen, Mississippi.

P&G had no expertise in this industry, but that did not stop it from becoming involved at the government's request. As Harvey Knowles, the company's General Manufacturing Manager pointed out at the time, "the principles of good management can be applied to problems in almost any field." That proved true in this case, as it has in so many others as far as P&G is concerned.

The company suffered some setbacks during the war. Its Philippines plant was practically destroyed. Factories in England and Java were damaged somewhat. Facilities in the United States suffered a bit since material shortages inhibited the repair of machinery. Sales of Drene shampoo suffered seriously due to a shortage of packaging materials. One product, Teel®, a new liquid dentifrice, disappeared altogether due more to consumers' dislike for it than the war effort. Consequently, P&G pulled it off the market completely.

As a paraphrase of the Kenny Rogers hit song, "The Gambler," says, "you've got to know when to hold it, or when to fold it." P&G knew when to fold Teel, and knowing when to quit on a product sometimes makes good business sense. It did in this case. Besides, the post-war years gave P&G plenty of time to develop a replacement and find new ones to add to its product line. The company wasted no time recovering from the effects of World War II. The one thing that remained constant, though, was its commitment to the founders' principles, ethics, and morals.

LET THE EMPLOYEES SHARE IN THE PROFITS

P&G's concern for their employees' welfare continued in the post-war era. The number of company stockholders had almost tripled from 15,669 in 1930 to 44,925 in 1945. A large part of this expansion was due to an increase in an employee stock purchase plan.

Effective July 1, 1944, all salaried company employees earning more than $3,000 per year became eligible to participate in a profit sharing trust. This marked just one more innovation in the company's symbiotic relationship with its employees. Deupree labeled the new plan as "one of the most forward steps" the company had ever taken. As he viewed it, the move would assist P&G's efforts to build and maintain "a strong, virile organization." As history has shown, he was right.

HEY, BUDDY, CAN YOU SPARE SOME CHANGE? P&G CERTAINLY CAN!

Historically, change has been one of P&G's salient assets. No matter how well the company is doing, it is always willing to make changes that will help it do better. To Richard Deupree, change was inevitable and there was nothing in P&G's operations that could not be altered. One of the elements of change in the company's way of doing business was an increased emphasis on brand management.

P&G no longer specialized in Ivory soap and Crisco. The company's product line had expanded to the point where the major competition for some of its products came from within! The battle between Ivory and Camay illustrated that aspect of the business.

Management decided that the two soaps would fight it out for sales. P&G used separate advertising agencies to promote each soap. Neil McElroy, who had control over all of P&G's advertising in the late 1940s, maintained that internal competition would "bring into play every ability, every tool, possessed by brand managers." This type of internal competition was a new concept in American industry. As one company brochure described it, "Brand management is the mainspring and moving force behind all our consumer marketing. The brand management concept assures that each brand will have behind it the kind of single-minded drive it needs to succeed." As events proved, the concept certainly worked at P&G, based in large part on the prescience of the company's management!

Deupree's philosophy was to look at the future and build on the idea that the interests of the company and its employees were inseparable. In his view, the company already had the best employees in the industry. He reasoned, though, and quite correctly, that the company could not sit still. It had to recruit more talented individuals, who were "smarter than average, hard working, and honest young people who wanted opportunity more than they wanted security." Then, he said, they should be trained and advanced to management positions offering more responsibility in traditional company fashion. In other words, Deupree advocated that open management positions be filled from within. This concept worked well for the company—and it created a monopoly the company had no trouble creating.

Traditionally, bureaucrats viewed monopolies as contrary to the best interests of business. However, there was a type of monopoly that government could not control at P&G: a monopoly of talent.

Historically, P&G management had looked at people as the company's most important asset. Neil McElroy summed up this approach when he met various managers in company plants. He seldom asked them to tell him about their plants or business. "Tell me about your people," he would say. They would! After all, it was people who develop, produce, and sell new products—all of which they did in abundance as the company headed into the 1950s!

THE ONLY PEOPLE WHO WANT TO STEM THE "TIDE" ARE P&G'S COMPETITORS

After World War II, P&G researchers devoted a great deal of time to developing more effective ways to combine mildness with cleaning power. They envisioned a line of soaps that would work well with the increasing number of technologically advanced washing machines being made available to consumers. The company's competitors were doing the same. Finally, P&G released such a product that would revolutionize the soapmaking industry: Tide®.

P&G had the detergent available, but little capital to finance its production. Management estimated that it would cost $10 million to refine the technology which led to the production of Tide. Part of the problem was that the existing machinery could not be used to produce the new class of detergent. Management did not ponder the problem long. They realized that if P&G did not risk the expenditure, a competitor would beat them to the punch. That was contrary to P&G's modus operandi. So, with little fanfare, the company test marketed Tide in six cities. After a bit of refining, Tide hit the shelves nationally. Despite severe competition, it soon became a best seller. Tide led to a flood of new products.

New products from P&G that appeared in the late '40s and early 50s included Prell® shampoo (1946), Joy® dishwashing detergent (1949), and Cheer® laundry detergent (1950). Not only did they all do well, but they increased P&G's internal brand competition, and placed on added strain on the company's production facilities.

THE WORLD STARTS SHRINKING, SO P&G STARTS EXPANDING

P&G expanded into Mexico, Venezuela, Belgium, and France in the 1950s. Negotiations to gain access to foreign markets were not always easy. Little obstacles like local customs, tariff and other trade barriers, and outright bribery often impeded negotiations.

In keeping with corporate philosophy, P&G refused to compromise its principles. Consequently, its overseas operations grew considerably. By1955, P&G's foreign subsidiaries provided net earnings of $8 million. During the next quarter century, the earnings increased to $149 million! The company would be selling over 200 brands in 24 nations, and it would have 20,000 employees working overseas, which was one-third of its entire workforce. (Currently, the company's overseas employees comprise roughly 45 percent of its total workforce.) Management did not ignore its domestic market or the development of new products, though.

One of the things that management was looking into was the development of the company's cellulose production. In 1951, P&G, spurred by the government's urgings to expand this type of business, had purchased slightly over 1 million acres of pine-growing land in northern Florida. Of course, the trees were of little value if the company did not have any place to process the pulp. So, P&G constructed a huge pulp mill at Foley, Florida. This was a new venture, one of the rare times P&G concentrated on a technology and product line with which it had little experience. But, risks had never stopped P&G before, nor would they now.

WE'RE MAKING ALL THIS MONEY: LET'S USE IT

In June, 1955, P&G reported record sales of $966 million! The earnings on this amount were over $57 million. This reflected a great deal of growth and led to speculation as to what direction the company was headed.

By this time, P&G was operating three major divisions: soaps, foods, and drug products. (Today, it has twelve.) Management debated whether or not the company should hold firm and not compete in other product areas. Some individuals said there should be no expansion; others opted for diversification. No one individual's opinion prevailed. As Vice-Chairman Brad Butler explained, "The final decision will be made on the basis of wisdom and knowledge rather than on the basis of individual opinion." The one thing that managers did agree on was that any expansion would require bold decision making, careful planning, and capital. For once, the company went outside to finance its operations.

In 1952, the company had issued $30 million in long-term notes to help finance the Foley pulp mill. Four years later, it issued $70 million in debentures. That same year, P&G introduced a new toothpaste, Crest®. This soon became the standard bearer for the company's toilet goods business.

Crest was unique. It included stannous flouride, which researchers at Indiana University claimed would provide the key to an effective anti-cavity toothpaste. They were right! Eventually, the researchers received a patent for the stannous flouride process. P&G paid royalties for an exclusive contract and received a few patents of it own for the process. More important, the company got the American Dental Association (ADA) to endorse Gleem. That marked the first time in the ADA's history it had granted the use of its name to promote a commercial product. Gleem's success led to a newly founded Professional Services Division to promote more new products such as Scope mouthwash and Head and Shoulders shampoo. It seemed like there would be no end to the products streaming out of P&G's factories. There was one factor that inhibited P&G's production, though: governmental regulations.

P&G had never really had to worry about obtaining government approval for its products. However, as the company became involved more deeply with applications of industrial chemistry, it also became more aware of the power of the government controls. For example, it took the FDA 18 months to approve Scope and a full year to clear Head & Shoulders shampoo lotion. To P&G management, government intervention was merely one of the hazards of business. They had overcome greater obstacles in their careers; they could do the same in this area. Besides, they had other business opportunities to consider.

ON PAPER, P&G LOOKS GOOD

P&G owned a million acres of trees and a pulp processing plant. It seemed only natural, then, that the company would involve itself deeply in the production and sales of paper products. After all, P&G had a firm understanding of consumers likes and dislikes and an excellent track record in research and development. Management realized, however, that they had a limited knowledge of tree farming and wood pulp production. Therefore, they chose to involve the company in paper products, but in a prudent fashion. They followed a business axiom that implied "in the absence of knowledge, acquisitions are best." The first step in their expansion plan was the 1957 purchase of the Charmin paper mills in Green Bay, Wisconsin.

It did not take long before P&G researchers improved on the company's paper products (Charmin®, White Cloud®, and Puffs®) through the application of a process that would dry pulp with a stream of hot air. High sales of these products prompted the company to go for broke. P&G expanded its plants in Green Bay and Cheboygan, Michigan, and announced plans to build a new one in Mehoopany, Pennsylvania. Meanwhile, the company was developing yet another product that would increase its revenues significantly. That was a disposable diaper, which came to be known as Pampers®.

P&G spent a lot of time and money developing a disposable diaper that users would consider the ultimate product in the line. Certainly, the idea was not new. In fact, competitors had been selling disposable diapers for generations. Yet, when P&G launched its developmental project in the 1950s, less than one percent of the billions of diapers used in the United States each year were disposables. Management saw an opportunity to change that percentage—and change it they did.

By the late 1960s, almost 25 percent of the diapers used in the U.S. were disposables, and most of them were Pampers. They were so well received in the country that parents in other countries started using them in great numbers as well. By 1980, the product was in use in over 75 countries. Pampers proved to be one of P&G's most successful products ever—and one more indication that the company is growing stronger as it grows older. They were so successful, in fact, that even the new plant in Mehoopany proved insufficient for production purposes.

The initial investment at Mehoopany amounted to about $150 million in 1963. Three years later, when the plant opened, a daily stream of trucks brought logs there, where they were processed into toilet tissue, papertowels (P&G had added Bounty to its product line in 1965), and Pampers. The company's need for wood was so great that over 125 local timber growers were selling their trees to the plant, which operated around the clock every day of the year. More important to the local economy, the plant employed 2,500 people. Still, the facility was not large enough!

Within a few years, P&G built new plants at Cape Girardeau, Missouri, Modesto, California, and Greenville, North Carolina. They even bought International Paper's Oxnard, California, plant. Not surprisingly, the new additions were not enough to keep up with the demand!

Lack of production space was only one of P&G's concerns. There was also the problem of pulp supply. The solution lay in Canada. P&G leased 7 million acres of prime Alberta woodlands. The acquisition was a tremendous help to P&G, especially since consumers' demands for its paper products continued to increase. As P&G battled to meet those demands, it also did more and more research to provide even more products. Today, the company's paper products are all leaders in their categories—as is about every product the company sells.

THERE ARE NO GROUNDS FOR CONCERN HERE

P&G management continued looking for new opportunities to expand. They considered the foodstuff industry a likely place. According to government statistics, American consumers were spending more than $95 billion per year on food in the mid-1950s. Of course, P&G had little expertise in the area, but, as usual, that did not faze anyone there. Management decided to enter the foodstuff field through acquisition. They wasted no time doing so.

P&G's first acquisition was in 1955, when they bought the W. T. Young firm in Lexington, Kentucky. Grant sold Big Top™ Peanut Butter. (Big Top eventually passed out of existence to be replaced by Jif® in 1956.) Next, they bought the Nebraska Consolidated Mills of Omaha in 1956. That added the Duncan Hines® cake mix line.

In 1957, P&G expanded its household products line by purchasing the Clorox Chemical Company, headquartered in California. (The government later forced P&G to divest itself of Clorox, which it thought "might tend to create a monopoly in the household bleach industry.") Six years later, on November 26, 1963, P&G exchanged 1,650,000 shares of its common stock, worth about $130 million then, for J. A. Folger & Company. It did not take long before Folger's became enormously successful. That proved damaging to P&G.

The government did not approve of the company's Folger acquisition. So, on June 22, 1966, the Federal Trade Commission informed P&G that it intended to seek the divestiture of Folger.

P&G had gone to considerable expense to defend itself from the government's lawsuits regarding Clorox. It did not wish to repeat the drawn out, costly court battles on behalf of Folger. Rather, it reached a consent decree with the FTC in which P&G agreed:

1. that during the next seven years, it would not acquire, without the FTC's prior approval, any business in the United States concerned with household consumer products which are generally sold through the grocery store

2. to sell its Folger plant in Houston, Texas, within five years, to a purchaser approved by the FTC

3. not to engage in price discrimination on Folger or promote Folger coffee jointly with other P&G products for the next five years (The company stressed that it had not done either of these things in the past anyway.)

That concluded the government's great "coffee caper," but at least P&G remained in the business. Unfortunately for P&G, that business was changing. The company, and its competitors as well, had to face new challenges to their traditional operating practices.

KEEPING THE ENVIRONMENT CLEAN

Suddenly, people realized that detergents, paper products, and other consumer goods posed threats to the environment. Naturally, activists focused on the manufacturers of such products for redress.

P&G's size invited protests against some of the environmental hazards, real or imagined, that their products caused. One ingredient in particular, alkyl benzene sulfonate, created problems.

Residues of the sulfonate did not break down completely during sewage treatment. As a result, a white foam formed against waterway banks. Protestors perceived this foam as a potential danger to their health. They approached the government which convened congressional hearings to ascertain the seriousness of the problem. Scientists testified that the foam was not a health hazard. Their claims were ignored, partly because the foam was so visible. That gave environmentalists something tangible on which to focus attention. To appease them, manufacturers developed an alternative. That had a somewhat positive effect on the protestors' claims, but the sulfonate was not the only target activists had.

Enzymes also created a storm of protests. P&G researchers, acting on a tip from the company's European Operations Supervisor, verified that enzymes helped eradicate stubborn laundry stains such as blood, grass, tea, and coffee. Consequently, P&G began marketing a pre-soak product, Biz®. Then, reports appeared claiming that a few workers in manufacturing plants were suffering allergic symptoms from enzyme dust. This led to concerns that people using products containing enzymes were doing so at the risk of their health.

The fears became an epidemic. The company's attempts to allay consumers' worries proved futile. Consequently, P&G removed enzymes from its products. After all, management reasoned, no business can survive by selling products that consumers will not buy. This lesson had served P&G well for over 100 years, and it had no plans to bypass it now.

Next came the phosphates controversy which arose in the late 1960s. Environmentalists claimed that phosphates, too, were detrimental to society. To circumvent any more adverse publicity, many manufacturers removed phosphates from their detergents. P&G refused to do so. It maintained that most of the phosphorous found in groundwater and the environment in general came from sources other than phosphates. Few people believed that—for which the company paid a price.

Consumers switched to competitors' phosphate-free products, which were, in many cases, of inferior quality. Even a few stockholders questioned the company's position on the use of phosphates. Management realized that they had to counteract the loss of business and placate their stockholders. They spent $130 million to develop a phosphate replacement. Researchers thought they had found a suitable alternative, called NTA (sodium nitrilotriacetate). The government thought differently and announced that NTA posed environmental threats of its own. P&G found itself between the proverbial rock and a hard place—and accused of polluting both. Eventually, the company bowed reluctantly to public and government pressure and developed alternatives to phosphates. Perhaps P&G wasted its money!

In 1979, a joint Canadian-American commission announced that 98 percent of all phosphorous entering the Great Lakes came from groundwater runoff, sewage, and airborne dust. That meant that no more than two percent stemmed from phosphates. The announcement vindicated P&G's claims that phosphates were not dangerous to the environment. It also substantiated the company's position summed up by President Ed Harness. "In difficult times," he said, "the company must continue operating on the principle of what it believes is right rather than what will make everyone happy next week."

Following Harness' advice was simple for P&G. It certainly helped the company through some trying times, including such upheavals as the civil rights movement of the 1960s, the Vietnam War, the women's movement, and rising environmental concerns and consumer aggressiveness. Despite the problems, P&G grew steadily.

P&G continued to develop new and/or improved products that matched consumers' health and environmental concerns. Among them were Bold-3™, a detergent with a built-in fabric softener, Cheer,® with a wrinkle-relaxing ingredient, and the fabric softener Downy®. Between 1957 and 1974, total sales increased from $1.1 billion to $4.9 billion. Net earnings on common stock grew from 86 cents to $3.85. More importantly, P&G's net assets went from $462 million to almost $2 billion! Such growth has continued ever since.

The company added several new products throughout the 1980s. In doing so, it did not forget the past. It used the hallowed name of Ivory on liquid soap (1982) and shampoo and hair conditioner (1983). It diversified into juice products such as Citrus Hill Select™ Orange Juice (1982) and Winter Hill™ fruit juices (1989). P&G acquired Tender Leaf™ bagged teas in 1982. There has been no shortage of plants and acquisitions to manufacture these deposits.

For example, P&G acquired Jetco Chemicals in Corsicana, Texas (1984), Richardson-Vicks, Hatboro, Pennslyvania (1985), and Maryland Club food products, Omaha, Nebraska (1989). It built a new pulp plant in Barnesville, Georgia (1982) and opened another food product facility in Edenton, North Carolina

(1989). These acquisitions and new plants were made possible by the company's outstanding earnings record.

There has been a steady growth in net sales throughout the 1980s. For example, the company had net sales of $13,552 in the 1984-85 fiscal year. That figure jumped to $21,398 in 1988-89. It has had two stock splits since 1980 (four since 1960). As of December 15, 1989, there were 324,423,921 outstanding shares of common stock with a dividend rate of $3.60 (effective November, 1989.) Significantly, dividend payments have been uninterrupted since the company's incorporation in 1890, and there have been 34 consecutive fiscal years of increased dividends per share!

Certainly, the company has come a long way since it began its operations in a single building in Cincinnati. Today, P&G has operations in 46 countries plus the United States. The company employs 43,600 people in the U.S. in 61 plants and 35,700 in other countries. It still sells Ivory soap and Crisco, but those products, which were once the company's mainstays, are but two of over 100 products ranging from all-fabric bleach to analgesics, gastrointestinal products, hair conditioners, and apple juice. There is no doubt that P&G is here to stay.

Currently, the company operates 17 research and development and engineering facilities in 8 countries. Many of P&G's other subsidiaries outside the United States also have product development laboratories and engineering facilities. There is no telling what these facilities will produce that will help strengthen P&G's status as a corporate giant in the world business arena. After all, a company can only grow old successfully if it concentrates on new products and their relevance to the future. Procter and Gamble's management has always balanced the past and the present well, with an eye to the future. It is this balance which has made P&G the success it is, and which it promises to be for a long time to come.

Proctor & Gamble CEO - Edward L. Artzt

Courtesy of Proctor & Gamble

Chapter 7

1853

Aetna Insurance Company

WHO ELSE WOULD START AN INSURANCE COMPANY WHEN THERE IS NO ONE TO INSURE?

The history of Aetna Insurance can be traced through its succession of presidents, most of whom spent large portions of their adult years in their positions. Aetna offers a classic example of how beneficial the practice of grooming high-level executives from within can be—and the company certainly owes its phenomenal success to the remarkable parade of well-trained presidents whose collective longevity defies all odds.

Life insurance salesmen in the first half of the 19th century were as popular as cockroaches in a sugar bowl. In fact, some people would have preferred to have the cockroaches in their houses! The concept of

151

life insurance was still new at the time, and Americans were experiencing too many problems with unscrupulous life insurance salesmen and companies to put any faith—or money—into the purchase of policies. That did not deter Eliphalet Adams Bulkeley. He was determined to begin a life insurance business that people could rely on to treat them fairly, and begin one he did.

BULKELEY FOR PRESIDENT—OF EVERYTHING IN TOWN

Bulkeley had a unique background. He was born in Colchester, Connecticut, in 1803. Twenty-one years later, he graduated from Yale University. Following that <u>milestone, young Bulkeley</u> spent four years as a law apprentice in Lebanon, Connecticut. Then, he grew tired of his home state. Being an adventurous soul, he moved for some unknown reason to Selma, Alabama, in 1828. Two years later, he returned to Connecticut to marry Lydia Smith Morgan.

Aetna's First Headquarters

Courtesy Aetna Life & Casualty Co. Archives, Hartford, CT

The newlyweds took up residence in East Haddam, only a few miles away from their native Colchester. Bulkeley established a successful law practice...organized a bank and became its first president...became a large stockholder and director of the Willimantic Linen Company, which manufactured cotton thread...earned election to the lower house of the Connecticut legislature....In short, Bulkeley exercised his organizational and political skills to the fullest. It was only natural, then, that he set his sights higher as far as his business interests were concerned.

The concept of life insurance intrigued Bulkeley. What interested him most was the opportunity life insurance offered individuals. He recognized that most people could not set aside enough money in their productive years to protect their futures. To his way of thinking, life insurance would help them do so. Of course, he was also aware of the fact that many other business people felt the same way and started life insurance companies—many of which had become financial disasters.

WHO IS GOING TO INSURE THE LIFE INSURERS?

A large number of life insurance companies had come and gone by the 1850s. Entrepreneurs saw the need for the insurance, but they could not always convince potential clients of its need. Worse, some of these entrepreneurs were terrible business managers. The combination of too few insureds and bad management caused many insurance companies to fail. The majority of these institutions were in England and the eastern United States. Bulkeley took note of these failures and looked for a way to avoid the mistakes that caused them. Judging by Aetna's longevity, he found the way.

BULKELEY'S FIRE EXPERIENCE HAS HIM BURNING WITH ENTHUSIASM FOR LIFE

Bulkeley had some experience in the insurance field. He had been the first president of the Connecticut Mutual Life Insurance Company founded in 1846, the same year he joined the 27-year-old Aetna Fire Insurance Company as a director and general counsel. As the name implied, fire insurance was Aetna's primary business. However, its charter allowed it to sell life insurance. Bulkeley took advantage of that provision, but not until 1850.

That year, Bulkeley and several associates formed a subsidiary of the fire insurance company. They called the affiliate, which had separate capitalization, a distinct board of directors, and proprietary ownership, the Annuity Fund. On June 6, 1850, Connecticut's Governor Thomas H. Seymour approved a bill which officially made Aetna a licensed life insurance company. Five days later, a committee charged with effecting the company's plan to insure lives offered a plan to do just that.

The plan provided that:
- the new life department would be called the Annuity Fund
- the department would have a capital of $150,000 to be made available to the shareholders of the Aetna Fire, to be divided into shares of $100 each
- the capital and business of the Annuity Fund were to be kept separate from that of the fire insurance company

- seven members of the Aetna Fire Board of Directors were to be entrusted with the Annuity Fund (They were to be called "Managing Directors" of the life department, and the chairman of the directors, one Eliphalet A. Bulkeley, would be a vice president of Aetna Fire.)

The company was in business, and stockholders rushed to participate.

WE HOLD A GREAT AMOUNT OF STOCK IN THIS COMPANY

By July 2, 1850, all the stock had been sold to 103 shareholders. There was a bit of shuffling in holdings, but things had settled down somewhat by August 12, when the official shareholder count rose to 105. Aetna Life had become a reality—such as it was!

The company did not rush to hire employees. That was certainly understandable. Prospective customers did not stampede to buy life insurance. The Annuity Fund simply did not need a large workforce at first.

The Aetna Fire provided one employee to do the Annuity Fund's accounts when necessary. Two of Bulkeley's sons, Morgan G. and Charles E., earned fifty cents per week to sweep the office and keep it clean. (That was a humble beginning for young Morgan, who would serve as the company's president for 43 years!) The company's medical examiner, G. W. Russell, and Consulting Physician, H. A. Grant, dropped in on the rare occasions when there was a prospective insured to be examined. The company even had an actuary, local attorney John W. Seymour. In truth, his appointment was nominal, since the company did not list a full-time actuary until 1868. That was probably because the directors were not even sure the Annuity Fund would survive that long!

THIS IS HARDLY THE TYPE OF BUSINESS FROM WHICH AN INSURANCE GIANT WILL ARISE

The Annuity Fund's early years did not fit the founders' dreams—unless they were the nightmare segments. The company sold only 537 policies between its opening and December 31, 1850. One agent, Curtis L. North, accounted for 320 of them. Unfortunately, North was not the most scrupulous man in the industry, He constantly violated remittance rules and territorial rights. By 1852, his career with the Annuity Fund was history. In fact, the Annuity Fund itself was almost history. One of the most significant factors that separates successful companies from those that fail is their ability to overcome problems. Every business experiences downturns; not every company survives them. Aetna was one of those that did, which is why it is an insurance giant today.

The life expectancy of a life insurance company during the early 1850s was about the same as that of a bleeding guppy floating among a school of hungry sharks. Sixteen life insurance companies failed between 1850 and 1854. Others teetered on the brink. Fortunately, the Annuity Fund hung on, but Bulkeley had his doubts as to how long it could do so.

Actually, the company's early fiscal picture was not bad for a start-up business. Within a year of its opening, the Annuity Fund's operations included most of the eastern states and eastern Canada. On June 30, 1851, the operation reported an income of $30,164 from premiums and other sources. The company had

1,003 policies in force, which translated into $1,285,710 of insurance. The costs of the operation up to this point were only $7,375. The company had paid out a total of $4,000 to settle two death claims. On the surface, it looked as if the Annuity Fund was in good financial shape. It was management's job to keep it that way. The Annuity Fund's directors took no chances on letting their initial success delude them into thinking they would make millions early in their venture. They were paying close attention to the negative things that were happening to their competitors with an eye to avoiding similar problems.

First, many life insurance companies were engaged in unsound life insurance practices. For example, they were paying out huge agents' commissions, which ultimately contributed to their insolvency. That in itself would not have been so bad if they had not been paying them to unscrupulous agents. (The Annuity Fund's directors had already manifested a distaste for such representatives when they parted company with Curtis North. This set a precedent which holds today.) Worse, legislators were boldly meddling in insurance companies' affairs.

Gideon Welles, best known as the Secretary of the Navy during the Civil War, then president of the Hartford-based Charter Oak Life Insurance Company, recorded in his diary just how deeply involved legislators were in the local insurance business. He wrote that legislators were openly presenting bills to companies asking for money in exchange for their influence. Principled businessmen like Welles and Bulkeley wanted nothing to do with such practices. Welles ultimately resigned—and the company failed. Bulkeley concerned himself more with what the New York state legislature was doing.

That august body mandated in 1849 that the same company could no longer carry both life and fire insurance in New York State. Just to make sure that the companies which decided to continue operating in the state knew the legislature was serious, they strengthened the law in 1853 and warned that it would be strictly enforced. Technically, Aetna Fire Insurance and the Annuity Fund operated as two separate entities according to the state law, but Bulkeley took no chances. The stockholders dissolved the latter and formed the Aetna Life Insurance Company. Significantly, on Independence Day, July 4, 1853, shareholders gathered to elect 10 directors, 1 president, and 1 secretary. To no one's surprise, they named Eliphalet A. Bulkeley as the "new" company's president. That still did not resolve the firm's problems in New York State, though.

Another law the legislature had passed in 1851 had an adverse impact on Aetna's ability to do business in New York State. The law declared that any company wishing to do business in the state would have to deposit $100,000 there. Faced with these new laws, all but three out-of-state companies withdrew that year. Aetna simply could not raise the required money. Its limited funds also precluded the company from operating in Massachusetts. The Aetna Life Insurance Company was in danger of collapsing. Fortunately, Bulkeley and his directors anticipated John Babsone Lane Soul's sage advice: they headed west.

GO WEST, YOUNG INSURANCE COMPANIES

Bulkeley refused to let his fledgling company die. He sought new opportunities to sell life insurance. In his estimation, the best place to do so was the western

United States. The place may have been right, but the timing was not. Nevertheless, Bulkeley moved forward with his plan to capture the West for Aetna.

The primary factor that prompted Bulkeley to direct his attention westward was the fact that insurance legislation there was limited in comparison to the eastern states. So, in August of 1857, Aetna assigned Dr. Thomas B. Lacey, of New Milford, Connecticut, to start selling life insurance in Michigan, Ohio, Indiana, and Wisconsin. The directors also granted him the power to hire other agents, which was a company first. Lacey, who historian Richard Hooker described as "another Curtis North, but a Curtis North who had well balanced judgment as well as enthusiastic enterprise," paid dividends immediately. More important, the timing of Lacey's assignment proved beneficial to Aetna.

1857 was a milestone year in U.S. and Aetna history. The country entered one of its periodic financial dry spells which became acute in October of the year. A serious depression affected the entire country. It was particularly acute in Aetna's home city of Hartford, where all but one of the city's banks closed on October 7 and suspended specie payments. Naturally, stockholders suffered as the economy worsened. Some of them pressed for the dissolution of the company so they could share in whatever proceeds resulted. Such talk intensified in 1858 as the depression continued. Bulkeley continued to resist. Perhaps even he would have agreed that the company's dissolution would be a wise move, except for one thing: Lacey continued to flood the home office with applications. That made Bulkeley believe that the company could succeed. His obstinacy paid off.

AETNA MAY NOT BE FINISHED, BUT ITS END(ERS) IS IN SIGHT

In 1854, Bulkeley hired a young man named Thomas Ostrom Enders as a clerk in Aetna's home office. Four years later, Enders was promoted to secretary, and even though the company was five years old by this time, he was still its only full-time employee. Enders had an immediate impact on Aetna's operations.

Enders devised a plan whereby insureds could buy life insurance as part of a participating strategy. Most policyholders at the time wanted mutual ownership, i.e., all the assets of an insurance company belonged to them. Bulkeley preferred the stock ownership approach. Enders recognized that the difference in the two strategies was a function of bookkeeping.

At Enders urging, Aetna combined the two ownership forms into a "participating" plan. Stockholders and policyholders shared in the profits. The only difference was that policyholders in the participating plan had no vote in company management, whereas the stockholders did. Enders' plan pleased everybody and gave Aetna a great deal of respectability in the life insurance industry. As luck would have it, the Participating Department became a reality in 1861, the year the American Civil War broke out.

Surprisingly, the war proved beneficial for Aetna. People, especially young males who were subject to military service, developed a higher appreciation for life and the potential for death. A quick glance at the dramatic increase in policies, income, and assets shows that people were indeed growing more insurance minded.

Aetna Life Insurance
Growth 1861-1867

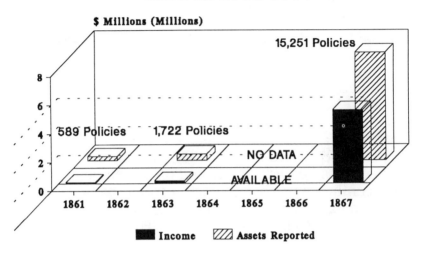

Naturally, the increase in policies and claim payments necessitated a larger staff. By 1868, the Aetna's full-time workforce consisted of 20 employees! That pales in comparison to today's workforce of approximately 45,500, but it was certainly large according to the company's 1868 perspective. It was so large, in fact, that Aetna Life Insurance had to move to new quarters. The future looked bright for Eliphalet Bulkeley and his company, and the optimism certainly was warranted.

OKAY, AETNA IS HERE TO STAY, BUT WHAT'S NEXT?

Aetna entered the post-war era as the fifth largest of the nation's 80 life insurance companies. During the war the company had secured more new business than any of its competitors. Jealous competitors accused Aetna of unjustly withholding dividends from its policyholders.

Most of these competitors were mutual companies and had no concept of the benefits of Aetna's participating plan. What the accusers failed to recognize was that Aetna's policyholders preferred the company's set-up! As a result, when competitors attacked Aetna, they actually gave the company publicity it was not getting elsewhere. That was a boon for the company, especially in the western states, where Aetna continued to do a landslide business despite losing Dr. Lacey's services. (He died in 1865, but the large volume of business he had established on the company's behalf continued unabated.) Aetna could thank its competitors for their help, but it did plenty of selling on its own by losing a bit of business. HUH?

NOW THAT WE HAVE YOUR INTEREST...LET'S DISPOSE OF IT

In the early days of life insurance, companies accepted premium payments in a combination of cash and interest bearing notes. Since the majority of the companies extant were mutuals, policyholders expected that the dividends at the end of the year would equal 50 percent of the premium, which would cancel the note. Although Aetna followed this practice, neither Bulkeley nor Enders were fond of it. They opted to end it after the war. They paid a small price for their bold move, but the decision proved to be the right one in the long run.

Bulkeley was an extraordinary risk taker. He realized that policyholders would switch to other companies in the belief that they were getting a better deal.

He also recognized that they would realize eventually that all-cash, rather than half-cash, half-interest policies were the best policy. Bulkeley was gambling that policyholders would rather associate themselves with a sound insurance company than one whose future could be in doubt due to a lack of cash reserves. Once again, he was right.

Initially, Aetna experienced a drop in the number of policyholders. The number dropped from 15,251 in 1867 to 13,337 in 1868 (the year Aetna became the first insurance company to introduce renewable term insurance plans) and 11,337 in 1869. By 1870, however, only one mutual company continued to operate on the half-cash, half-interest note basis. This pleased the prescient Bulkeley. Unfortunately, adopting an all-cash premium program was his last major decision as Aetna's president. On February 13, 1872, Eliphalet Bulkeley died. However, he left the company in good hands.

Thomas O. Enders assumed the presidency of Aetna after Bulkeley's death. Even though he had sufficient experience to run the company alone (the company was not at that time the giant it is today), he did what so many other successful CEOs have done throughout history. Enders surrounded himself with experienced, knowledgeable people who were experts in their particular specialities. More important, *he relied on their counsel.*

YOU DON'T NEED SHEMP, MOE, AND CURLY TO RUN YOUR COMPANY

Enders' three top aides were Dr. Gurdon W. Russell, the company's Medical Director, Howell W. St. John, Aetna's first real actuary and a renowned mathematician, and Joel L. English, secretary, whose career with the company spanned 60 years (1867-1927). Even that distinguished record for longevity barely exceeded St. John's 56 years (1868-1924). Russell *only* lasted 49 years (1853-1902). They applied their experience wisely.

The Enders team concentrated on developing new types of policies designed to serve the real needs of policyholders. St. John and Russell in particular proved their value to Aetna through their reputation outside the company. St. John earned a national reputation as an authority in the actuarial field. Russell, too, was recognized throughout the industry as an outstanding medical examiner. Their reputations drew attention and provided Aetna with a lot of publicity, which certainly did not hurt the company's business.

YOU GOT A MINUTE? LET'S EXCHANGE INFORMATION

One of the things that this team did to improve Aetna's position in the life insurance competition was to build *esprit de corps* among its agents. The team members reasoned that happy agents would sell more insurance. This was certainly not a startling revelation, but the communications lines between the agents and senior management did open up to everyone's benefit.

The agents plunged into the open communications effort. The vehicles for the exchange of information had been in place since 1868. That year the general agents established an association and a magazine called simply "The Aetna." The secretary of the association functioned as the liaison with senior management. This led to a beneficial exchange of ideas and suggestions that gave executives and agents alike a new insight into life insurance operations. This rapport between the two entities was extremely important at the time, since the insurance industry was undergoing a severe shakeup.

Between 1868 and 1878, a total of 102 life insurance companies failed. The country suffered through yet another financial downturn in 1873, from which Aetna did not escape.

The company suffered declines in the amount of insurance in force throughout the 1870s, but it weathered the storm. In fact, in 1878, the Connecticut State Legislature overrode the governor's veto and authorized an increase in capitalization from the original $150,000 to $750,000. Thus, Aetna's first quarter century of business ended on a high note. Enders had done his job well. But, the stress of the 1870s took a lot out of him. He decided to step down as president in 1879. His replacement carried a familiar name: he was Morgan Gardner Bulkeley, Eliphalet's son.

THE BULKELEY STOPS HERE

Morgan Bulkeley began his service with Aetna in 1872 at the age of 35 as a member of the Board of Directors. Obviously, he was being groomed to assume the company's presidency at some point. Even at this time in the company's existence, management (basically the Bulkeley family) was realizing the importance of training and promoting its top executives internally. So, by the time young Bulkeley became president he was well versed in the company's operations.

Bulkeley remained in office for 43 years. Was he successful? Look at a comparison of the company's finances between his first and last year of service.

Morgan Garner Bulkeley

Courtesy Aetna Life & Casualty Co. Archives, Hartford, CT

YEAR	ASSETS	ANNUAL PREMIUM INCOME	INSURANCE IN FORCE	CAPITAL STOCK
1879	$ 25,636,195	$ 2,494,187	$ 77,738,038	$ 750,000
1922	207,041,779	55,934,645	1,334,026,507	5,000,000

Dollar figures do not tell the whole story, though. The remarkable expansion the company experienced is equally impressive.

Toward the end of the 19th century, Aetna began selling accident coverage through a newly formed subsidiary, Aetna Accident Insurance Company, formed in 1887. The company began health insurance coverage in 1899. In 1902, Aetna branched into employers' and other types of liability coverage and workers' collective insurance. The company created the Aetna Accident and Liability Company in 1903 to handle these new lines. And, with an eye to the future, the company added auto property damage coverage, protection for drivers against damage to horse teams (horses and autos were sharing the road at the time), and other types of coverage. Significantly, Aetna wrote the country's first auto insurance policy in 1912. One year later, the company formed the Automobile Insurance Company of Hartford to write fire insurance on the "horseless carriage." Development did not stop there.

In 1913, Aetna became one of the first insurers to write group coverage for businesses. Four years later, the company changed Aetna Accident Insurance Company's name to Aetna Casualty and Surety Company to match its broader scope—and phenomenal growth—of business.

By the time World War I began, Aetna was insuring people for practically every purpose, ranging from life to workers compensation to elevator liability to ocean marine. The latter line in particular grew as a result of the war. Fortunately, the U. S. government assumed the responsibility for war risk insurance for uniformed personnel during this war. That left Aetna free to concentrate on its other insurance interests, which it did with alacrity. (There was one sad note to Aetna's war contributions: 1,154 Aetna employees joined the armed forces. Twenty of them were killed.)

Managing growth was one of Bulkeley's strongpoints. He exercised careful control over expenditures during his years in office and adhered closely to a well-developed growth plan.

The tone for Bulkeley's leadership appeared in an 1884 editorial in *The Aetna*. As it said, "We do not expect to make Aetna the largest company in the land. We do, however, expect it will, and intend it shall, maintain its enviable reputation for strength and fair dealing." That it did—and has continued to do.

What makes Bulkeley's achievements even more remarkable is his political record during his presidency. He did what no CEO of a large company can do today. Between 1879 and 1911, he served 4 terms as the mayor of Hartford, 2 terms as Connecticut's governor, and 1 as a United States senator! He still found the time to steer Aetna in a successful direction. He was a remarkable man in charge of a remarkable company—and one whose record as an executive will never be rivaled.

THERE'S MORE MORGANS HERE THAN IN A HERD OF WORK HORSES (MORGANS, THAT IS)

Morgan Bulkeley died on November 6, 1922, at the age of 85. His successor was another Morgan: Morgan Bulkeley Brainard, Eliphalet's grandson.

Morgan Bulkeley Brainard

Like his predecessor, Brainard was well prepared to take over the presidency. While still a law student at Yale in 1902 (he graduated in 1903), Brainard's father, a member of Aetna's Board of Directors, died. Morgan, only 23 years old at the time, succeeded him.

Courtesy Aetna Life & Casualty Co. Archives, Hartford, CT

In 1905, after two years of legal apprenticeship in the law office of Aetna's general counsel, Brainard joined the company as assistant treasurer. Two years later, he became treasurer. In 1910, he rose to a vice president position. This put him in a close working relationship with Morgan Bulkeley and stamped him as a likely successor to the company's presidency. When that time came, it was by default. The presidency had been offered to 76-year-old Joel English, who had been a vice president since 1905. English declined the position because of age and faltering health. Enter Morgan Brainard. Brainard admitted that "I have got to surround myself with as able a group of men as I possibly can." He said it apologetically, as if most successful leaders did not operate that way. (Indeed, not all did. For example, Brainard's style of leadership was different than Morgan G. Bulkeley's, which was more autonomous in nature.) What he did not apologize for, though, was Aetna's size—and its potential.

A newly appointed Aetna director told Brainard at a meeting early in his career that a competitor had labeled the company as a "sleeping giant." The remark caught Brainard's attention. As he explained, "It was the word 'giant' that opened my eyes....All at once I became aware of the latent power in the Aetna family....Apparently everyone recognizes that we have within ourselves a giant's strength that only needs to be called on to awaken." Brainard took it as his mission to awaken that giant.

The new president immediately created a closer bond between the home office and the field force. He made it a point to appear personally wherever he could to deliver information, policies, etc., to agents. He made it clear that the home office was in complete control of the company's business, but he helped in every way he could. The company established uniform agency contracts, simplified procedures, and insisted upon sharp reductions in the average costs of soliciting new business. His inspiration prompted company agents to intensify their search for new business. His participation paid off quickly.

Business improved for Aetna throughout the 1920s. Shortly after World War I ended, Aetna reached $1 billion in life insurance in force. Brainard felt the company could do better, both in life insurance sales and expanding its lines. He was right on both counts, as figures prove. Increases in other lines complemented the unprecedented growth.

Aetna Life Insurance
Growth 1922-1929

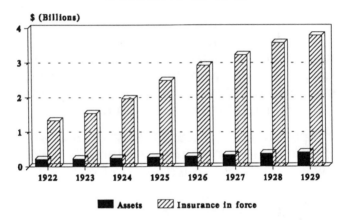

IS THERE A FIRE SALE? IF NOT, THERE "AUTO" BE

In 1924, Aetna purchased the Standard Fire Company to strengthen its presence in property-casualty insurance lines, e.g., fire, windstorm, riot, explosion, civil commotion. Concomitantly, the company experienced problems with its automobile insurance business, which caused grave concern.

The Automobile Insurance Company faced serious problems in the mid-1920s. (This may sound familiar to contemporary policyholders.) Even though this autonomous affiliate was experiencing an astronomic increase in premiums and new business, it was also suffering high losses and a serious drain on reserves. A great percentage of the losses could be attributed to deficiencies in the company's ocean marine business, which was a part of the automobile insurance affiliate's operation.

As happens at every company from time to time, a high-ranking management individual was guilty of negligence. He failed to come to grips with the mounting losses or to notify Brainard of them. Losses accumulated to such a high level that the affiliate's financial structure grew unsound. That led Morgan Brainard to write in Aetna's 1926 annual report that "through its efficient agency plant, [the affiliate] has for several years been given more business than it could digest." He did not want to see it driven to financial disaster. He acted to resolve the problem quickly.

One part of the problem resolved itself when the negligent executive resigned on March 8, 1926. Another was directly connected to World War I.

THE AETNA HAS A SINKING FEELING

Heavy losses of allied shipping during the war resulted in high premiums which had a positive effect on insurers' bottom lines. This proved beneficial to insurers who watched profits roll in. On the other hand, the high premiums cut into shippers' profits and prompted some to defraud the insurance companies even to the extent that a few sunk their own vessels! After the war, insurers had to reduce their premiums, but shippers did not necessarily stop their fraud. It required great vigilance on the insurers' parts to detect fraud. Unfortunately, the Aetna's special marine office in New York City continued to pursue new business, often at inadequate rates, and failed to screen its new policyholders carefully. Oddly enough, Aetna's ocean marine premium income almost tripled between 1918 and 1924 despite the reduced rates. It increased from $2,217,000 in 1918 to $6,305,000 in 1924. The bad news was that the new policyholders who accounted for much of this business through the New York office were not always well chosen. Thus, Aetna had well justified cause for concern.

Brainard's first step was to appoint E. E. Cammack, a vice president and actuary, to examine closely the impact the ocean marine disaster had on the Automobile Insurance Company's affairs—and the company's image. Brainard had two choices: let the automobile insurance company go into bankruptcy or refinance it and retain consumers' and shareholders' faith in Aetna. To him, the second option was the most viable.

Cammack recommended that the company reduce its automobile insurance business temporarily and increase its capital in order to restore the affiliate to a sound fiscal status. Brainard agreed and followed up on the recommendations.

Quickly, automobile insurance premiums dropped by almost 75 percent between 1924 and 1927, from $30,085,000 to $7,931,000. Also, the Automobile Insurance Company's directors voted at a March 31, 1926,meeting to issue 10,000 additional shares of stock at a par value of $100 at $1,200 per share. Aetna Life took the issue in its entirety. This resulted in the addition of $1 million to the affiliate's paid-in capital of $4 million and $11 million to its surplus. That left one more step to take.

The parent company increased its own capital and surplus to ensure a resolution to the affiliate's problem. The Board of Directors authorized the issue of 50,000 additional shares of stock, par value of $100, to be offered at $200 per share. The stock sold

Aetna Headquarters

Courtesy Aetna Life & Casualty Co. Archives, Hartford, CT

quickly. As a result, the company's paid-in capital rose from $10 to $15 million. An additional $5 million went into Aetna's surplus. The problem was resolved, the company's reputation was intact—and the Great Depression lay ahead.

IF THE OCEAN MARINE DISASTER WAS DEPRESSING, TRY 1929 ON FOR SIZE

Aetna had been building its business for a little over 75 years. The company required new facilities to accommodate its expansion. In anticipation of consolidating all its operations in one location, Aetna began constructing a magnificent new headquarters building in 1929. The building proved more reliable than the economy. It opened in 1931, just about the time when the roof caved in on Aetna's business.The Great Depression had a profound impact on Aetna. Total annual premium income for the entire company dropped from $132,511,000 in 1929 to $117,725,000 in 1933. That year marked the first time since 1862 that Aetna did not pay a dividend for an entire year. Even though the dropoff in the company's total annual income was small, an increase in the number of policy loans necessitated the decision to discontinue dividends.

The number of policy loans in 1932 rose to 87,100 which, in dollar figures, amounted to $55,121,000. (By comparison, there were only 22,367 loans in 1927 at a value of $13,695,000.) In addition, the money that would have been paid out in dividends represented an important source of revenue to the company in a credit-short economy. Nevertheless, the situation was short lived. Aetna resumed paying dividends on July 2, 1934.

On the plus side, Aetna did not lay off or dismiss any workers at the home office during the period. The company did institute a ten percent pay cut, but that was far less than the 25 percent pay cuts most companies put into effect during the depression. One of the reasons the workers fared so well had to due with Aetna's investment practices. While many companies invested heavily in common stocks during the 1920s, Aetna had resisted the temptation. Thus, when the market collapsed in 1929, it had only 11.7 percent of its assets tied up in common stocks—5.22 percent of that in its own affiliates! This helped Aetna weather the storm, although not all of its investments were as prudent.

AETNA BECOMES A FARMING CONCERN—WITH A GREAT DEAL OF CONCERN ABOUT FARMERS

The number of defaults on farm mortgages rose considerably as a result of the depression. Whereas in 1920 Aetna owned only one piece of foreclosed farm property, it found itself in possession of nearly 1,000 by 1930 at a value of $7,000,000. Four years later, the company owned 3,105 at a value of $22,677,000. Surprisingly, Aetna was not caught unaware of the problem.

With remarkable foresight, Home Office management had planned for the acquisition of farms as early as 1926. It organized a group of personnel in strategic branch offices in farming states to handle the company's farm business. Brainard made several visits himself to inspect some of the farms. Not long after the depression ended, agricultural recovery alleviated

Aetna's farming burden. That was indeed fortuitous, since Aetna needed all its resources to help it through yet another war.

DIDN'T THE COUNTRY JUST GET THROUGH ONE WAR?

Once again, the federal government assumed responsibility for war risk insurance as World War II unfolded. Aetna, as were its competitors, was left with the problem of underwriting risks that had never been underwritten before. For example, there were thousands of civilian workers not covered by war risk insurance who had to be transported by contractors over submarine-infested waters. They had to bond contractors whose volumes of business increased by as much as 20 times their normal loads. And there were the unusual things that had to be bonded such as ammunition storage igloos at the Arctic Circle and special foods for the Russian armies. The Aetna Casualty and Surety Company even became involved in the "Manhattan Project," which resulted in the development of the atomic bomb, when they were asked to insure workers constructing the buildings at Oak Ridge, Tennessee, in which the research was carried out.

This created a unique problem for the company. The army would not—and could not—reveal what the project was supposed to accomplish. Thus, Aetna had no idea of whether it would be underwriting insurance against fire, mechanical, explosive hazards, or all of the above. The company worked out a complicated deal with the army "by making modifications of the War Department Insurance Rating Plan; the result of-which was insurance coverage on the basis of obtaining the claims service of the insurance carriers on a cost basis with no possibility of loss to the carriers." Under these terms, the Aetna did not need to know what claim it was paying for. It simply relied on the "Manhattan District" as to whether or not it should pay a claim. This was a unique resolution to a unique problem—but developing plans to cover such situations was nothing unique to The Aetna.

Aetna's contributions to the war effort were not restricted to insurance. As was the case with so many other businesses, the company supplied another precious commodity: people.

At the onset of the war, Aetna employed about 30,000 people, 3,025 of whom served in the armed forces at one time or another during the conflict. A total of 76 of them lost their lives. That was a terrible price to pay, but, as history shows, it is sometimes the price required if individuals and businesses are to operate in an atmosphere of freedom. After all, no matter how big an insurance company grows, there is one thing it can never insure against: that people's right to freedom will never go unchallenged. Companies, like countries, must fight to protect their freedom, even when the risk of personal losses is involved. The people of Aetna did just that, and their contributions will never be forgotten.

AETNA IS LIKE WILT CHAMBERLAIN—IT REBOUNDS QUICKLY AND STRONGLY

The end of the war brought about a sharp drop in the amount of group life insurance in force, which had, since its introduction in 1913, become a company mainstay. The reductions were attributed to cancelled contracts for war supply production and the change to a peacetime economy. The decrease was only temporary, as the company's figures demonstrate.

The dramatic increase in group insurance premi-

Aetna Life Insurance
Growth of Group Insurance

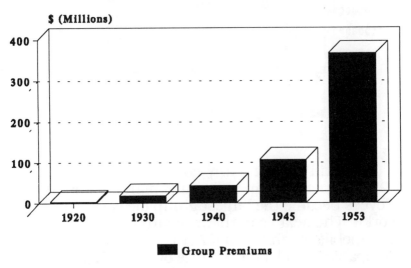

Group Premiums

ums and the continuing expansion of Aetna's overall business presaged a promising future—and management took steps to make sure that the company would continue to grow according to a well-designed long-range plan.

The 1950's were a period of exceptional growth for Aetna. To be sure, the company had been growing steadily since its founding in 1853. How much? Let's compare the insurance in force in 1953 to the 1853 figures as Aetna marked its 100th birthday.

Aetna Life Insurance Company
Growth 1872-1953

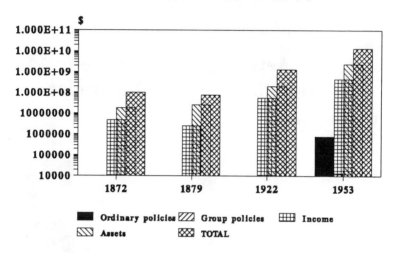

And still the company continued to expand. In 1954, Aetna's group insurance plan on federal employees became the largest group life coverage in the world. The next year, there occurred a merger of the Automobile Insurance and Aetna Casualty and Surety Companies—and a rare change of leadership.

President Brainard announced late in 1955 that he was stepping down after 43 years in the position. They certainly had been good years for Aetna. Brainard could be proud of what he had done, but he realized that it was time for new blood to run the company. He knew that he could not go on forever, but that the company could under the right leadership. And that right leader was available. He was Henry S. Beers.

Like his predecessors, Beers had plenty of experience with the company before assuming the presidency. He began work in Aetna's actuarial department on April 15, 1923. By 1937, he had been promoted to vice president. He was well prepared to lead the company at a time when it was undergoing rapid, positive changes.

By 1958, Aetna had reached two important milestones: annual premium income surpassed $1 billion for the Aetna Life Affiliated Companies, and life insurance in force reached $20 billion. The company's growth was phenomenal, but undeveloped markets still existed. Aetna turned its attention to international opportunities.

Aetna entered the international arena in 1960 when it purchased the Excelsior Life Insurance Company of Toronto, Canada. Six years later, it signed agreements with Assicurazioni Generali, a Milan, Italy-based insurance company which had operations in over 50 countries. These were but a couple of Aetna's many highlights in the 1960s.

For example, in 1966, the same year Aetna made its first benefits payment for the Medicare program, the life and casualty branches turned in record earnings. They accounted for $89.56 million in net earnings, a 7.4 percent increase over their previous high set in 1963. One year later (and this had no connection with Medicare), Aetna reorganized its corporate structure and formed a parent company, Aetna Life and Casualty. Later in 1967, Aetna purchased the Participating Annuity Life Insurance Company, which gave it the honor of being the first major insurance organization to enter the variable annuity field. The growth did not stop there, however.

That same year, Aetna formally stated its intention to expand into related insurance fields in both national and international markets. To accomplish this, it began a corporatewide restructuring program that would facilitate the acquisitions of other companies through cash and property transactions or stock swaps. This was a major step forward for the company, as it was Aetna's first move towards enlarging its influence and utilizing the full potential of its considerable resources. A decline in earnings in 1967, 1968, and 1969 put a slight damper on the company's ambitions, but for only a short time.

Aetna, like all insurance companies, is subject to cyclical swings and inflation rates that can have dramatic effects on earnings. Insurance companies are especially hard hit in the casualty and property lines when natural disasters like hurricanes and tornadoes strike. Companies' responses are generally to increase rates, concentrate on sales lines with the most potential for profits, and improve underwriting procedures. Aetna applied these measures during this period with satisfactory results.

Although the company had to add $30 million to its reserves in 1968 and another $29 million in 1969, it reversed the downturn. In fact, President Olcott Smith wrote in his March 1970 letter to Aetna's shareholders that, "for the casualty and property industry, as a whole 1969 appears to have been the worst year in history." Yet, management did not simply accept that situation. Rather, it applied the lessons of the past to prevent, or at least ameliorate, future downturns. Aetna innovatively redesigned its procedure for calculating reserve needs, switching to a monthly system that eliminated large year-end adjustments. Consequently, the company entered the 1970s in excellent financial shape.

There occurred one final major milestone in 1968, when, for the first time, Aetna was included on the New York Stock Exchange. That gave more people access to the company's stock, and encouraged management to become even more innovative in an effort to return healthy dividends to investors. They were all on the same team, and Aetna's senior managers were proponents of the team approach.

THE TEAM GOES TO BAT FOR ONE ANOTHER

A new company president, Donald M. Johnson, took over in 1972. He and his counterparts believed a new form of company management was in order. Thus, they implemented the "corporate office" style of management.

Four men, Chairman John H. Filer, Johnson, and executive vice presidents William O. Bailey (who would move up to become company president from 1976-1987 and Vice Chairman from 1987-1988) and Donald G. Conrad, set up a team style of management referred to as the corporate office. These were high-powered individuals, all of whom were outstanding decision makers. The idea behind the corporate office was to make decisions based on group discussions. They drew upon their diverse backgrounds to draw a complete analysis of issues concerning the corporation.

Each man was still responsible for making decisions affecting his own department. After all, the corporate office was not designed to replace individual decisions with group consensus; it was intended to enhance the individual decision-making process. The feeling was that the corporate office would maximize senior management's effectiveness, especially since the company had grown too complex for any single individual to keep track of everything that affected the entire corporation. Alas, the experiment lasted only

183

four years. Although there is no printed documentation, rumors attribute the failure of the experiment to ego conflicts among Johnson, Conrad, and Filer.

The promise the corporate office held was shattered, but the company really did not lose anything. That management was even willing to try such a radical approach was testimony to the fact that even though the Aetna, which, by tradition was as conservative as any other insurance company, was receptive to new ideas. Eliphalet Bulkeley had set a standard for innovative management back in 1853. His successors were following that standard over 100 years later. No doubt, their successors will be doing the same another 100 years from now.

THE PENDULUM SWINGS IN AETNA'S FAVOR

Filer and Johnson took over the company's leadership at a good time. Aetna's earnings record in the first half of the 1970s was admirable. In 1971, for instance, the company's net earnings were $136.49 million. The property and casualty lines showed a profit for the first time in seven years. No wonder Smith wrote in his final annual report as Chairman that, "While fluctuations will continue to be inherent in [the insurance business], we believe that the controls, management information systems and other programs [we] developed in recent years should minimize these fluctuations in the future." They did, but only for a short while.

Earnings continued to increase under Filer's leadership. There were several reasons. Among the principal ones were improved returns on the company's diversified investments, led in large part by real estate gains, the implementation of employee incentive plans, and the expansion of innovative marketing policies and programs. These new programs were responsible for *doubling new business sales* between 1971 and 1973. Then came the insurance industry's perpetual nemesis, inflation. This time it came with a new enemy: an oil crisis.

One of the major factors in the mid-1970s downturn was the fall in the real estate market. Aetna, like many of its competitors, invested heavily in real estate as a means of diversifying its portfolios to minimize insurance business fluctuations. The strategy backfired in the mid-1970s.

Real estate and land development values fell dramatically during the mid-1970s due to rapid inflation, exorbitant construction costs, and high interest rates. This created a serious downturn which lasted throughout 1974 and 1975. Once again, though, the company weathered the storm. Finally, in 1976, the company more than doubled its 1975 operating and net earnings. Earnings aside, more problems loomed ahead.

Aetna was a participant in a real estate development partnership with the Kaiser Company. As with many of its other real estate dealings, this one caused difficulty. Aetna's diversified business division recorded a $50.4 million loss, most of which could be attributed to a $49 million write-down of the partnership's assets. Consequently, the Aetna ended its relationship with Kaiser in January 1977. Once again, the company learned a valuable lesson: real estate was not a dirt cheap investment, and losses in such investments were a sure-fire way of bringing insurance companies' notions of offsetting losses through them down to earth. Once Aetna learned that lesson, its financial picture brightened again.

Earnings almost doubled again in 1977. Although every area of the corporation contributed to the rosy financial gains, one division in particular stood out. The diversified business division, which had lost more than $50 million in 1976, actually contributed earnings of $16.55 million! The turnaround was due to the dissolution of the Aetna-Kaiser partnership. That lesson was not lost on Aetna's management as it planned the company's future investments.

AETNA HOLDS A SALE—ANYBODY'S MONEY IS WELCOME

Management's optimism for a strong company future grew as Aetna's earnings increased. So, in 1977, the company took advantage of its healthy operations to hold its first-ever debenture sale. Aetna sold $250 million worth of the notes, which were payable on a fixed schedule and not attached to assets. The proceeds from the sale were used initially to purchase investment securities. Analysts lauded the move, especially since the company's financial picture strengthened even more as the 1970s came to an end.The 1980s got off to a bad start. Once again, inflation, high and unsettled interest rates, and intensified competition combined to lower operating earnings. Despite the downturn, the company began planning for expansion.

Aetna anticipated building new office facilities in Hartford, Middletown (about 15 miles south of Hartford), and Fall River, Massachusetts. Filer and Bailey wrote in their 1979 annual letter to shareholders that "the expansion is designed to strengthen operational efficiency at the divisional level, enable Aetna to draw on a broader labor pool, and enhance the economy of our home region." Their optimism typified the Aetna's philosophies regarding growth and commitment to the community.

The slump continued almost unabated during the first half of the 1980s. Slump or no slump, Aetna continued to expand.

Aetna reorganized its divisional arrangement in 1981 to create a structure that was more marketing oriented. The arrangement's purpose was to better situate the company in the marketplace in order to capitalize on emerging business trends and needs. The company's longstanding ability to take advantage of the changing marketplace had stood it in good stead since 1853. There was no reason to change the company approach in the 1980s.

Although operating earnings continued to decline, Aetna made three major purchases in 1982 in an effort to diversify into non-insurance fields. It spent $775 million in a three-month period to acquire Geosource, Inc., Samuel Montagu and Co., and Federated Investors, Inc. (Aetna divested itself of these companies in 1989 and retreated from its expansion into non-insurance fields.) These acquisitions, combined with the ongoing expansion program, created a need for capital. Consequently, Aetna sold $350 million of new securities that year.

A COMPANY LITERALLY ON THE MOVE

Aetna had been expanding its physical facilities for years. It had added to the home office complex in 1958, 1962, and 1964. Despite these additions, the company still suffered from a lack of space. So, in 1972, it opened yet another addition of seven stories to the home office building. This made Aetna's headquarters one of the largest office buildings in the northeast. But, guess what! The addition was no sooner completed than it was time to grow again.

Part of the reason that Aetna needed so much space was to house its computer facilities. The company had begun an ambitious computerization program in 1954 when it ordered its first computer, an IBM 650 Magnetic Drum Data Process Machine, which was installed in 1955. Over the years, it added more equipment and implemented a variety of state-of-the-art software systems. As early as 1971, the company had created its own computer network, SAFARI. As it added more and more equipment and personnel to program and operate it, Aetna realized its need for additional space to house them all. The solution was twofold:

1. build a new facility in nearby Windsor

2. move 550 employees and some data processing equipment to company offices on Brainard Road in the southeast section of Hartford.

The moves took place in 1980. Aetna moved 1,000 employees and some, but not all, of its computer equipment into the Windsor building and followed up on its Brainard Road plan.

The dual computer moves demonstrated Aetna management's awareness of the dangers inherent in centralizing its computer facilities. The company had become so reliant on computerization that power outages, sabotage, or other catastrophes could have a devastating impact on its business operations. The moves to Windsor and Brainard Road were aimed at decentralizing computer facilities, just as the other personnel moves taking place were designed to do for space purposes.

The company simply did not have enough room to expand in the city of Hartford. It had to look elsewhere. "Elsewhere," in this case, consisted of Middletown, southwest Hartford, and Fall River, Massachusetts.

1983 was a strange year for Aetna. It had to institute a hiring freeze in October to streamline the payroll, improve efficiency, and avoid layoffs. Management emphasized retraining extant employees and maximizing in-house human resources. Yet, with all the moving going on, it was almost impossible for management to count noses!

That year, the company moved into its new 900,000 square-foot office complex in Middletown designed to accommodate 5,000 employees, which was one-quarter of Aetna's workforce! There were other moves that same year that reflected Aetna's commitment to Hartford and its appreciation of history.

Aetna had purchased several old buildings on Capitol Avenue in Hartford that had lasted longer than the industries they housed. At one time the area had been the city's manufacturing center. Aetna bought and renovated buildings that had been home to businesses like the Pope Manufacturing Company, which built the short-lived Pope-Hartford automobile, and Sharp's Rifle Manufacturing Company. The new office buildings were designed to accommodate 2,000 employees. The end result of all these moves was to disperse the unprecedented number of company employees geographically. This presented problems in the training area.

EMPLOYEES CANNOT LEARN IF THERE IS NO PLACE TO TEACH THEM

Management realized that a well-trained workforce was essential if the company was to compete successfully in the insurance industry. It chose not to trust this training to chance. Consequently, the company constructed the Aetna Institute for Corporate Education, a model for businesses interested in employee training programs.

The building, which is located directly across the street from Aetna's corporate headquarters, was originally intended to be a dormitory for people attending insurance training programs. Aetna purchased the land on which the facility is built for $1.9 million.

By the time John Filer broke ground for the new building in May, 1981, plans had changed. The building would be used as a facility in which would be conducted on-site education for home and field office employees, representatives from foreign corporations interested in creating programs similar to Aetna's, and citizens of the Greater Hartford community. The classes offered would include the relevant insurance and technical courses, as well as some in the humanities and cultural areas. Aetna's philosophy towards education was that its comprehensive, diverse program would provide employees with the sophisticated world view necessary to allow them to compete in the expanding insurance market. Aetna has met that goal—and continues to expand upon it.

The $42 million building included overnight accommodations for 380 people, two dining rooms, a library, a fitness center, and numerous classrooms and lecture halls. Construction was funded partially by a 20-year, $4 million, 3 percent loan from the city of Hartford and also by a $5.7 million Housing and Urban Development grant from the federal government. By the time it was completed, Aetna had a facility that was the envy of many a competitor—and a model for businesses everywhere to follow.

John Filer had some cogent comments regarding the construction of the education facility at a time when the insurance industry struggled through one of its cyclical downturns. He said, "Some people may think that our timing was not perfect in terms of building a $42 million building at a time when the earnings were turning down to stay down for a while. But the emphasis on training and education is crucial; if we hadn't created it now we would have had to do it later." Filer put his finger on Aetna's commitment to education and the company's longstanding willingness to act with an eye to the long run. There is no doubt that Aetna will be around in the long run, as its continuing expansion indicates.

The final phase of the 1980s expansion program occurred in 1984 in Fall River, where Aetna had opened its operation in 1965 with 35 employees. By 1981, that number had grown to over 800 spread out through four offices. Once again, consolidation was in order. Aetna constructed an $8 million building in Fall River which was completed in 1984. That put an end to the company's ambitious program for the time being, and gave it a chance to concentrate on the main business of selling insurance.

THE LATE 1980S: NOT THE BEST OF YEARS

The last few years have not been particularly memorable for the insurance industry. Nevertheless, Aetna is continuing to maintain its position as an industry leader in all aspects of its business. As of August 1, 1990, the company had assets of $87.1 billion, which makes it the largest investor-owned insurance/financial services organization in the country, as well as the 11th largest U. S. corporation. Statistics regarding its business reveal just how major a force the company is in the insurance and financial services industry.

INSURANCE STATISTICS

- TOTAL LIFE INSURANCE IN FORCE $351.3 billion [1]
- TOTAL GROUP LIFE INSURANCE IN FORCE 301.0 billion [1]
- TOTAL INDIVIDUAL LIFE INSURANCE IN FORCE—50.3 billion [1]
- UNIVERSAL LIFE IN FORCE—26.5 billion [1]
- NUMBER OF PERSONAL AUTO POLICIES IN FORCE —2,074,455 [2]
- NUMBER OF LIVES COVERED UNDER GROUP LIFE —8,681,885 [2]
- (EMPLOYEES ONLY) NUMBER OF LIVES COVERED UNDER GROUP HEALTH 10,244,640 [2] (DISABILITY, MEDICAL AND DENTAL: EMPLOYEES ONLY)

[1] AS OF 6/30/90

[2] AS OF 12/31/89

To keep track of these policies, premiums, payments, etc., connected with the company's business, Aetna employs approximately 45,500 people throughout its home and field offices (17,500 at home and 27,000 in the field). The company's impact on the community is significant.

For example, it made charitable contributions of $3.1 million in 1989. A separate entity, the Aetna Foundation, Incorporated, made charitable contributions of $9 million. The company paid a total of $432 million in state and local taxes to states and communities in which it has offices and holdings. Connecticut state and local taxes alone amounted to $55 million! There is no doubt that Aetna is a significant contributor to the nation's economy, and a leading player in the business world. Aetna's steady growth since its founding in 1853 is a marvel of consistency. Come to think of it, so is the company. No wonder Aetna is a survivor—and promises to be one for some time to come.

Chapter 8

1856

Atlanta Gas Light Company

A LONG GAS LINE TO BE PROUD OF

The Atlanta City Council decided in the 1850s that it was about time for the citizens of the fledgling city to see the light. The method it proposed to shed light on Atlanta was to build a city-owned gasworks. Two things prevented the Council from going ahead with its project: no money and no expertise. The Council did not see either as a problem.

A committee headed by Jared Irwin Whitaker told the Council on March 3, 1854, that:

> While most of our citizens are desirous that a Gas Works should be established in this city, we are of the opinion that funds enough could not be raised by private subscriptions and

> that the financial condition renders it
> inexpedient for any subscription to be
> made on the part of the city.

In the Council members' eyes, however, if city residents wanted a gas works, they would have one. After all, the City of Augusta had an operable gas plant already. (The first gas lights in that city were lit on June 24, 1852.) The Council saw no reason why Atlanta could not have one, too. So, in 1855, council members contacted William Helme of Philadelphia, who had previous experience as the engineer of the Augusta Gas Company. Helme was happy to help the good citizens of Atlanta.

In early 1855, Helme proposed that within 10 months he would erect a coal-gas plant and lay at least 3 miles of pipe. All the city had to do was install 50 street lights and pay $30 a year for the gas to light them. The system would cost $50,000; the city would become a stockholder to the tune of $20,000. Helme and the city would work together in getting the new company incorporated. Finally, he proposed that the council would grant the company the exclusive privilege of lighting Atlanta for 50 years. The city accepted the terms.

The involved parties wasted no time putting the agreement into action. They drew up an act of incorporation and introduced it in the Georgia state legislature. The governor signed the act on February 16, 1856—approximately eight weeks after the first gas lights in Atlanta went on! His signature marked the official establishment of Atlanta Gas Light Company, which has one of the more unusual histories in American business.

IF YOU ARE GOING TO SEND A BIRTHDAY CARD, YOU HAD BETTER BUY TWO

Atlanta Gas Light Company actually has two birthdays. Even though the official incorporation act is dated February 16, 1856, the first lights glowed on December 25, 1855. People connected with the company simply could not wait for the government to act to turn on the lights. Someone suggested that the company hold a special ceremony on Christmas Day that year to mark the introduction of gas lighting to Atlanta. The suggestion was adopted. On that day, the first gas lights in the rapidly growing city flickered on. They did more than illuminate the streets; the lights also provided an omen of the bright future that Atlanta Gas Light Company would enjoy. There were a few dark spots along the way, though.

ATLANTA GAS LIGHT COMPANY HAS SEEN MORE TWISTS THAN A PRETZEL FACTORY

Atlanta Gas Light Company has gone full circle from an independent company to an out-of-business company to the "gas department" of a power company to a component of a holding company and back to an independent company. It has gone through wars, a depression, takeover bids, and hard times of all sorts. The company has bounced back from near extinction more times than a ball slams off the wall in a fast-moving jai-alai game. Today, Atlanta Gas Light Company is both a viable company with a bright future and a model for entrepreneurs with an eye for survival to study.

WHO IS GOING TO TURN ON THE LIGHTS?

Gas lights may have turned on the citizens of Atlanta, but it was difficult finding someone in the company's early years to turn on the lamps physically. The "Old Lamplighter" of song certainly would not have topped the hit parade in Atlanta in the late 1850s.

The night watchmen in Atlanta had no desire to turn the lamps on and off. Even though then Mayor Ezzards paid them $1.50 per month extra to light and extinguish the street lamps every day, they did not relish the job. According to the February 1 and 15, 1856, City Council minutes, Ezzards contracted one Russell Crawford "on the best terms possible" to handle the lamps. It was not long before Crawford was charged with improperly performing his duty. The Council acquitted him, but that left it with the problem of finding someone who would carry out the lamplighting and extinguishing duties faithfully. The job fell to the police. They, too, received extra money for the service, earning 20 cents per lamp per month! This experiment did not work out well, either. The police had better things to do than lighting and extinguishing lamps. The problem of who would light the lamps became a thorn in the Council's side, and remained one for decades. That was the least of the company's problems, though. In November 1864, the company's lights went out completely.

THE CIVIL WAR WAS NOT VERY CIVIL FOR THIS COMPANY

Atlanta Gas Light Company had hardly gotten its corporate feet wet before the Civil War erupted. Despite the ravages of the war, the company managed to keep Atlanta lit between 1861 and 1864. The task was not easy.

The company had undergone considerable growth during its formative years. Sales and profits soared as the city itself burgeoned. The coming of the Civil War marked Atlanta's emergence as a metropolitan center. The Confederates turned the city into a strategic supply and military center. Ironically, this almost ended the company's history before it even had one!

With few exceptions, Atlanta Gas Light Company continued to supply its customers throughout the first half of the war. There was a problem late in 1863 due to dwindling supplies of coal from which the gas was made and a lack of transportation for nonmilitary goods. Apparently, the company overcame the problem. The word "apparent" fits here, since Sherman burned Atlanta in November of 1864—and the gas company's records along with it. In general, 1864 was a difficult year for the company.

City Council minutes of April 22, 1864, record at least a temporary lack of gas. They read "Atlanta Gas Company has made a proposition to the Mayor and the Council to resume the making of gas if the city will pay the advanced rates proposed." A few days later, the mayor met with company officers to discuss the gas situation. What happened then—and from that

point on—is not known. The company's gas plant
went up in flames on Sunday, November 13, 1864. It
was almost two years before it resumed business.

ATLANTA GAS LIGHT COMPANY RISES FROM THE ASHES—LITERALLY

The company resumed activity on September 15,
1866. At first, it focused on restoring service to previous customers. By March of 1869, the company
turned its attention to expansion, which seemed to be
well managed, judging from City Council minutes in
January 1872. A committee on gas and lamps reported that "We believe the works to be well managed,
the various officers exhibiting fidelity and skill in the
discharge of their duties. The books are neatly kept,
and the officers of the company have been courteous
and obliging to your committee." Those words notwithstanding, there existed problems between the
Council and the company, most of which were in the
Council members' minds.

THE COUNCIL HAS A GAS PROBLEM FOR WHICH THERE SEEMS TO BE NO RELIEF

Council members felt that the company was charging too much for its products. They instructed the gas
and lamps committee to "inquire into the possibility of
chartering a new gas company." That request went by
the wayside as the severe economic depression of
1873 set in.

The depression, often referred to as the "Panic of
1873," created economic hardships for just about
everyone. How hard it affected Atlanta Gas Light Company is reflected in the fact that between 1871 and

1875 gas rates dropped four times! Between 1873 and 1880, the company and the city government wrangled continuously over rates.

The Council demanded lower rates and even threatened to drop the company's services if it did not comply. At the same time, the City Council acted to relight lamps that had been shut off due to excessively high rates and looked to add new ones. The company seemed amenable to the Council's idiosyncrasies. Both sides recognized that they had to work closely together for the good of the citizenry. So, by 1880, the two entities were on good terms again.

In the city's 1881 annual report, the committee on gas and lamps thanked the company for voluntarily reducing the annual cost of supplying gas for each lamp. "For this," the committee wrote, "the city is indebted to the officers of the Gas Light Company to whose uniform courtesy your committee desires to bear testimony." The officers were no doubt pleased, but not half as much as they were with a significant development in the cooking arena.

May 1881 marked the introduction of widespread gas cooking in the United States. Gas cooking stoves had been around for decades prior to 1881, but homeowners still preferred coal and wood stoves. Atlanta Gas Light Company sought to change this state of affairs.

Company officials saw gas as an economical cooking medium. They began a large-scale advertising campaign to promote the benefits of gas for cooking purposes. Never reluctant to seize on a new opportunity to expand the company's product line, they offered a special rate for customers who would use gas for cooking or any purpose other than lighting. This was a wise move, which paid off quickly. Within 25 years, the combination of a steadily improving standard of living in the U. S., increased advertising and sales promotions, and a major coal strike in 1902 pushed homeowners to use gas more and more for cooking. The changeover could not have come at a better time for Atlanta Gas Light Company.

A new form of competition, electricity, threatened the gas lighting industry toward the end of the 19th century. It also prompted an innovative rate reduction strategy necessitated by increasing competition.

ATLANTA GAS LIGHT COMPANY FACES A NEW POWER STRUGGLE

On June 21, 1881, the Atlanta City Council granted permission to a company to erect poles on which to suspend wires for electricity. The company never actually produced any electricity. The gas company rested easy, but not for long.

In December 1883, the Council awarded the Georgia Electric Light Company a similar franchise. Four months later, the city contracted with the company for the installation of six street lights in the center of Atlanta. To its credit, the Council tried to protect the gas company by ordering that any gas lights displaced by the electric ones be used elsewhere in the city. The question was which gas company would benefit from the repositioning.

Yes, there was another gas company in Atlanta! The Gate City Gas Light Company petitioned the City Council for a franchise in May 1883. Atlanta Gas Light Company wasted no time lowering its rates in anticipation of the competition. Perhaps the company jumped the gun a bit, since the Council rejected Gate

City's application. Shortly thereafter, the Council reversed its decision. Early in 1884, the Gate City Gas Light Company began building a system in Atlanta. In response, Atlanta Gas Light Company reduced its rates yet again and set the tone for intense rate wars between the two firms.

Gate City made tremendous inroads between 1884 and 1889. In fact, a local newspaper, the *Atlanta Capitol*, claimed in an 1885 article that Atlanta Gas Light Company had fallen behind in the competition. The issue was moot at the time, though. Both companies were losing ground to the electric company! In October 1888, the City Council ordered that the gas lighting system be superseded by 32-candlepower incandescent electric lights. That was a blow to Atlanta Gas Light Company, and a prelude to its being swallowed up.

THE YANKEES STRIKE AGAIN

In 1889, for the second time in 25 years, Northerners dealt a blow toAtlanta. This time, they did not burn the city. They simply swallowed up its gas companies.

The United Gas Improvement Company (UGI) of Philadelphia bought both Atlanta gas companies. First, it purchased Gate City. Next, it concentrated on Atlanta Gas Light Company. UGI solicited stock from the company's shareholders at $31.25 per share. At that price, it had no trouble gaining control. In fact, UGI paid the staggering sum (for the time) of $520,000 for its majority stock, which was more than ten times the total capitalization of Atlanta Gas Light Company at its inception. The new ownership made little difference as far as the company's service went, though.

203

Other than losing local control, the company went about its business as usual. At that point in Atlanta Gas Light Company's history, the usual was giving way rapidly to the unusual, i.e., rapid changes in technology.

More and more people realized the advantages of electricity over gas. It looked for a while at the turn of the 20th century like gas would lose its popularity. As so often happens, though, an unexpected event reversed the trend toward electricity and breathed new life into Atlanta Gas Light Company's existence. That was the coal strike of 1902.

Anthracite coal miners initiated what would be a 23-week strike that severely curtailed the availability of coal throughout the nation. At the time, despite Atlanta Gas Light Company's push for cooking with gas, homemakers were still heavily dependent on coal for heating and cooking purposes. Without it, they reverted to wood or gas. As a result, gas ranges grew in popularity. Concomitantly, people found new uses for gas, e.g., heating water and fueling small space heaters. In retrospect, the coal strike of 1902 was a boon for the gas industry in general—and Atlanta Gas Light Company in particular.

Although gas range sales had not been anything spectacular up to 1902, there was a sudden spurt in sales after the coal strike. As a result, an estimated 8,000 ranges were in use in Atlanta in 1903. There was also another owner of Atlanta Gas Light Company.

On July 1, 1903, Georgia Railway and Electric (GRE) acquired ownership of the company from UGI as part of the consolidation of all the street railway, electric light and power, and steam operations in Atlanta into one company. GRE was financed mostly by northern money. Basically, Atlanta Gas Light Company could no longer be considered a local company. Its owners had lost a great deal of their control over everyday operations. They lost even more a few years later.

REGULATION REARS ITS UGLY HEAD

Government officials decided in 1906 and 1907 that local utilities needed state regulation. The Railroad Commission of Georgia, which already had jurisdiction over railroad and telegraph companies, seemed to be the logical regulatory agency. On November 6, 1907, the commission directed utilities to file their rules, regulations, rates, charters, and franchises. That did not bother Atlanta Gas Light Company officials. In fact, they welcomed regulation!

R. C. Congdon, company manager, said:

> We regard the commission as a body which we need not fear, for they are looking after our interests as they are looking after everybody else's. They protect us as well as others. They are elected by us and you. We feel as much at liberty to carry our troubles to them as anybody, if we can't adjust them ourselves. We have nothing to conceal and fear.

Congdon was a wise, perspicacious manager who epitomized the company's attitude toward business and the customer. As he said in that regard, "The most successful gas company is the one which is most popular. We are popular now, and are growing more so every day." The company took advantage of its popularity to increase customer trust and confidence. Apparently the strategy worked. Congdon noted that "Gradually, the people are learning, by our persistent efforts to please them and to dispel every suspicion in their minds that we are trying to rob them."

Congdon certainly recognized the need to please customers and provide them superior service, which had been the company's goals since its inception (and continue to be today). According to him, "They are learning that we consider it in our interest as well as theirs that they feel free to tell us their troubles with our service and have good reason to believe that we will remedy them at once." Those words summed up Atlanta Gas Light Company's approach to service —and the reasons for its success! An editorial in the *Atlanta Journal* summed up the company's philosophy best when it said "Improved ideas and active progress are the slogans of the local company, which is rapidly winning the confidence and favor it deserves." Company officials vowed to continue the search for new ideas and progress. While they searched, the company ownership changed hands again.

After its formation in 1912, Georgia Railway and Power (GRP) assumed ownership of Atlanta Gas and Light in a roundabout way. Since GRP did not have a market for the electricity it would generate, it sought a partner. That partner turned out to be GRE, which had a market but not enough electricity to supply it. So, GRP leased GRE's properties (a classic case of not being able to tell the players without a scorecard), which included Atlanta Gas Light Company. Even though Atlanta Gas Light Company lost its independence, it gained a new market. For the first time, the company expanded operations outside Atlanta.

The expansion began with a whimper in 1913 when the company supplied gas to the Suburban Gas and Electric Company in Decatur. Technically, the companies were distinct entities. However, since GRP owned both, it mattered little whether the companies were separate or one and the same. Regardless of who owned them at any given time, Atlanta Gas Light Company did one thing well: it continued to "pump" gas.

THE GAS LINES EXPAND

Atlanta Gas Light Company expanded into College Park and East Point in 1916, despite the fact that it did not have authorization. The company's original charter did not allow for service outside Atlanta. That did not deter the company, though. Company officials sought an amendment, which they received in 1929— 13 years after the company began service outside the city. The intervening years were far from easy for Atlanta Gas Light Company .

World War I was a difficult time for gas suppliers. Because of the military's demands for products, shortages occurred in the quantity and quality of gas available. As compensation for both, the public demanded lower rates. Outspoken company vice president P. S. Arkwright told the railroad commission investigating the need for a rate change, "You're lucky to be getting any gas at all." To emphasize his point, he said "as for a reduction in rates, they are already too low." His candor did nothing to mollify the public's dissatisfaction. Nonetheless, the company did take steps to improve the quality of the gas and refund a part of the customers' payments.

At the commission's order, the company purchased gas and kerosene oil to enrich its gas. Then, it offered a rebate to the customers. The moves placated customers and the commission alike. The company had weathered another storm, and the country survived the war. Unfortunately, Atlanta Gas and Light had a war of its own to fight.

THE MAYOR LAUNCHES AN OFFENSIVE

Newly elected Mayor James L. Key took office in January 1919. He might as well have moved into Atlanta Gas Light Company's corporate suite, since it was in that direction that his aspirations leaned. Key felt that the City of Atlanta should have control of the company. He attacked immediately to gain it.

On March 2, 1919, Key announced that he would investigate the company because it was selling gas for cooking without authorization. (In fact, that was not true. The company's charter had been amended in 1889 to allow it to furnish gas for any purpose.) Then he "uncovered" a scheme through which the company had been using steam from the city crematory to make gas. Arkwright vehemently denied the charge. The mayor and the company wrangled over the issue, which created quite a stir among the media and the public.

Key hoped the controversy would lead to a city takeover of Atlanta Gas Light Company. It did spark a debate that reached the state legislature in the form of a bill that would allow the takeover. The legislature soundly defeated the bill and thwarted Key's ambitions, at least temporarily, but the company got a new owner anyway.

A series of consolidations involving the Southeastern Power and Light Company, the Georgia Railway and Power Company, and assorted others resulted in the formation of the Georgia Power Company. Once again, Atlanta Gas Light Company served a new master, but it was simply business as usual as far as the company's staff was concerned.

Atlanta Gas Light/Georgia Power Billboard, ca 1927

Courtesy Atlanta Gas Light Company

WE'LL CONTINUE TO SUPPLY GAS AT ANY RATE

The period between the end of World War I and the onset of the Great Depression was one of constant rate haggling for the company. For example, rates went up for the first time in decades in 1918. They increased again in 1920 and 1921 due to inflation. Then, in 1928, they dropped. To compensate for the reduction, Arkwright pushed for the "wider use of appliances and a more generous enjoyment of electric and gas service" in a memo that appeared as part of an advertisement in the December 12 *Atlanta Constitution.* He concluded the memo with the assurance that "as much as we want to sell appliances, our Salesmen are instructed never to sell a customer anything the customer can't use to his advantage." This last statement summed up the company's attitude toward its customers—and explained in part its business success.

Another significant event in 1928 was the arrival of natural gas in Atlanta. Ever since its inception, Atlanta Gas Light Company had manufactured its own gas. The newly formed Southern Natural Gas Company of Birmingham, Alabama, announced that it had received all the permits necessary to begin delivery of natural gas to Atlanta. That was good news for the company and its customers, but there was some doubt as to whether or not there would be an Atlanta Gas Light Company to make use of the gas!

Georgia Power had practically relegated the company to little more than a "gas department" in its organization. It came as no surprise, then, when Georgia Power announced in March 1929 that it had sold the company and several of its counterparts to Colonel A. E. Peirce and his associates of Central Public Service Corporation of Chicago in order to concentrate on its electric power interests. The sale turned out to be positive for the company.

The new directors all lived in Chicago and had little interest in visiting Atlanta. This meant that the local management was free to run the company pretty much as it saw fit. More important, it was free of its bonds to any electric companies. For the first time in a long while, the company was able to concentrate on its gas business. It made the most of the opportunity.

NATURAL GAS BECOMES A FACT OF LIFE

Actually, Southern Natural had no plans to include Atlanta Gas and Light in its operation. The company's intent was to obtain a franchise, then operate its own distribution system. Atlanta Gas Light Company would have been trying to compete against Southern Natural's cleaner, cheaper, and more efficient natural gas with its manufactured gas. No doubt that would have meant the end of the company. However, Atlanta Gas Light Company had been backed up against the wall before and survived. It did so again.

Natural Gas Arrives Feb.3, 1930

Courtesy Atlanta Gas Light Company

A long struggle for the power to supply Atlanta's natural gas ensued. Southern Natural had the gas but no distribution system. Building a new system would be costly, not to mention that the city's streets would be torn up for a long while. On the other hand, Atlanta Gas Light Company had a distribution system but a limited supply of gas. Compromise seemed to be the best solution to the impasse. There was one other major obstacle for Atlanta Gas Light Company to overcome before it could receive the right to serve the city exclusively.

From the *Atlanta Georgian* 1930

Courtesy Atlanta Gas Light Company

There was a question as to whether Atlanta Gas Light Company's charter permitted it to distribute natural gas. The original document did not. But, legal experts ruled that the aforementioned 1889 amendment did. Once that issue was settled, it seemed natural that Atlanta Gas Light Company should serve the city. Thus, on March 29, 1929, it signed a long-term contract with Southern Natural that assured the company a steady supply of gas. The agreement opened a business relationship between the two companies that exists to this day. It also ushered in a new era for Atlanta Gas Light Company .

Of course, the introduction of natural gas into Atlanta meant the inevitable squabble over rates. The company petitioned for an increase. The City Council argued against it. Eventually, the Railroad Commission reduced the rates to be charged. That did not please company officials. They did not dwell on the setback, though. Rather, they aggressively pursued new business to attract more revenues. Unfortunately, their timing was not the best.

MANAGEMENT IS DEPRESSED—BUT SO IS THE REST OF THE COUNTRY

Natural gas arrived in Atlanta on February 2, 1930, at about the same time as the "Great Depression." The depression gripping the nation did

1930s Ad for Gas Hot Water Heat

not faze Atlanta Gas Light Company management, though. The company launched a huge expansion project to greet the worst economic downturn the country had ever experienced!

While the economy shrunk, gas consumption increased. Between 1917 and 1930, the company experienced a fifty percent increase in consumption. Its plans for the 1930s

Courtesy Atlanta Gas Light Company

included an expansion to meet twenty times that demand! There was no thought of turning back despite the depression. Of course, if the company planned on supplying the projected gas load, it had to have customers to consume it. So, while the rest of the country struggled with the depression, Atlanta Gas Light Company intensified its efforts to sell gas.

Innovative management pushed gas cooking and launched a campaign to find the oldest gas stove in use in Atlanta. Unfortunately, its search did not succeed, as an editorial in the February 23, 1930, *Atlantan Georgian,* revealed:

WHO HAS ATLANTA'S OLDEST GAS RANGE

Atlanta Gas Light Company, Atlanta's oldest public utility, would like to find out....it may be yet in service—continuous service, since the last time Atlanta's gas service was interrupted, even momentarily, was when Sherman burned Atlanta.Now, with the introduction of natural gas...gas company officials are digging in the files yellow with age and compiling a history of this company. But they have not found yet who used the first gas range, and they would like to know.

Atlanta Gas Light Company also expanded its Home Service Department, the first in the South, which had been started in 1910. Significantly, the formation of that department led to the beginning of the Home Economics curriculum in the Atlanta school system. It was another example of the company's importance in the city.

Yet another innovative campaign was the "Old Stove Round Up." Under this plan, the company took in old ranges in partial trade for new ones. The program still operates, although it was suspended temporarily during World War II. The most important aspect of the company's aggressive campaign, though, in-

Gasco Bill Rides for Old Stove Roundup 1930

Courtesy Atlanta Gas Light Company

volved rates. The company voluntarily lowered them effective October 1, 1930. Despite its efforts, the depression caught up with the company, which suffered from a gradual loss of customers. The numbers dropped from 49,238 customers at the end of 1930 to 46,089 in 1932. The downturn reversed itself quickly. By 1936, the company had 56,204 customers—and the opportunity to expand its service area tremendously.

A NEW STATE OF AFFAIRS: THE ENTIRE STATE OF GEORGIA SIGNS ON

On July 1, 1937, Consolidated Electric and Gas Company, the holding company for Atlanta Gas Light Company, bought Southern Natural's interest in the Georgia Natural Gas Corporation. This merged eight other gas companies with Atlanta Gas Light Company. Then, in 1941, Consolidated combined Georgia Public Utilities, Macon Gas Company, and Atlanta Gas Light Company into one corporation. That meant that all the gas companies in the state were now part of one organization, for which Atlanta Gas Light Company was the continuing corporation. The company was almost back to where it had started as an independent corporation. Of course, by this time it was much larger than its founders envisioned. So, too, was the war that prevented the company from achieving its independence—at least for the time being.

ANOTHER DECADE, ANOTHER WAR

World War II had a serious impact on Atlanta Gas Light Company. Almost half of the approximate 700 employees who worked for the company at the onset of the war entered the military. They may have been gone, but the company certainly did not forget them. As far as management was concerned, the employees may have been scattered physically, but their spirits remained in Georgia. That being true, management innovated once again. It founded a publication, the *Blue Flame News*, to keep the employees apprised of what was going on at home. The newsletter bolstered employee

Blue Flame News 1945

Courtesy Atlanta Gas Light Company

morale at home and abroad, and exhibited the importance of continuous management-employee communications.

Of particular interest was the September 1944 issue of the newsletter. It carried the news that the company was developing its post-war plans. More important, it carried a notice reporting that:

> Every man and woman who left the Company to enter the Armed Forces will have a job when they get back, as good or better than the jobs they left. We are counting on the return of every one of you.

The company's loyalty to its workers was admirable, and explained in part its success and longevity. Almost all the employees who entered the military returned (six company employees died in the war)—and they came back to a much stronger Atlanta Gas Light Company .

THE LIGHT KEEPS GROWING STRONGER

In 1941, shortly before the war started, there were 28 towns in the company system. That translated into 102,859 customers. By the end of the war, there were 123,309. The increase in business made the company a prime candidate for a takeover. Sure enough, Southern Natural moved to purchase Atlanta Gas Light Company. The plan encountered serious opposition.

The primary arguments against Southern Natural's takeover were that the purchase would constitute a conflict of interest and that control of the company would once again rest outside Georgia. Knowles Davis, chief engineer for the Georgia Public Service Commission, was especially outspoken on those ideas.

First, he revealed an intricate connection among major stockholders of Southern Natural and other holding companies that would be involved in the purchase. Second, he addressed the concept of regional pride in ownership of the company.

Davis said:

> I am of the opinion that the common stock of Atlanta Gas Light Company Company should be owned entirely in the South, and if at all possible, it should be owned in Georgia. In this way, earnings on invested capital would remain in this section of the country, which would be of ultimate benefit to the South.

His arguments swayed the members of the Commission, who told Southern Natural they preferred that the company not buy Atlanta Gas Light Company. To its credit, Southern Natural dropped the plan. According to C. T. Chenery, president and Board of Directors member of the Federal Water and Gas Company, which owned and controlled Southern Natural, "We wanted to make the transaction, but not if there is opposition to it in Georgia." Atlanta Gas Light Company was safe again. Soon, it would become completely autonomous.

FREE AT LAST

Regardless of who owned it, Atlanta Gas Light Company continued to grow. In 1946, for example, the first full year after World War II, Atlanta Gas Light Company added 10,000 customers. It continued to add storage facilities and sendout capacity. Then, in 1947, it finally attained complete independence. Effective November 1 that year, its affiliation with any holding company ended as the Central Public Service, parent company of Consolidated Electric and Gas, relinquished control of Atlanta Gas Light. The company had come full circle—and was on its own once again!

THERE IS STRENGTH IN NUMBERS—AND THE COMPANY HAS THOSE NUMBERS

The company was in good shape to set out on its own. At the end of 1947, Atlanta Gas Light Company had 146,079 customers in the 33 incorporated cities it served. Revenues that year were a bit more than $14 million. Georgians held most of the stock in the company and full-time local directorship. The future looked promising as growth became a full-time industry for the company.

At the end of September 1950, Atlanta Gas Light Company had added two more communities to serve, along with an additional 39,000 customers. (For fiscal 1950 the monthly customer average was almost 185,000.) The company had grown so much, in fact, that it had to contract with a new supplier to obtain more gas, since the company's sendout rate set new

219

records that strained its facilities. Atlanta Gas Light Company was entering a new era, to which it adapted well.

TECHNOLOGY ENTERS THE PIPELINE

Atlanta Gas Light Company's customer base continued to grow rapidly throughout the 1950s. So did its use of technology!

In 1950, the company air conditioned its general offices building. A year later, it began sponsoring two local television programs to advertise its services. Then, in 1952, Atlanta Gas Light Company opened its first data processing office. The company was quick to take advantage of all the innovations technology had to offer. By the time it celebrated its 100th birthday in 1956, Atlanta Gas Light Company was well on the way to attaining a position as one of Georgia's most significant corporate citizens—and a nationwide pioneer in technology. Nevertheless, its existence as a company was far from guaranteed.

Savannah's World-A Unique Storage Tank Built 1956-7

Courtesy Atlanta Gas Light Company

COULD GAS BECOME A THING OF THE PAST?

There was a bit of irony in the company's introduction of air conditioning. After World War II, air conditioning consumed the bulk of the energy supply in the United States, most of which was provided by the electric companies. The demand heightened the competition between Atlanta Gas Light Company and electric power companies, which threatened the existence of their gas counterparts. Fortunately, the gas companies survived the challenge. Atlanta Gas Light Company grew stronger despite of, or perhaps because of, the competition, as ensuing events proved. One of the company's proudest achievements was the opening in 1957 of the nation's first refrigerated propane storage plant. The plant, which cost one-third the price of conventional storage facilities, manifested the company's commitment toward providing more service at the lowest rates possible. The timing was perfect considering the never-ending increase in the company's customer base.

By 1960, Atlanta Gas Light Company boasted of 356,147 customers in 67 communities. Yet, company management would not rest on its laurels. President W. L. Lee, the first native Georgian to head the company, instructed all employees in 1961 that "We cannot stand pat in the face of changing times and intense competition. For this company to be successful—a condition which is important to every employee—every employee must assume some responsibility for selling the company and its product."

To ensure employee involvement, he expanded the sales department and initiated customer surveys. Even though the results of those surveys showed that

221

more than 95 percent of the customers consistently expressed satisfaction with service, Lee kept pressing for even higher percentages. (A 1981 survey reflected the continued pressure. That year, 97.7 percent of the company's customers reported that they were satisfied with the service provided. Perhaps the company will not be satisfied until it achieves a satisfaction rate of 100 percent—which may not be impossible if history is any indicator.)

By 1965, Atlanta Gas Light Company was serving more than 460,000 customers. Merchandise sales had risen to $4.2 million. And still the company expanded!

A substantial event occurred effective January 31, 1966, when Atlanta Gas Light Company merged with the oldest gas system in the state, Savannah Gas Company. That merger added another 60,190 customers. In retrospect, 1965 was a superior year for the company as it extended service to 10 new towns and acquired 11 more through purchase and merger. By 1969, Atlanta Gas Light Company served 191 communities and 586,135 customers. The question was whether or not there would be enough gas available to serve everyone as the 1970s unfolded.

IS THE COMPANY FINALLY RUNNING OUT OF GAS AFTER 114 YEARS?

The 1970s were terrible times as far as gas supplies were concerned. Actually, the shortages that materialized should not have come as a surprise, since experts began predicting them during the 1960s. There were several reasons for the shortage. Chief among them was the artificially low price structure for gas imposed by federal regulations, which removed any incentive to drill for new supplies. This factor did not pose major concerns for Atlanta Gas Light Company's customers. They had confidence that the company's management would provide gas regardless of supply problems. As usual, the company did not disappoint its customers.

An entry in the company's 1970 annual report assured customers and stockholders that "Atlanta Gas Light Company is in a better situation with respect to gas supplies than many gas distribution companies in the country." The reason was simple: management foresaw the shortages and contracted for future increases in supplies. It expanded the company's storage facilities in the West End of Atlanta by adding 30 liquid propane tanks with a total holding capacity of 4.3 million gallons. Of course, these moves incurred increased costs, but the company compensated for them through petitions for rate increases and a concession to economic reality. For the first time in its history, Atlanta Gas Light Company started charging for service calls. Not all the company's customers were pleased, but most acknowledged the need for the move. Fortunately, they also did their part to conserve fuel.

SAVE WHILE YOU CAN, OR THERE WON'T BE ANYTHING TO SAVE AT ALL

As energy prices climbed throughout the 1970s, so did the public's awareness of the need to conserve. Atlanta Gas Light Company and its customers worked together to find new ways to save gas and hold down costs. One of the problems that concerned the company was the growth in its customer base at a time of uncertain supply. The fact that its residential customers reduced their consumption by four percent in 1974 and 1975 eased its concern somewhat. More important, the reduction demonstrated that the company and its customers could—and would—work closely together to resolve a mutual problem.

The close working relationship between the two entities reflected Atlanta Gas Light Company's longstanding tradition of loyalty to its customers, which was actually the foundation of the company's (or any company's, for that matter) success. There had never been any doubt that the employees who personified Atlanta Gas Light Company valued their customers. Their growing alliance with customers, however, introduced a new element of success into the company's efforts to serve its public. The relationship carried Atlanta Gas Light Company into the 1980s, and will no doubt continue to influence the company's growth well into the next century. Wisely, management chose to strengthen the company's relationship with its customers. New Chief Executive Officer (CEO) Joe T. LaBoon had a great deal to do with that.

HAIL TO THE CEO—AND TO A HALER AND HEARTIER COMPANY

Joe T. LaBoon epitomized Atlanta Gas Light Company's commitment to managers who worked their way up through the ranks. He began work with the company in 1939 as a co-op student from Georgia Tech. Gradually, he took on greater responsibilities such as Vice President in the Rome and Atlanta divisions (1962-69) and Senior Vice President of Operations (1974-76) before assuming the company's presidency in 1976. (He was elected CEO in September

1980.) LaBoon was the consummate CEO who recognized the value of the company's employees and strong public relations.

LaBoon told shareholders in the 1980 annual report that Atlanta Gas Light Company's dedicated employees were one of "the company's most valued assets." He said that "For their loyalty and fine work, they earn the admiration and appreciation of the officers and directors." The words were more than lip service. He invited employees to visit him whenever they felt the need. Many employees took advantage of his open door policy and phoned or visited LaBoon. So did a few customers! LaBoon was a nontraditional CEO. He answered his own phone and handled some customer complaints himself. No doubt that surprised a few customers. More important, it strengthened customers' trust in the company, as did many of LaBoon's innovations. For example, he:

- set up a customer relations committee charged with finding and resolving the causes of customers' complaints
- installed a state-of-the-art telephone system to improve the handling of customer calls
- decentralized the handling of customer relations by appointing consumer affairs personnel in each of the company's operating divisions
- improved termination problems by introducing Third Party Notification, whereby an interested third party received notification when a customer's gas service was about to be shut off

- initiated the "Pat-on-the Back" award in which
  the company president sends a certificate of appreciation to each employee about whom the
  company receives a complimentary customer
  letter or telephone call.

In short, LaBoon fostered an open environment in
which employees at all levels became part of the decision making process. Moreover, he expanded the
company's training programs, raised pay scales, improved facilities and buildings, upgraded the gas delivery system...in short, LaBoon positioned Atlanta Gas
Light Company to grow bigger and more financially secure during the 1980s. That was not an easy task.

YOU CAN'T SPEND MONEY YOU DON'T HAVE

LaBoon realized that his improvements would cost
money. In fact, the company's financial position in the
early 1980s was not strong. Several factors, e.g., inadequate rate relief, bans on the use of gas for some
industrial purposes, and rapidly increasing costs of
gas, reduced the company's earnings. To make matters worse, the country experienced yet another depression in the early 1980s.

Many of those situations were a fact of life for gas
companies. Atlanta Gas Light Company had battled
against the odds for survival for much of its corporate
existence and won. LaBoon certainly would not let a
few minor hindrances deter his plans for the continued growth of the company. He sought and received
rate increases every year. Of course, the commission
never granted the full amount the company requested,
but that too was a fact of life for Atlanta Gas Light
Company . The company issued 2,771,682 shares of

common stock between May 1983 and November 1984, part of it in exchange for $20,059,000 of First Mortgage Bonds. (Many of those shares have ended up in employees' hands. By the end of the 1980s, employees owned nearly 2.5 million shares of stock through the company's stock ownership plans.) This reduced the company's proportion of long-term debt significantly. As an additional bonus, the recession

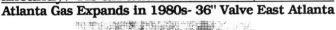

Atlanta Gas Expands in 1980s- 36" Valve East Atlanta

Courtesy Atlanta Gas Light Company

ended. By mid-1985, the company's common stock had risen to 33 1/4 from 15 7/8 on September 1, 1980. LaBoon's leadership paid off, as the company's growth during the 1980s attests.

Between 1980 and 1989, Atlanta Gas Light Company added 394,850 new customers to raise the total number to more than 1.1 million. The average number of customers during the decade rose from 799,499 in 1980 to 1,163,402 in 1989. (The company celebrated the addition of its one millionth customer in 1986.) The company added 1,052 new employees during that same period. That made a lot of people happy, since Atlanta Gas Light Company has—and always has had—an outstanding reputation as an employer.

As of 1989, the average employee's length of service with the company was almost 14 years! That was due in part to the company's long-term commitment to its workforce and the community. Atlanta Gas Light Company's stock prices also reflected that commitment.

There was a significant increase in the value of Atlanta Gas Light Company's stock during the decade. It jumped from a year-end price of $7.38 in 1980 to $27.63 at the end of 1989. Annual dividends went from $.75 in 1980 to $1.88 in 1989. When the company listed its stock on the New York Stock Exchange in May 1988, institutional ownership had increased more than three times. People in all 50 states and several foreign countries held company stock. That growth was the direct result of the company's aggressive expansion program.

In 1983, Atlanta Gas Light Company acquired Chattanooga Gas Company's gas facilities in north Georgia. Five years later, it bought the whole company! Even though its new customers were outside the state, Chattanooga is much closer to Atlanta—the heart of the company's distribution system—than towns served by the company in South Georgia, including Brunswick and Savannah. Other acquisitions during the 1980s included the City of Montezuma's natural gas system and two Georgia retail propane operations: Hinesville Gas Company and Satilla Gas Company in Waycross. Those acquisitions reflected the unprecedented growth in Georgia's population during the 1980s. They also exacerbated an old problem: where to get natural gas.

The company solved that problem handily. It coordinated the installation of 85,000 feet of 24-inch steel main in the Atlanta area in 1982. The following year, Atlanta Gas Light Company worked on 16 miles of new pipeline in Cobb County and began replacing cast iron mains with new plastic ones. In 1985, the company announced plans to build its third liquefied natural gas (LNG) plant, to be located in Cherokee County. One of the most important moves took place in 1987, when Atlanta Gas Light Company signed a contract with East Tennessee Natural Gas Company, its third major supplier. Of course, the two companies had to have a way to get the gas to Atlanta Gas Light Company's facilities. That was not an easy task.

Very little had come easy to Atlanta Gas Light Company during the company's existence. So, the problem of getting gas from East Tennessee's system to Atlanta Gas Light Company's facilities was nothing more than a minor aggravation.

The hardest part of the job was obtaining the proper permits and a review of the company's construction plans from the Federal Energy Regulatory Commission. There were also environmental impact studies and reroutes to contend with. Obstacles and delays aside, Atlanta Gas Light Company constructed a 78-mile, 16-inch transmission line from the Tennessee state line to the Cherokee LNG plant in only 77 days! That accomplishment typified Atlanta Gas Light Company's determination to succeed—and demonstrated why the company has remained in business for so long.

Atlanta Gas Light Company capitalized on technological developments in the 1980s, too. The company went from 100 terminals and personal computers in 1980 to 1,000 in 1989. During the same period, it began using a variety of computerized systems to take advantage of the latest technology available. For example, it introduced an on-line material management system (1984), a human resources system to track personnel and payroll (1985), and an on-line bad debt system (1988). The company also brought load control, telemetry, and pressure control on-line in 1987. The move to automation paid off: the company needed only 2.7 employees in 1989 to serve each 1,000 customers. That figure was well below the industry average, which was about the only aspect of the company's operations that could be considered below average.

One of the most telling statistics pointing to Atlanta Gas Light Company's growth is revealed in the number of computer hardware updates in the 1980s. One major update involved the installation of a new mainframe computer in 1986 that was 4 times larger and 4 times faster than the two the company had used previously. In 1989, information systems needed 65 software packages to maintain and control the information the company used in its jobs. New equipment installed that year was able to process 44 million instructions per second! That certainly improved the company's ability to handle everyday transactions and logistics!

Unfortunately, not all of the news was good for the company during the 1980s. W. L. Lee, chairman of the board and CEO, died in 1980. Joe T. LaBoon, his successor, died in 1988. Their deaths left holes in the company's history, but their spirits lived on. Atlanta Gas Light Company has a history of cultivating strong managers from within, and the succession of David R. Jones as CEO just prior to LaBoon's death continued the parade of outstanding leaders.

HEADING FOR THE TURN OF THE CENTURY WITH A FULL TANK OF GAS

Atlanta Gas Light Company is in excellent shape as it heads for the 21st century. Under the leadership of new CEO David R. Jones, it expects to continue expanding in the future to keep pace with Georgia's growth. (The population of the state today is approximately 5.5 million people. Some forecasters expect it to increase to 9 million by 2010.) And who knows where else the company will expand? It has already moved into Tennessee, so it is not inconceivable that the company will expand into other states, too. Atlanta Gas Light Company will be ready to accommodate growth, no matter where it takes place.

CEO David R. Jones (right) with 1,000,000,000 James and Susan Jordan January 1986

Courtesy Atlanta Gas Light Company

As President and CEO Jones says, "We've got to be ready for the growth. The future looks bright for our industry because environmental concerns have focused positive attention on natural gas, and because

gas reserves in this country are in abundant supply."
(Experts predict that there are at least another 60
years of gas reserves available today in the lower 48
states.) Certainly, Jones' outlook on the future does
not entail any unrealistic expectations, especially
based on his company's past success. Atlanta Gas
Light Company has come full circle—and is fueled for
yet a longer trip into the future.

Chapter 9

Laclede Gas

1857

Laclede Gas Company

**A COMPANY THAT SHOULD HAVE RUN OUT OF
BUSINESS LONG AGO**

Whoa: not another gas company! Why not? Laclede Gas and Atlanta Gas Light may have a principal line of business in common, but other than that, their histories are dissimilar. Laclede's problems have been completely different than Atlanta Gas Light's and are deserving of special attention. It is a wonder that Laclede is still in business today, as this chapter shall demonstrate. In truth, the only common traits these two companies share are that they are gas companies—and CHAMPIONS.

A MARVEL OF MISSOURI MANAGEMENT

The fact that Laclede's present management is willing to concede that the company's history has not always been distinguished sets it apart from many businesses. Lee M. Liberman, Laclede's Chairman and CEO, admitted in a November 18, 1987, speech to a Newcomen Society group in St. Louis that the company has had some problems in the past. He then outlined a company history that would make any corporation proud. (The author is indebted to Mr. Liberman for his contribution to this chapter.)

Laclede Gas Light's history began on March 2, 1857, when the Missouri Legislature passed an act incorporating the company. There was already one gas company in the city, and had been for 20 years. That was the St. Louis Gas Light Company, which had opened for business in 1837. (Actually, since Laclede eventually swallowed up the older company, it could lay claim to being 20 years older than it really is. Either way, Laclede is a survivor.) Ten years later St. Louis Gas Light started gas flowing through its mains on the streets of St. Louis. On November 6th of that year, St. Louis became the seventh city in the nation to have its streets lit with gas.

The primary purposes of the gas lights were to make St. Louis' streets safer and to introduce a bit of night life. The lights must have impressed the city's residents considerably, but not numerically, because 20 years later *two* new gas companies formed: Laclede and Carondelet Gas.

Laclede, whose original capitalization totaled $50,000 of stock, set a promising management precedent from its inception. The company's first president, a flamboyant former steamboat captain, John Keiser, presided over Laclede for 32 years. That is the longest term of any president to date. In fact, the company has had only twelve presidents in its history, seven of them between 1889 and 1938. Management longevity is obviously one of Laclede's strongpoints.

It did not take long for Laclede to deviate from its original business of street lighting. There was no regulation in the mid-19th century, so companies were pretty free to do what they wanted in order to make a profit. Laclede began to install indoor house lighting. Sales and revenues grew considerably as a result. Keiser was also attuned to the power of advertising to increase sales even more.

The company participated in a new and growing sport, ballooning, by furnishing gas for the balloons, sometimes for free. As early as 1859, the company supplied gas to a pioneer balloonist, John Wise, who flew his balloon from St. Louis to Hendersonville, New York.

Laclede needed all the help it could get to solicit new customers. Competition between it and St. Louis Gas was cutthroat. (Carondelet was not a major player at the time.) In many cases, both companies installed mains on the same street and made all sorts of deals, not all of them ethical, to entice new customers. The best deal was to get a new customer hooked up to the competitor's main without its knowledge, which was done quite often.The competition became so severe the city administration had to intervene. In 1873, the city and the two companies reached an agreement whereby Laclede served everything north of Washington Avenue and St. Louis Gas everything south.

The system worked well for a while. There seemed to be enough customers to go around. This was the "Golden Age" of gas illumination, highlighted by such massive undertakings as the 1882 "Carnival City of America," which featured gas-lighted arches with 21,000 globes of various colors. There was a parade lit by gas and the routes were decorated by gas lit trees. Ten years later there was another extravaganza, the Columbia Exhibition of 1892, at which the center-piece was a gas-lit arch featuring each president of the United States.

Gradually, though, the agreement broke down. Ironically, the primary cause was the expanding use of gas. The answer to the problem lay in consolidation. That was good news for Laclede.

Laclede acquired Carondolet and the St. Louis Heat and Power Company in the summer of 1889. Later that year, with the help of a New York invest-ment firm, H. B. Hollins Company, it acquired St. Louis Gas. These acquisitions added to Laclede's problems, because the larger company attracted out-side interests. Consequently, control left local hands. For the next several years, Laclede bounced from owner to owner as often as a bigamist adds wives. The timing could not have been worse.

Electric lighting, which was in its infancy towards the end of the 19th century, was cutting into the use of gas lighting. Although it did not replace gas light overnight, it still made steady inroads into Laclede's business. At the turn of the century, 90 percent of Laclede's revenues came from gas lighting. By the mid-1930s, less than one percent did. That is due in part to the fact that St. Louis did not begin to replace its gas lights until 1920. The last gas light on a main thoroughfare in the city flickered off in 1938!

WHO OWNS THE COMPANY TODAY?

Laclede had so many owners between 1900 and the onset of World War II that it was hard to keep track of them. The North America Company acquired Laclede in 1903. Six years later, a group of New York investors purchased Laclede. This was the beginning of the holding company era, which was marked by chicanery, deceit, exploitation, and a badly blemished reputation for the entire utility industry. Regardless of who owned the company, Laclede made several changes for the better in the early 1900s. One prominent move was the construction of a new headquarters building. It goes without saying that most corporations do not occupy new and larger facilities if they do not plan to stay in business for a while. Also, such moves are indicators that a company is healthy and expanding. Such was the case with Laclede.

Laclede had entered the electric business by forming a subsidiary called Laclede Power and Light. Gas remained its principal business, however. That was apparent to anyone who came upon the sprawling, newly built coke oven gas manufacturing plant the company erected at the intersection of the Mississippi and Meramec Rivers.

The new plant loaded 1,100 tons of coal per day into 64 ovens to produce coke, ammonia, light oils, fertilizer, tar, and 11 million cubic feet per day of 550 BTU gas. Laclede needed the additional capacity because it had started branching into selling gas for cooking, water and home heating, and industrial uses.

237

Laclede began selling gas for home heating as early as the winter of 1911-12. It added the cooking and water heating later. By 1925, industrial uses for gas had grown to the point that the company had a separate sales force aimed at promoting such sales. That side of thebusiness was hardly worth being involved in, though.

For example, as late as 1931, Laclede had only 525 or so home heating customers. What the company did have, though, was unbounded optimism for the future of the service, and optimism reined in is survival denied. More than a new manufacturing plant, though, Laclede needed a source of more efficient gas.

The process of making gas in those days involved passing steam over hot coke to form carbon monoxide and hydrogen. This was a relatively new process which replaced the old one in which gas from burning coal was driven into small ovens called retorts. Then, impurities were eliminated and the gas was collected and pumped. Neither process was particularly effective when compared to the use of natural gas. The heating value of gas produced by either of these methods ranged from 300-500 BTU per cubic foot, compared to natural gas' 1000 BTU per cubic foot. Eventually, the company would convert to natural gas, but the changeover was cumbersome and fraught with litigation. In the interim, it had to put up with holding company management.

The concept of holding companies was brilliant in theory. In reality, owners took advantage of the idea to bury companies under a myriad of layers. They pyramided company upon company with leverage in each successive layer so that a small amount of investment like $50,000 could control ownership and management of a billion dollars or more of assets. Utility companies in particular were folded into holding companies.

Holding companies of the era (indeed, of any era) exercised considerable control over prices and production in a given industry. They also affected investments and the rate of technological innovation. Of utmost importance, they took away local control of utilities. As John Galbraith says tongue-in-cheek in *The Great Crash,* they did so "not to eliminate competition, but rather the incompetence, sonambulance, naivete, or even the unwarranted integrity of local managements." Consolidation under a centralized leadership in a distant city could accomplish this purpose.

PEEL AWAY THE LAYERS, AND WE STILL HAVE NO IDEA OF WHO OWNS OR RUNS THE COMPANY

Holding companies in the 1920s often controlled other holding companies. The layers of bureaucracy and ownership were so complex that local managers were not sure to whom they were reporting. There were few, if any, local power, gas, and water companies in the United States which avoided falling prey to a holding company. Some were better than others. Although Laclede passed through several owners during this time, it did so without any major incidents for the most part. Unfortunately, in 1927, Laclede came under one of the "others," i.e., Harley Clarke's Utilities Power and Light Company, a vast holding company based in Chicago.

Only one man of the time, Samuel Insull, could claim more notoriety when it came to deviousness and power. It has been said that Harley Clarke kept in his desk an undated but signed resignation from each of his directors—which were given to him by the directors when they were first elected! Sure enough, Clarke created problems for Laclede.

In 1929, the Mississippi River Fuel Company constructed the first natural gas line joining Louisiana's gas fields to St. Louis. The company's principal purpose was to serve the industrial market on the east side of the city, but Mississippi River Fuel did view Laclede as a prospective customer. Laclede was reluctant at the time to convert strictly to natural gas. The company's plan was to maintain its coke plant and the market for that plant's by-products. Of course, Laclede also wanted to expand its gas sales. Management compromised.

Management decided to convert the company's natural gas distribution system to a product consisting of a mixture of natural gas and coke oven gas. This hybrid raised the BTU of the gas sold from 550 to 800 BTU. One of Laclede's competitors, the St. Louis County Gas Company, a subsidiary of Union Electric, did the same. In 1932, both companies began to sell the new mixture.

The conversion to the higher BTU provided for the expansion of the house heating market. This was good news for Laclede. There was bad news to offset it, though. The specter of environmental activism loomed large.

Local industries created a great deal of pollution caused mainly by the soft Illinois coal they burned. Hence, there was a growing amount of political pressures on these companies to reduce the smoke and grime that coated the area. Then mayor Bernard Dickmann and future mayor Raymond Tucker, who was a professor at Washington University, mounted a campaign which resulted in restrictions on the use of Illinois coal. The lack of coal hurt Laclede.

The smaller the amount of coal available, the less gas Laclede could produce. This, in turn, inhibited its growth in the house heating market. The political pressure pushing industries to clean up the environment focused on Laclede. Environmentalists wanted the company to convert strictly to the distribution of straight natural gas. To do so would cost money, which Clarke was reluctant to spend.

Utilities Power and Light had two choices: it could convert to straight gas or continue to produce the hybrid gas in defiance of the mounting pressure. It chose to do neither. City officials viewed Clarke's refusal to cooperate with their demands as unacceptable. They began calling for the elimination of the holding company and the formation of a municipal gas company to replace it. The timing was all in favor of the politicians, since the "Great Depression" was chipping away at Clarke's financial empire. Ultimately, bankruptcy forced him to sell Laclede. One of his principal lenders foreclosed on the company and sold Laclede to Floyd Odlum's Atlas Company. This put the management of Laclede back into local hands.

THE LOCAL "YOKELS" ARE BACK IN CHARGE

Odlum recognized that Laclede was badly in need of reorganization. The first step took place in 1938 when prominent local citizen Wade Childress assumed chairmanship of the company. Several other well-known local people became directors of Laclede. Three years later, management filed a reorganization

241

plan with the Missouri Public Utilities Commission and the SEC. The company was growing stronger, but there were still a few obstacles to overcome.

One event that occurred in 1945 did not seem significant at the time, especially since management was trying to rebuild the company. It was the introduction of propane as an additive to the gas supply. Managers put that aside as they wrestled with their restructuring plan.

The plan called for the divestiture of Laclede Power and Light. The divestiture occurred in 1945 when Union Electric bought Laclede. There was also a complex financial reorganization to be worked out. The heart of the plan required bondholders with maturing bonds to agree to extend their maturities. This, too, was accomplished by 1945. As a result, the old common stockholders were squeezed out—and a new company emerged.

A NEWBORN AT 88 YEARS OF AGE

The new Laclede was a financial lightweight, but management had one major thing going in its favor: it was energetic and dedicated to restoring Laclede's spoiled reputation.

Wanting to build a strong, rebuilt company was one thing. Overcoming the roadblocks to doing so was another. The roadblocks facing the new management were formidable—but not insurmountable, as subsequent events proved.

One of Laclede's problems was geographic in nature. The Mississippi River hemmed it in on the east side of St. Louis. St. Louis itself hemmed in the company elsewhere. City officials had set boundaries in

1876 that applied to Laclede's operations 70 years later! Management decided to eliminate those restrictions. They turned to acquisition as one step.

In 1947, Laclede bought the St. Louis County Gas Company from Union Electric, outbidding the St. Louis County Water Company in the process. The financing arrangements for the purchase inflicted a very restrictive debt on the company, but that was secondary in importance to the growth potential the acquisition made possible. The company's new president, Robert W. (Bob) Otto, who had been with Laclede since 1932, had the courage and foresight to make the acquisition despite the tremendous financial strain it created.

Otto's background included several years as a prosecuting attorney and a justice on the Missouri Supreme Court. Like so many successful executives, he compensated for his own weaknesses, such as they were, by picking capable lieutenants. Liberman says that Otto also had "intuitive skills that were the finest I have ever encountered."

The company's upper management in 1947 was not particularly strong. Otto recognized this and compensated for it. He hired two extremely capable young senior executives (they were both in their late 30s at the time), Henry A. (Tex) Eddins from Stone and Webster Company to be Vice President of Operations, and Lovett C. (Pete) Peters as Financial Vice President. Hiring Peters was a coup of sorts, as Otto lured him away from Bankers Trust Company, where, according to Liberman, "he had tied Laclede up so cleverly and tightly in financing the purchase of County Gas."

Liberman recalls that "it was exciting around here. You can't picture how little resources we had and yet how bold our plans were." Therein lies another of the major keys to success for many survivors: the ability to turn dreams into plans—and plans into reality.

Now that Laclede was back under local management and ready to expand, it aimed at converting to straight natural gas. This would be a three-step process:

1. There would have to be a massive strengthening of the company's city and county distribution systems in order to handle the inevitable expansion in sales made possible by natural gas.

2. Company employees would have to enter virtually every home in the area to adapt each gas burner to accommodate the higher BTU gas. (Remember, straight natural gas operated at 1000 BTU.)

3. Mississippi River Fuel would have to construct a second pipeline from its fields in Monroe, Louisiana, to the St. Louis area.

Accomplishing all these steps cost money, which Laclede did not have in abundance. What management did have was a great deal of persuasiveness. It was able to convince bankers to finance the company's ambitious projects based primarily on its tremendous growth potential.

EVERYTHING'S IN PLACE—EXCEPT FOR THE MOST CRITICAL ELEMENT

Management had planned thoroughly for the expansion. The company had taken thousands of applications from customers wishing to convert to gas heating. Liberman was responsible for reviewing the adequacy of the local street mains to see what additional reinforcement was needed there. Meanwhile, employees reviewed each application to make sure adequate local capacity existed. The employees involved put in long hours in anticipation of the actual conversion. Then, Tex Eddins inadvertently threw a monkey wrench into the plans.

Eddins casually asked Liberman how many applications had been accepted. Liberman admitted he did not know. His job, he said, was to "determine whether or not the system can deliver the gas." Then, Tex asked "Did it ever occur to you that we might have enough distribution capacity but not enough gas?" The two executives pondered the question and realized they were in trouble. In between the summers of 1949 and 1950, Laclede had expanded from 16,000 to 80,000 househeating customers and had expanded natural gas purchases from 165,000 MCF per day to 268,000. Yet, that was not enough. Simply put, the company was out of gas. It had to stop attaching new homes to its lines, cancel approval of thousands of applications, and discontinue taking on additional conversions to househeating until it could find more gas. The prospects of doing so were bleak.

There began around 1950 a long period of strain between Laclede and Mississippi River Fuel. That year, Laclede sold its coke oven plant to Great Lakes

Carbon Corporation. The sale cut into its ability to produce gas, even if the methods used there were archaic by gas company standards. Fortunately, management had the foresight to sell the plant, but not all the land surrounding it. The retention of the land notwithstanding, Laclede still wanted an ever-expanding supply of gas.

Mississippi River Fuel had reservations about the growing needs because of their seasonal nature. Since Laclede wanted most of the gas for househeating purposes, that meant it would have large demands in the winter and low demands in the summer. Mississippi River did not want to deal with Laclede on that basis. That led to a serious struggle between the two companies.

Mississippi River actually went so far as to acquire a substantial stock interest in Laclede. It even managed to place one of its candidates as one of Laclede's nine directors. In turn, Laclede held its real board meetings the night before the scheduled meetings while this director served. Laclede took some strong retaliatory measures against Mississippi River, which ultimately sold its interest in the company. Relations between the two corporations remained strained, however, and Laclede still had the problem of an insufficient gas supply.

IT CAN GET MIGHTY COLD IN A MISSOURI HOUSE WHEN THERE"S NO GAS TO HEAT IT

Laclede did manage to increase its purchases somewhat during 1952 because Mississippi River Fuel added compressor stations along its system. As a result, Laclede approved several thousand more conversions to househeating. It was also able to attach new homes, which it had been unable to do since the 1950 shutdown. Despite these significant steps, the company still had to find other ways to increase its supplies. As the old saying goes, where there's a will, there's a way.

Management decided in 1950 to install 57 large propane storage tanks on the land adjoining the old coke oven plant. The additional storage, added to preexisting capacity, totaled about 2,000,000 gallons. At the same time, Laclede contracted with Phillips Petroleum for a total winter delivery of 8 million gallons of propane. This supply expanded even more in ensuing years.

EXACTLY HOW IMPORTANT IS PROPANE?

A steady supply of propane had a bit more significance to Laclede than it did to other gas distributors. Most gas companies had a large number of industries mixed into their customer base. This was not true in Laclede's case. A great deal of the industrial strength in the St. Louis area is concentrated across the Mississippi River in Illinois. Since Laclede does not serve that state, industry potential was limited. (This actually worked to the company's benefit in the long run, as we shall see.) Add to that the limited capacity of pipelines, and Laclede had a unique problem.

Pipelines have fixed capacity which means there can be very little variation in throughput at different seasons of the year. There is a natural inconsistency between the characteristics of the fixed investment in pipeline facilities such as those owned and operated by Mississippi River Fuel and Laclede's need for gas, which varies almost directly with the weather. Propane manufacturing capacity as a supplement is one way to deal with this mismatch, but the ability to utilize propane is limited. The answer to Laclede's problem of supply and demand was being worked out in Chicago.

Peoples Gas Company in the "Windy City" shared this uncommon problem with Laclede. They had begun to experiment with underground storage in aquifers, i.e., water-bearing formations that had never previously contained hydrocarbons. Propane had been stored successfully underground in depleted gas fields, but the aquifer experiment was a first. The early signs of the tests indicated that they would be successful.

According to Liberman, "We who are engineers, realizing the unique requirements of underground aquifer storage—and believe me, they are unique—would not have thought that any chance existed to find such favorable geology in eastern Missouri where no previous oil or gas had ever been discovered." That did not deter President Otto.

Otto was a man willing to take a chance. He decided that anything that could be done in Illinois could be done in Missouri. Otto called in the state's geologist, Ed Clark, who agreed with Liberman et al. Nevertheless, he decided to investigate.

By the end of 1951, the investigation had zeroed in on an area north of the town of Florrisant. The geology looked promising. More important, if it proved workable, the area could not have been better located, since it would provide Laclede the opportunity to feed its distribution supply from the north end of St. Louis. This supply, when added to the traditional Mississippi River Fuel feed from the south side, would add immeasurably to the company's system distribution capacity.

There were two drawbacks to Laclede's search for underground storage capacity. First, the company had only one executive, Al Burgess, with an in-depth knowledge of geology. When Burgess realized that Otto was serious about the project, he hired a young geologist, Rex Bannister, to help. Second, Otto insisted on carrying out the Laclede project exactly as Peoples was doing its own. This created a new set of problems.

Otto wanted to hire all of Peoples geological consultants, of whom there were three principals, none of whom could get along with one another. After Laclede started drilling a few shallow wells to determine what the geology looked like in the area, Burgess suggested that the company take oil and gas leases. His reason was simple: if the company did discover any hydrocarbons, it would be able to produce them *if they had the leases.* The consultants said that was ridiculous. They argued that no gas or oil had ever been discovered in Missouri. Their argument prevailed, much to the company's chagrin.

OUR SORROW IS AS DEEP AS AN OIL WELL

Early indications of the shallow testing proved favorable. The next logical step was to drill deeper. So, in the early summer of 1953, the company drilled a deep test from the top of the earth to bedrock, which is granite, at 3,500 feet below the surface. Lo and behold, the test encountered oil at about 1,100 feet! Ironically, that *did not* make the Laclede executives happy.

Liberman describes a meeting of executives when the oil was first discovered as a "wake." As he relates the story:

> On July 10, 1953, which was a Sunday, I was called off the golf course to come to the office. It looked like a wake when I got there about 3 p.m. When I asked what the problem was, I was advised that our deep test had encountered oil at about 1,100 feet. I thought that was good, and when I said so, I found out it wasn't good if you didn't have any oil and gas leases.

Bob Otto wanted to know how to get such leases, and Al Burgess said you had to get some lease hounds. Bob said, "What in the hell is a lease hound?" Al advised him that a lease hound is a professional who secures oil and gas leases. Bob asked Al how to get some and Al said he would get some to drive here from Oklahoma and be here by the first thing the next morning.

That settled one issue. Then, a second one involving business ethics arose. The question revolved around whether the company should inform the public about the discovery of oil. Otto said yes; everyone else said no. A long argument over the issue ensued.

Otto maintained that since the company had already announced to the public that they were developing storage, they were morally bound to let them know the results of their efforts. No one else agreed with him. But, as Liberman says, "Bosses prevail," so local newspapers headlined the news the next day.

The *St. Louis Globe Democrat* announced in its July 11, 1953, edition that Laclede had discovered oil and that it would be taking oil and gas leases. More important, the paper reported, anyone else who wanted to could. This led to more complications for the company.

The discovery of oil demonstrated the presence of a gas field, but the company's announcement to the public complicated things enormously. Laclede was able to lease only about half of the field; the rest went to interests not compatible with storage development. The company had to buy out these interests after considerable trouble and expense. Meanwhile, the project moved along rapidly.

On December 2, 1955, Laclede injected the first gas into storage. About two years later, it began using the storage field to deliver gas back into the system. The storage was a decided boon to the company. By 1959, the equivalent of 85,000 additional househeating customers had been added due solely to the new storage capacity.

Gas distributors cannot underemphasize the importance of storage facilities. The development of Laclede's improved facilities did not change its supply picture overnight, but it did in the long run. By 1987, the company could deliver as much as 350 million cubic feet of gas per day and sustain deliveries over the winter of about 8 billion cubic feet, a substantial portion of its heating requirements.

The new storage development program was not the only step in Laclede's drive to upgrade its service. At the same time as the exploration was taking place, Laclede continued its pursuit of Mississippi River Fuel in an attempt to get additional flowing gas. Mississippi resisted Laclede's requests. Consequently, in

1959, Laclede filed a complaint under the Natural Gas Act based on the fact that there existed unused capacity in Mississippi's system. There followed a substantial amount of litigation, which worked eventually in Laclede's favor.

Mississippi River Fuel finally agreed to build a line to connect its system to the trunkline system located about 90 miles east of St. Louis. This added about 85 million cubic feet per day of delivery into St. Louis and ended years of squabbling between the two companies.

Laclede also located additional sources of gas in the next two years. By 1963, it could supply gas for househeating for every customer who wanted it. That was a major milestone for Laclede, and proof positive that a well-run company can achieve its goals through a combination of effective, foresighted leadership and persistence. Laclede exemplifies these principles.

THE LEADERSHIP CHANGES, BUT THE PROGRESS DOES NOT

Bob Otto stepped down as president and up to chairman in 1956, at the height of the major expansion effort. (Otto retired in 1962). H. Reid Derrick, former president of the Alabama Gas Company, succeeded him. Progress continued unabated.

In 1963, Laclede acquired the St. Charles Gas Corporation, and with it the right to supply gas to St. Charles County, which is the company's fastest growing territory today. Until the acquisition, Laclede had served only the environs of the City of St. Charles, but the purchase allowed it to serve Wentzville, in which was located a General Motors plant. This was a major step for Laclede.

The next year, Laclede moved into Jefferson County and formed a new company with Missouri Natural Gas. This gave the company a foot into northern Jefferson County. That foot turned into a giant step several years later, when Laclede bought out Missouri Natural entirely. This gave Laclede access to a service area that extended about 170 miles south of St., Louis, all the way to Poplar Bluff. Then, an old problem resurfaced to challenge management's optimism.

OH NO, NOT THOSE DREADED GAS LINES AGAIN

In the late 1960s, after a lot of study, Laclede began participating in the revitalization of downtown St. Louis by becoming a prime tenant in a new building bearing its name. For a short time, this 30-story Laclede Gas Building was the tallest in downtown St. Louis. The company took up occupancy in 1970, the same year Lee Liberman became its 12th president. Unfortunately, Liberman inherited an unwanted problem. (How many problems are wanted?)

The beginning of the 1970s brought with it a gas supply problem that was related to resources rather than capacity. The natural gas industry had long been expanding its sales, but not its reserves. This did not bode well for Laclede or any of its counterparts, all of which were growing concerned. As usual, management did not waste time in acting to resolve problems.

Laclede took two important steps:
- expand and solidify its storage capability and enter new contracts for expanded supply
- enter the exploration business to discover its own gas reserves

The company proceeded with both immediately.

Laclede made geological studies and embarked on construction of an 800,000 barrel (33,000,000 gallon) cavern mined out of the limestone about 300 feet deep, which was about 1,200 feet above its underground gas storage stratum. It also solidified new contracts which would provide the company with 70,000,000 gallons of propane per year. (Not surprisingly, Laclede currently owns one of the major propane storage facilities in the nation and is one of the nation's largest propane users.)

Laclede launched an exploration program in late 1971. As luck would have it, the results were incredibly successful. In the company's *first* venture, it participated in one of the largest on-land discoveries of that decade (the Mills Ranch Field)! This discovery not only benefited the company, but its ratepayers as well.

The company's ventures at the time were conducted on behalf of the ratepayers. Accordingly, Laclede properly sought and received the approval of the Missouri Public Service Commission to include the activity in its rate base and to give the benefits to the ratepayers. During the first ten years of Laclede's involvement, the company participated in the drilling of 81 test wells. Forty-one were productive. By 1981, Laclede had its supply problem well in hand. Since that time, it has conducted gas exploration on an unregulated basis, with a moderate success rate. Moderate or not, the fact that Laclede took the problem of its supply shortage into its own hands prepared it favorably for the critical supply disruptions in the mid 1970s.

Many gas distributors were forced to curtail supplies during the oil embargo in 1973. Laclede was not. It weathered the period despite some extremely cold winters. However, Laclede, like its counterparts, was affected by the profound changes in the industry brought about by the embargo.

Curtailment of gas caused customers in some areas to lose faith in gas as a source of heating. It also prompted the Federal Energy Regulatory Commission and Congress to loosen their control over gas prices. The combination of factors caused a substantial decline in the market for gas. Consequently, between price-induced conservation, including increased insulation and improved plant efficiencies, and switching to other energy sources, the nation's demand for gas declined from about 22 trillion cubic feet in 1973 to about 16 trillion feet in 1987. History helped Laclede in this respect somewhat. Its sales did not drop as dramatically as did some other companies because of its smaller percentage of industrial sales. Nevertheless, the situation did halt the company's sales growth—but it did nothing to check its battle against the regulations and legislation affecting the gas industry today.

WE MIGHT AS WELL TAKE ON THE GOVERNMENT, TOO

During the 1980s, Laclede became very active in fighting regulation aimed at gas distributors and legislation affecting its business. In effect, Laclede became a champion of the consumer. The company became particularly active in Washington DC.For example, Laclede opposed the 1978 passage of the Natural Gas Policy Act, and almost succeeded in defeating it. Laclede predicted that passage of the act would double the cost of gas to the nation's consumers, which it did. According to experts' estimates, the Natural Gas Policy Act has cost consumers about $30 BILLION annually, with little, if any, countervailing benefit.

Laclede also opposed producers' attempts to pass on heating value upward price adjustments to distributors and consumers. The company failed with the Federal Energy Regulatory Commission (FERC), but pushed the case all the way to the U. S. Supreme Court, which ruled on the company's behalf.

Another area in which Laclede became active was in fighting special marketing programs introduced by producers and pipeline companies. It was Laclede's belief that these programs took low-cost gas away from consumers and made it available to boiler fuel customers. The FERC did not agree with Laclede once again. Once again, the courts did, and threw the special marketing programs out.

Laclede's battles did not end there. It opposed producers and the FERC when they sought permission to adjust prices upward to compensate for their own production and gathering activities. Subsequently, the DC Appellate Court found such charges illegal. Laclede's most serious struggle, however, was against two other FERC actions.

The FERC operated under the assumption that the natural gas industry can become workably competitive. Based on this belief, the commission aimed at making pipelines common carriers with the responsibility for acquiring gas supply transferred to the distributors. This goal was based on the FERC's conviction that there was a surplus of natural gas in the late 1970s and 80s, and there would continue to be one. Therefore, the commission said, distributors and other end users should rely upon this surplus and fill their gas requirements through spot market purchases. Laclede did not agree.

As Liberman said, "We think the spot market is ephemeral and unreliable. We caution that if the industry moves in that direction, there could be disaster as gas supplies tighten up, which we are confident they will. We foresee those distributors who rely on the spot market having serious difficulty in meeting their obligations to their customers." Laclede's arguments went unheard. Discouraged, but not beaten, the company has continued to battle with the FERC over the issue.

One other area in which Laclede fought the FERC was in appealing its attempt to deregulate and thereby raise the price of a good part of the nation's gas supply denoted as "old gas" under the Natural Gas Policy Act and forever regulated by it. Liberman indicated that Laclede would have more success in overturning the commission in this area, albeit it only after protracted court battles. The important thing in this regard, though, is that Laclede is a leader in fighting what it considers to be oppressive government regulation. In the process, Laclede has become a champion of consumers' rights and a company that acts on its convictions, even if being one requires that it fight an opponent as formidable as the United States government. That has long been Laclede's style; the company's consistency in its approach to regulation in its consumers' and industry's best interests has contributed to its ability to survive.

There is no doubt that Laclede will be around for a long time to come. Look at the growth between 1945, when the "new" Laclede emerged, and the present. As World War II ended, Laclede served 215,645 customers. Only a few thousand of them used gas for househeating. The investment in the company's plant was $36,551,000 as of December 31 that year, and the company's revenues were $9,461,000. Compare that to the figures four decades later.

In 1987, revenues were about $450,000,000. The company was serving 571,000 customers, of whom about 520,000 used gas for househeating. Plant investment had gone up to $476,000,000, and the company could send out 1,100,000,000 cubic feet of gas in a 24-hour period. That was 30 times the company's sendout rate in 1945! These figures indicate that Laclede has overcome many of its problems and is in a position to resolve any more that arise in the future. That the company has a future is assured. After all, any company that has overcome the problems Laclede has in its 134-year existence is bound to survive for considerable time more.

Chapter 10

1873

Adolph Coors Company

PRODUCTS THAT ARE GOOD FOR WHAT "ALES" YOU

It's easy to brew beer in Colorado. You merely fill a vat with water running off the Rocky Mountains. Then, you add some malt, hops, yeast, barley, other selected grains, a few chemicals, and wait a couple of days for it to ferment. That is, unless, you own the Adolph Coors Company!

Coors has mastered the art of brewing—and growing. What started out in 1873 as a small local brewery is now the fourth largest brewery in the nation. Significantly, it ranks among the top 250 companies on the Fortune 500 list of American industrial corporations. The company's products are sold in 49 states and the District of Columbia. The only state in which it is not sold is Indiana. That is simply because Coors ships *all* its beer in refrigerated railroad cars and trucks. Indiana state laws mandate that all beer shipped into the state must be warm. Coors refuses to change its shipping procedures, which would violate its strict quality control policies. Indiana may soon change its laws to allow Coors into the state, however.

Coors has been a model of consistency since its inception. That is not surprising. The Coors name is everywhere in the management structure. Coors management today includes several third and fourth generation family members. Five of the nine Board of Directors members are Coors. William K. (Bill) Coors is Chairman and President, Joseph Coors is Vice Chairman, and several other Coors head subsidiaries. All three of its major subsidiaries, Coors Brewing Company, Coors Technology Companies, and Coors Ceramic Companies, are headed by a Coors. Yes, this is one business that has stayed in the family since the day it opened its doors—and which promises to continue that way for a long time to come.

Basically, Coors' history falls into three distinct periods. The first included the company's formative years, which lasted from its foundation in 1873 through the Prohibition era (1914-33). The next period (1933-55) was relatively uneventful from an historical standpoint. It involved recovery from prohibition, strengthening of subsidiaries, and stabilization of regional sales. The third, which began in the mid-1950s and is still in progress, has been marked by national and international expansion and incursions into new technologies. This has been Coors' most significant and sets the company apart from its competitors. People who believe that Coors is only a beer maker will be surprised to learn that it is much more. Let's look at these periods one at a time.

1873-1933: LIFE UNDER ADOLPH, SR.

AWAY, AWAY, ADOLPH'S A STOWAWAY

Adolph Coors' brewing career began in Dortmund, Germany, in 1862, when he signed a three-year apprenticeship contract with the Henry Wenker Brewery. He fulfilled his contract with Wenker, then moved onto other breweries in Kassel, Berlin, and Uelzen. Young Adolph learned a lot about making beer in his early years. He also learned that he did not want to be a soldier. The Franco-Prussian War was in full swing during the 1860s, and Adolph had no desire to become a participant. So, he joined half a million other Germans who emigrated to America between 1866 and 1870.

Coors began his trip across the ocean in the spring of 1868. He embarked aboard a ship outbound from Hamburg to Baltimore. He did not have a ticket, but that was no obstacle as far he was concerned. Adolph manifested his determination to get to America by stowing away aboard the vessel. Unfortunately, crew members discovered him aboard the ship. But, instead of arresting him, they allowed him to work in Baltimore long enough to pay for his ticket. Work was one thing which did not scare Coors. During the year he was in Baltimore, he toiled at various times as a bricklayer, a stone-cutter, a fireman, and a laborer. Soon, his wanderlust caught up with him and he emigrated from Baltimore. He arrived in Naperville, Illinois, in late 1869 and found a job as a foreman at the Stenger Brewery.

Coors remained with Stenger for a little more than two years. Between January and April of 1872, he worked his way to Denver. It did not take him long to make his mark there. By the end of the year he became sole owner of a company which sold bottled beer, ale, porter, cider, imported and domestic wines, and seltzer water. That was certainly a diverse line of products, but diversity would become a hallmark of the Coors business in the future—especially during the United States' brief experiment with prohibition.

The bottling business was a success, but it did not quite satisfy Coors' ambition of owning his own brewery. He dreamed of opening one in the town of Golden, primarily because of the presence of clear, cool water running down from the Rocky Mountains. Coors was a man who believed in turning dreams into reality. It was only a matter of time, then, before he opened his own brewery.

THIS MAY NOT BE A BAKERY, BUT COORS STILL NEEDS SOME DOUGH

Coors had the perfect place in mind for his brewery. He found an abandoned tannery on the banks of a river at the base of Table Mountain. The most important topographical feature of the site was several clear springs and a stream named Clear Creek. If there was one thing that Coors had learned about brewing beer, it was that the quality of water used made a big difference in the taste of the product. So, Coors had a location; all he needed was money to build his brewery. A backer was not hard to find.

One of Coors' customers, Jacob Schueler, invested $18,000 in the brewery. Coors contributed $2,000 from his own savings. They spent $2,500 for the land, remodeling the tannery, and initial purchases. Coors was by nature a frugal man, but he spared no expense in buying the finest ingredients for his beer. He believed that in order to provide a superior beer, he had to use the best ingredients available. Apparently, his customers agreed. In less than a year, Coors Brewery was turning a profit. Within seven years, Adolph was able to buy out Schueler's interest. That left him free to begin careful long-term planning and devise new ways to distribute his beer.

WHAT GOOD IS BEER WITHOUT A BOTTLE?

At the same time as he established the brewery, Coors also built the Colorado Glass Works to manufacture the bottles for his beer. Shortly thereafter, he leased the glass works to his friend J. J. Herold, who began making china cooking utensils. A few years later, Coors regained the lease and entered the field of pottery production. The ceramic and brewery businesses grew considerably as the years went by. Eventually, the ceramics work would play an important role in the company's survival.

Virtually all of Coors' profits in the early years went right back into the plant for expansion and equipment. (There was also a bit of personal expansion involved. In 1879, Adolph married Louisa Weber of Denver. By 1893, he was the father of three sons and three daughters!) Coors was shrewd enough to realize that expansion was based on his ability to market the product—and he had a lot of product.

Between 1880 and 1890, Coors' output rose from 3,500 barrels a year to 17,600. (That's a lot of beer! One barrel equals 31 gallons, or 13 3/4 cases, each holding 24 12-ounce cans or bottles.) The company had no problem with its distribution. Consumers clamored for more.

By 1900, Coors output rose to 48,000 barrels annually. From an historical standpoint, that was amazing, since the company went through a national depression, a devastating flood, and, worse, the growing threat of prohibition during the 1890-1900 decade. The increase in production pleased Adolph, but he knew well enough that there was more to life than brewing beer. He was also a firm believer in not putting all his hops into one vat. With these ideas in mind, he immersed himself in community affairs and made sure his offspring were well trained to operate and diversify the family business.

YOU HAVE TO HAVE THE RIGHT CHEMISTRY TO RUN A BREWERY SUCCESSFULLY

Adolph sent two of his sons, Grover and Adolph, Jr., to Cornell University. The third, Herman, joined the company at a later date. After graduation, the younger Adolph went to Germany and pursued graduate studies in chemistry. All his education paid off. His father named him superintendent of the company in 1912. This began a strong family tradition of placing the company under family members' leadership and effectively ended the senior Adolph's 39-year rule over his brewery. It also put his sons in a rather tenuous position.

The nation was flirting with prohibition in the early 1900s. Although the 18th Amendment did not make national prohibition constitutional until 1919, one quarter of the states were dry well before that. World War I did not help brewers and distillers, either. For example, the Lever Act of 1917 outlawed the use of grain in the manufacture of alcoholic beverages. Ironically, ethnic heritage affected the production of beer and alcohol, too.

Many Americans directed the anger over the war toward people of German and Italian descent. Even though Coors had left Germany 49 years before that country went to war with the United States, he suffered indirectly from the conflict. Americans identified certain alcoholic beverages with ethnic preferences. Since the Germans were stereotyped as prodigious beer drinkers, and the Italians were considered to be heavy wine drinkers, some Americans decided to punish them by prohibiting *all* alcoholic beverages. So, by 1914, Colorado was dry. The Coors family did not look at that as being the death knell for their business. After all, the word "quit" was not in their lexicon. They simply saw prohibition as an excuse to diversify.

THE WATER IS STILL FLOWING, BUT THE STATE IS DRY

As current President William K. Coors wrote in a November 19, 1990,letter to a consumer:

> Any company in the alcohol beverage industry which is not actively driving diversification is not being realistic about its long-range future. We regard diversification as a vital strategy to our long-range survival.

These words may have been written three-quarters of a century after Coors first experienced the need for—and the benefit of—diversification, but they certainly sum up one of the primary reasons the company has been so successful throughout its existence.

If the Coors had any doubts that prohibition would really come, they were dissolved in 1914 when the company had to dump more than 17,000 gallons of beer into Clear Creek. That would have meant the end of business for many brewers. (In fact, it did. Of the 1,568 American breweries operating in 1910, only 750 reopened when prohibition was repealed in April 1933.) Adolph Sr. and his three sons had long since decided to diversify either until the prohibition experiment ended or it became permanent. Either way, they intended to be in business in some capacity. The four Coors put their heads together to find some way to get through the dry stage. The results of their brainstorming sessions were a new cement manufacturing operation and a heavier concentration on the porcelain plant. These companies were as much the product of their foresight as their pragmatism. The Coors had an eye to the future. Whatever business they went into, they intended to stay in. With that in mind, they continued to use their brewing equipment to produce foodstuffs related to beer and developed their porcelain business with the help of the United States government.

The porcelain plant fit in well with the government's plans during World War I. At the beginning of the war, the Allies blockaded Germany. This meant that they would suffer shortages. The United States in particular would be deprived of its primary source of chemical and laboratory ware. The government asked Coors to develop porcelain ware that would meet laboratory needs. Coors was ready and able to do so.

The government work gave Coors a boost at a time when it desperately needed one. Since that time, the company has acquired a reputation as a leader in the ceramics industry. In fact, in 1989 it had sales of $166,749,000 and has attained a position as the leading advanced high-temperature materials company in the United States. More important, its future bottom line should improve each year, if past performance is any indicator.

Coors Ceramics
Growth

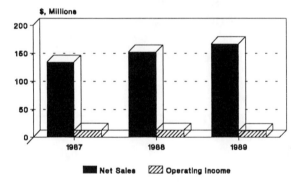

One thing that will help sales is the fact that Coors Porcelain Company is the sole manufacturer of porcelain chemical ware in North America! Joe Coors, Jr. envisions it as becoming the world's premier technical ceramics company. That's not bad for the third-largest business of the Coors Company! Porcelain aside, Coors had other products to carry it through the prohibition era. During the 17-year prohibition period, Coors produced several food products. One was a near beer, Mannah®. The process by which it was made included a step in which the alcohol was condensed out of the product. The condensed alcohol was stored in government-bonded cellars and then sold to drug companies, hospitals, and other approved markets. Consequently, the younger Coors kept their hands in the brewery business so they would be prepared for the end of prohibition.

Coors also became a leading producer of malted milk during the period. This was as natural a step as brewing near beer, since making malted milk entails the same process and equipment as the production of malted barley for brewing beer. The company continued to make malted milk until 1955, when it discontinued the process in order to concentrate on internal production demands.

1933-1955: A RETRENCHING PERIOD

PROHIBITION IS OVER, AND IT'S TIME TO MAKE SOME MORE BEER

The company survived prohibition very nicely. Unfortunately, its founder did not. Adolph Coors Sr. died in 1929. His son, Adolph Jr., succeeded him as president. Little changed in the way the company operated.

The senior Coors had made it a practice to make high-quality products by the most modern and efficient methods available. He followed four primary rules to achieve this goal:
- reinvest profits in the company to expand production facilities and improve the product
- improve his products constantly

- investigate new ideas continually
- institute practices and innovations that were unheard of elsewhere in the industry

The last in particular resulted in applications of new technology that set the pace for the brewing industry. Among them were tinplate and aluminum cans, a special malting process, the sterile-fill process, and constant refrigeration. Two other concepts that the senior Coors taught his sons were to be involved in the community and be aware of employees' views on matters pertaining to the corporation. Those practices have been handed down to today's generation of leaders.

COORS MOVES OUT OF THE ROCKIES

Coors concentrated primarily on improving its products and refining its marketing and distribution strategy and techniques between the end of the Prohibition Era and the 1950s. It was a regional brewer for the most part, but the company's executives did not plan to stay that way. After all, they had the largest single-site brewery in the world—which is the way the Coors family wanted it. They felt that they could exercise better control over the quality of their beer, on which they had built their reputation. They were afraid they could not duplicate the water anywhere else. So, while they expanded gradually throughout the second half of the 20th century, they continued to rely on their Golden brewery.

In the first year after prohibition ended, Coors sold only 90,000 barrels of beer in two states. It took 22 years, until 1955, for them to reach the million barrel mark in annual sales. By comparison, they shipped

17.7 million barrels in 1989. The company's growth has been steady. That growth is projected to continue, but the pattern for it was set in that 1933-55 time-frame. It was during those years that the Coors family realized exactly how much potential lay in that one brewery in Golden.

One of the amazing things about the Golden brewery is its capacity to supply almost the entire United States with Coors beers and ale. As much perspicacity as Adolph Coors, Sr., possessed, he could not have foreseen the day when his company would be operating in 49 states, the District of Columbia, and several foreign countries. Yet, that did happen—but it was the confidence his descendants had in their product that prompted them to expand nationwide.

Coors constant research and application of its findings are more evident in the products some of its other subsidiaries generate. The company's history is replete with subsidiaries and products that have been developed in response to the United States' ever-changing needs and environmental concerns. In fact, people may be surprised to see just how diverse Coors really is. Even though the brewery continues to be Coors' mainstay, the portion of the company's assets in non-beer business has increased from less than 25 percent in 1980 to more than 38 percent today. That percentage will more than likely grow as Coors positions itself for the 21st century.

1955-TODAY: COORS' GOLDEN YEARS

COORS MOVES OUT OF THE ROCKIES

The 1950s were particularly good years for Coors. It was during this period that the company began to diversify on a large scale and build a "cradle to grave—and back" operation. These were the years when Coors began to not only manufacture its own cans and bottles, but bring them back again and reuse them. Although the company has always been headquartered in Golden, its true "Golden" years did not begin until the mid-1950s.

COORS STARTS A NEW BUSINESS CYCLE WITH ITS CONTAINER RECYCLE

Coors recognized the need for a recyclable, energy-efficient can for its beer. The tinplate cans the company used were not recyclable. Hence, the empty ones frequently ended up as litter in open spaces, along highways, on park grounds and beaches....In other words, they contributed heavily—and inadvertently—to a growing litter problem. Company researchers sought a way to resolve this problem.

Coors owned its own container manufacturing plant. As far as there searchers were concerned, all they had to do was develop a better beer container. The Container Manufacturing Plant could produce the new product. On January 22, 1959, Coors manufactured the result of that research: the industry's first all-aluminum cans.

271

In typical Coors fashion, the development and production of a new product did not mean the end of the search for an even better one. Over the next few years, Coors developed new processes whereby it manufactured even more advanced cans. Today, Coors not only makes these cans, but it sells them to other companies. The company has experienced similar advances in bottle making. Coors runs the only glass plant in existence that has an operating, all-electric powered furnace that produces amber glass.

RECYCLING MAY BE A PAIN IN THE CAN AND THE GLASS, BUT COORS DOES IT ANYWAY

Coors made bottles and cans, filled bottles and cans, and then ceased to worry about them. That all changed in 1959 when the company pioneered the use of aluminum cans.

The company encouraged aluminum can recycling from the time it introduced these containers. There were not enough cans on the market at the time to make the effort worthwhile. However, as more and more companies followed Coors' lead and packaged their products in aluminum cans, recycling became more feasible—and profitable. The increase prompted Coors to begin a full-scale recycling program in 1970. The response was so great that Coors eventually established a separate subsidiary, the Golden Recycle Company (now known as Golden Aluminum Company), in 1980 to recycle its bottles and cans. That has been a successful venture.

Look at these numbers. In one 13-year period, Coors reclaimed 913 million pounds of aluminum cans, for which the company paid the public more than $192 million. In 1987 alone, the company collected

80 million pounds of aluminum cans for which it paid the public $21.5 million and 8,300 tons of glass for which it paid $166,000. The cans recycled amount to 80 percent of all aluminum cans produced at Coors' can manufacturing facility.

Coors not only buys its cans back, but it processes them. Golden Aluminum, which is the largest of the Coors Technology Companies, operates a $44 million aluminum recycling center in Fort Lupton, Colorado, northeast of Denver. The plant produced 60 million pounds of recycled aluminum in 1989, supplied all of the end and tab stock used by the brewery, and still sold over 30 percent of its production to other beverage and food can manufacturers. The business has been so successful Coors has built a second plant in San Antonio at a cost of $155 million which will have the capacity to produce 130 million pounds of aluminum sheet stock per year. Certainly, the formation of this subsidiary has proven beneficial to Coors—and a cost saver besides.

EXPANSION: AT WHAT COST?

There is no doubt that Coors is cost conscious. That is not surprising. Businesses simply cannot survive if they are not. After all, attention to the bottom line is what makes a company successful. But, company officers must never sacrifice quality while striving to make a profit. Bill Coors, Chairman and President of the Adolph Coors Company, makes that clear when he sums up the corporation's philosophy.

"Our strategy is to develop new businesses or expand existing ones based on our proven technologies and market experience," he says. "We expect these businesses to manufacture distinctive products of su-

273

perior quality and to provide a reasonable return on investment." The key words there are "a reasonable return on investment." The way Coors does business, if there is no reasonable return, it does not hesitate to divest itself of unprofitable lines.

Again, Bill Coors sets the tone for Coors' philosophy regarding the bottom line. "We will participate in only those businesses where we have a quality or marketing advantage, or those that supply cost-advantageous strategic materials for our operations and have the potential to earn a substantial return," he says. Certainly, the company adheres to that philosophy.

Coors adheres to the words in a Kenny Rogers hit song, "The Gambler": "You've got to know when to hold them, know when to fold them." In the past four years, Coors has ended its involvement in several businesses, including snack foods, rice milling, power semiconductor devices, ceramic dental supplies, and coal mining. Its reasons are simple: management either did not see a return to shareholders or had other less-expensive sources of supply. To this might be added a third: Coors saw more profit in investing in its core businesses.

THE COUNTRY MAY BE RUNNING OUT OF ENERGY, BUT COORS ISN'T

Coors desire to be as self sufficient as possible is reflected in some of its subsidiaries. Four of them, Coors Energy Company, Golden Technologies Company, Inc., Graphic Packaging Corporation, and Coors BioTech, Inc., operate under the umbrella of Coors Technology Companies. We'll look at them one at a time.

Coors' Energy Company

The Coors Energy Company came into being in 1980 to assure that the corporation would have access to an uninterrupted supply of energy to its numerous facilities. The company has been successful.

In 1989 alone, Coors Energy drilled ten successful new wells which added significantly to the company's reserves. By the end of that year, proved reserves amounted to 37.4 billion cubic feet of natural gas and 6.5 million barrels of oil. That's not bad considering that in 1980 the reserves amounted to 15.8 cubic feet of natural gas and no oil!

Today, Coors buys and sells energy. Virtually all the gas it produces on its Western Slope fields is sold to pipeline companies. (Perhaps Atlanta Gas Light and Laclede should give Bill Coors a call.) Coors Energy has an interest in and operates hundreds of oil and natural gas wells. It also leases land for future evaluation and drilling. The company produces several hundred barrels of oil each day from wells in Utah and western Colorado. The company not only produces it, but delivers it, too.

Coors Energy delivers more than 4 million cubic feet of natural gas per day to the Golden area through its own 65-mile pipeline. The gas goes to Coors' power, porcelain, can manufacturing, and glass plants. Coors also uses a lot of coal. Its coal-fired plant in Golden provides enough electricity for a city of 120,000 people. Now, if that isn't enough to get steamed about, Coors uses its power production to heat the Colorado School of Mines, which is located in Golden.

In the fall of 1982, Coors constructed a 3,000-foot-long underground steam line between its plant and the college. The school purchases steam from Coors and uses it as its primary heating source. The water derived from the condensed steam is collected and piped back from the campus to the brewery, where it is reheated for steam! The entire process provides the school with heat at affordable prices, which is critical in light of today's energy situation.

Despite all the energy use, Coors is careful to maintain a concern for the environment. Air quality throughout Coors Industries is monitored by highly sophisticated equipment which takes round-the-clock readings to ensure compliance with required air standards. This attention to the environment is a high priority for Coors—and a benefit for the communities in which it operates.

Never complacent, Coors is quick to recognize changing market conditions in the energy field. Consequently, the company has sold some natural gas properties and discontinued mining coal at its two mines. Nevertheless, Coors plans to stay in the energy business and maintain its independence. Its commitment is certainly fuel for optimism regarding the future of the Coors Energy Company and its related subsidiaries. Speaking of the future, Coors is preparing itself already for the 21st-century technology through the Golden Technologies Company.

Golden Technologies Company, Inc.

Golden Technologies, formed on January 1, 1990, is designed to commercialize in-house developed technologies. The company is focusing on high-technology surface finishing, cleaning materials developed through biotechnology, a unique system for wooden pallet replacement, and a newly developed liquid dispensing system. Coors anticipates this subsidiary as being one of its "stars" in the next few years as it continues to turn innovative applications of engineering and technological expertise into business opportunities.

Graphics Packaging Corporation

Just as Adolph Coors, Sr., recognized early in his business career that he might as well make his own containers, his successors realized that the next logical step would be to manufacture packaging in which to hold them. Coors has gone into packaging in a big way.

Graphics Packaging is the result of a 1988 merger between Coors Packaging Company and Graphic Packaging Corporation. The company is a leading manufacturer of high-performance folding cartons and flexible packaging for several industries, e.g., beverage, soap and detergent, pet food, and chemical industries. Graphics Packaging operates plants in four states currently. In its brief history, the company has become an industry leader. Not surprisingly, they are a major supplier to Coors Brewing Company, but outside sales are expected to increase in the future. That is also the case with another major subsidiary, Coors BioTech, Inc.

Coors BioTech, Inc.

Coors formed BioTech, Inc., in 1983 to take advantage of its extensive experience in fermentation technology, biochemistry, and chemical engineering. The move was a throwback to the pre-prohibition era when the company applied its brewing knowledge to create products that would help it survive the period.

Among BioTech's major products are high-fructose corn syrup used in juice and soft drinks and riboflavin, aka Vitamin B2. These products are made at the company's plants in Johnstown, Colorado, and Winchester, Kentucky.

BioTech applies a unique, patented process to produce riboflavin for food and pharmaceutical industries. It also makes a feed-grade riboflavin, called BioRibo, which promotes optimum growth in livestock, swine, poultry, fish, and pets. Customers are flocking to the company for BioRibo, which offers unmatched purity compared to riboflavins sold by its competitors. Consequently, BioTech is growing.

Coors is expanding its Kentucky plant where the product is made. The expansion effort began in 1989. After its completion in mid-1990, the plant offered more than four times its former capacity for the commercial production of organically produced riboflavin. Obviously, Coors is well positioned for the future based on the success of its subsidiaries. It has not, however, neglected the product which led to its success: beer.

LET'S NOT PUT ALL OUR KEGS IN ONE BASKET

No doubt Adolph Coors, Sr., did not plan on producing riboflavin for goldfish or cleaning materials developed through biotechnology. He knew beer. So do his successors. They may have had the foresight to diversify, but they have not forgotten their roots. Coors is still heavily involved in the brewery business, but even there the company has by no means remained stagnant.

As recently as 1972, Coors sold beer in only 16 states. The line was limited to Coors Lager. Somehow, the company's beer developed a mystique outside of Colorado and people on the East Coast began to develop a taste for Coors' products. The company capitalized on this mystique and gradually expanded its territory—and its product line.

The first new product to hit the market was Coors Light. It was introduced on April 24, 1978. Consumers accepted it immediately. Its growth rate was nothing short of amazing.

In 1979, the first year of its availability, Coors Light was the 14th best selling beer on the market. Ten years later, it was the fourth—and growing fast! From 1984 to 1988 alone, sales of the product increased by more than 17 percent. According to recent beer industry reports, Coors Light is the fastest growing light beer on the market. It is *the* number one light beer in Canada, where it is brewed under license by Molson Breweries. Emboldened by the success of Coors Light, the company expanded its product line again.

The next new beer—actually an ale at the time—to be introduced by Coors marked a radical departure from its traditional lagers. That was Killian's Red®. (Killian's really is red. It derives its color from a special roasting process that carmelizes the malt.)

Coors entered an agreement with George Killian Lett, the last independent brewer in Ireland, and the Pelforth Brewery of Lille, France, to brew and distribute Killian's Red. Coors introduced the product in a test market in 1981. Marketwide expansion began the following year.

Although the ale was well received, Coors felt that it could improve the product. So, in 1988, and in violation of the business maxim "If it ain't broke, don't fix it," Coors converted it to a lager beer to improve its drinkability and to appeal to a larger customer base. In the process,and in keeping with the company's commitment to responsible use of its products, it reduced the alcohol content from approximately 4.3 percent by weight to approximately 3.9 percent—and retained the ale taste in the bargain! That kept Killian's drinkers happy—and continued the beer's viability as a popular seller. Killian's experienced double-digit growth in 1989, despite the fact it competed in a declining segment of the beer market. Maybe there are times when it is wise to defy business logic and tinker with an already popular product. That's risk taking—which is one of the keys to long-term survival.

1985 was a benchmark year for Coors. Not only did it introduce yet another new beer, Coors Extra Gold®, but the company expanded outside the borders of the United States for the first time. It entered an exclusive licensing agreement with Molson Breweries of Canada Ltd. to brew and distribute Coors and Coors Light in Canada. Still, Coors was not through.

In 1986, Coors expanded its market for Extra Gold entered an agreement with Asahi Brewers Ltd. of Japan to brew and distribute Coors and Coors Light in that country. It also introduced Winterfest. (The actual introduction of the beers in Japan began in April, 1987 when Coors became available. Coors Light was introduced in March, 1988.) Winterfest®was brewed originally for Colorado residents only. It is a special-seasonal beer brewed once a year. It was received so well that a year later, Coors expanded sales of the product nationally (except for Utah and Oklahoma). 1987 turned out to be a busy year for Coors.

Coors began selling beer in two important states that year, New York and New Jersey, and expanded its market yet again for Coors Gold. The impact of those moves became evident in 1988, when beer business sales and barrel shipments rose 9.1 percent and 5.6 percent respectively compared to the 1987 figures. Not surprisingly, the increase in production necessitated a new brewery. Coors had already planned for this eventuality. In 1987, the company completed a new brewery in Elkton, Virginia. That marked a major step forward in Coors marketing strategy, removed once and for all its image as a regional brewer, and launched a flurry of expansion.

Currently, the Elkton brewery is a packaging facility only. Beer is shipped there via specially insulated tank cars. Each car carries 660 barrels (85 tons) of beer. The journey takes seven days during which the temperature of the beer changes less than 1/2 of a degree. From there, the beer is packaged and distributed. Eventually, Coors plans to brew beer in Elkton. As originally constructed, the Virginia brewery was capable of processing 2.5 million barrels annually. (That's 3,788 railcars per year!) The design will allow it to expand its function from packaging to complete brewing, with an annual capacity of 10 million barrels. Even that will not be enough to produce all the beer that the company anticipates brewing in the next few years. In fact, Coors projected that beer shipments in 1990 were expected to utilize nearly all of the current packaging capacity at the beer business facilities. In light of that, the company announced in mid-1990 the addition of a new brewing and packaging capacity in

Golden, expanded packaging capabilities in Elkton, and increased beer shipping capacity—all at a cost of more than $100 million in that year alone. Still, that was not enough!

As another step toward future expansion, Coors purchased a Memphis, Tennessee, brewery and packaging facility. The purchase was based on Coors traditional criteria of quality.

Coors Brewing Company President Peter H. Coors noted that management selected the facility in part because of "its own source of top-quality water." Shades of Adolph Coors, Sr.!

The Memphis facility will be extremely important to Coors' carefully controlled growth plan. Management anticipates that it will add approximately 7 million barrels of packaging capacity and 5.5 million barrels of brewing capacity. Combined with the plants at Golden and Elkton, this will give Coors the overall capacity to produce approximately 26 million barrels per year. That may sound like a lot, but, at the rate the company is expanding, it may not be enough. After all, Coors is still adding new products and expanding into new territories. Let's get back to some of them.

1988 began auspiciously for Coors. In February, Extra Gold became available in the company's entire marketing territory. In its first full year of national distribution, Extra Gold sold more than one million barrels. The increase was due in part to Coors expansion into two more eastern states, Pennsylvania and Delaware. That same year, Coors introduced two super-premium beers, Herman Joseph's (named after the company's founder and his father, Johann Joseph) Original Draft and HJ Light, to most of its marketing territory. (The company took them off the market in 1989 due to disappointing sales and the consistent decline in their market segment.) At that time, they were the only bottled super premium draft beers available in the U.S. And, Coors took a major step forward in July when it began exporting its products to Bermuda. The non-stop expansion and introduction of new products positioned Coors well for an even busier 1989.

Perhaps the most salient event in 1989 was a further expansion of Coors export market. The company began expanding its products to the British and U. S. Virgin Islands and U. S. military bases around the world. Coors also introduced two new beers, Keystone and Keystone Light, in order to assure that it had a full line of products for its 613 independent and 6 company-owned distributors. This marked a major step forward for Coors.

Management recognized that beer drinkers' tastes were changing and that the time had come for Coors to break with tradition accordingly. It acted to take advantage of the change. Since Keystone falls into the "popular-priced" market segment, which accounts for 13 percent of the total U. S. beer sales, its introduction marked a radical departure for Coors.

The company had never produced a beer for the popular-priced market segment before. Prior to 1989, Coors had offered only premium and super-premium beers. Coors entered the popular-priced competition even though margins on these products are lower than on premium-priced products. Consequently, they offer a lower gross margin and provide a lower contribution to earnings in relation to sales than premium beers. To offset this, they do serve a larger consumer base, and no company can afford to ignore any market segment as high as 13 percent—which is growing considerably.

There are only two segments higher: Premium beers, e.g., Coors, Coors Extra Gold, Budweiser, Miller's High Life, at approximately 40 percent, and low-calorie premium, e.g., Coors Light, Bud Light, Miller Lite, at approximately 22 percent. Analysts estimate that the premium segment may actually be on the way out!

Premium beer sales slipped 20 percent between 1980 and 1989, while overall beer sales remained fairly flat. Light beers, however, became more popular. The nation's second, third, and fourth most popular beers are light beers. Coors Light is one of the fastest growing. In 1989 alone, it had a growth rate of more than 15 percent and was the fastest growing premium light beer in the United States. More significantly, it set a record by exceeding the 10-million barrel mark in annual sales for the first time. It is not surprising, then, that Coors shifted gears to take advantage of these changes.

Coors did not enter the popular-priced market segment quietly. The company provided an extremely high level of marketing support, which paid off immediately. The Keystone brands have already proven to be two of the most successful new beer products in recent years. This demonstrates Coors' boast that "regardless of which market segment they address, all of our brands reflect our uncompromising dedication to offering the highest-quality products possible." That has long been the secret to Coors' success—and the primary reason it is a survivor.

Coors also took another major step in 1989 by decentralizing most of its sales operations and initiating a strong regional marketing capability. This allowed the company to place a substantial number of sales and marketing personnel in offices closer to its customers. This, in turn, lets it work more closely with distributors and develop specific, regionalized strategies for marketing, pricing, promotions, and media placement. According to the company, this "emphasis on quick and responsive grass-roots marketing is designed to give Coors Brewing Company a competitive advantage in the 1990s."

THE SECOND COMING OF THE "Gay '90s"

Coors entered the 1990s filled with optimism for the decade and the century beyond. The company introduced Coors Rocky Mountain Sparkling Water, its first non-alcohol beverage since the Prohibition era. During the second quarter of the year, Coors set two new records: amounts of beer shipped and net sales of $475,510,000, a 12 percent increase over the same period in 1989. Beer sales in particular were good.

Coors Brewing Company had record net sales of $374,859,000 during the second quarter. There was a 14 percent increase in beer shipments to a record 4,831,000 barrels, compared to only 4,252,000 in the second quarter in 1989. Not surprisingly, the increase put a strain on the company's brewing capacity. Consequently, Coors plans significant capital expenditures to increase it. But the beer figures represent only a part of Coors' success during the period.

The company's second-largest business unit, Coors Technology Companies, experienced net sales of $100,346,000 during the second quarter, a 17 percent jump above similar 1989 figures. There was continued substantial improvement in earnings trends by Golden Aluminum, Graphic Packaging, and Coors BioTech. Not to be outdone, Coors Ceramics Company had record sales of $45,114,000 in the second quarter, up from $38,379,000 a year earlier. (Notice that the word "record" keeps appearing in these figures.) Why the spate of records?

HOPEFULLY, WE'LL PLAY THE SAME BROKEN RECORD THROUGHOUT THE DECADE—AND BEYOND

Bill Coors attributes the company's growth in part to its quality people and products. He also cites "aggressive growth, fiscal responsibility and courageous risk taking." We have seen evidence of all these claims. Of course, Coors' products speak for themselves. But how Coors treats its employees is worth emphasizing.

Coors employs about 10,600 people today, compared to only 9,600 two years ago. People are almost knocking down the doors to work for the company, since Coors receives approximately 35,000 job applications per year! That is not surprising.

According to 1988 figures, the average production employee earned more than $39,000 annually. Full-time, active employees receive a benefits package worth more than $11,000 per year. The workforce comprised 23 percent women, 16 percent minorities, and nearly 33 percent veterans. The company provides them with a modern health and exercise center which accommodates all work shifts, family members, and retirees. Participants receive exercise and diet programs, cholesterol testing, low-cost mammograms, stop-smoking classes, and stress reduction programs. The enduring philosophy at Coors is that a healthy workforce leads to a healthy company. That is certainly true in Coors' case.

Bill Coors reports that the company "could not have accomplished these changes without a flexible, experienced and talented team of senior managers and an outstanding group of dedicated employees worldwide. We will continue to rely on their superior talents in the years ahead." Based on Coors' history, the years ahead promise to be every bit as exciting and profitable as the century plus that has passed.

Bill Coors understands that people are essential to the company's future. He expects that Coors will be around for a long time to come. As he says:

> In looking to the future, our primary goal for the 1990s is to build on our leadership position in technology, quality products and customer satisfaction, as well as to enhance shareholder value. Our solid financial foundation and exceptional people give us confidence that we can make this goal a reality.

If history is any indicator, Coors will reach this goal. Its approach to the future, willingness to adapt to a changing technology, and successful past blend into a recipe that augurs a bright future. Coors' recipe is guaranteed to brew success.

One of the keys to business survival is to avoid bankruptcy—Chapter 11. Since the companies discussed in this book have done that successfully, we will avoid Chapter 11, also.

Chapter 12

ELGIN·BUTLER
"Butler Brick since 1873."

1873

Elgin — Butler

BUILDING A BUSINESS BRICK BY BRICK

M ost successful companies build themselves figu-
ratively brick by brick. The Elgin-Butler Brick
Company (EBBCO) of Austin, Texas, has done so literally.

THE FIRST BRICK

When Michael Butler established a brick company
on the north bank of the Colorado River in Austin,
Texas, in 1873, he no doubt expected a flood of busi-

ness. He got a flood, all right, but not of business. Two years after his plant opened, the river overflowed its banks and destroyed Butler's plant. That might have discouraged a lesser man, but it did not faze Michael Butler. He simply rebuilt his plant in a different location and carried on.

Butler was no stranger to bad luck or hard work. He left his home in Limerick, Ireland, in 1866 at the age of 24 to go to New York City. One source, the *Indian Wars and Pioneers of Texas*, suggests that he left Ireland at the age of 21 and arrived in New York in 1865. (These dates may be a little off, since the same publication states that he arrived in Austin in 1874—which was a year after he opened his company there!)

Michael Butler, Circa. 1874

Courtesy Austin History Center, Austin Public Library #PICB 13013

One thing is not subject to debate. Once he arrived in New York, Butler learned the rudiments of the brickmason's trade. Apparently, he was a fast learner. He spent only one year in the city, but that was long enough for him to actually lay bricks in several buildings there. But Butler did not envision a life spent laying bricks for other people. He had a desire to open his own business, and New York City did not offer the opportunities he wanted. The city became the first of many stops in an odyssey that eventually took him to Austin—and the realization of his dream.

Butler left New York City in 1867 to move to Tomah, Wisconsin, where he continued his trade and began contracting masonry work. Like so many men seeking their niches in society, he could not settle down until he reached the right place. Tomah was not that place for Butler.

In 1868, Butler moved on to St. Louis, Missouri, to work on a job as a masonry contractor. The following year he moved to Little Rock, Arkansas, with the same contractor he worked with in St. Louis to work on another job. He did not spend much time there, either.

By the time he finished in Little Rock, Butler felt that he had learned the trade enough to open a business of his own. He recognized that the time for doing so was right, especially in the southern states, which were still rebuilding after the destruction caused by the Civil War. So, he left Little Rock in 1869 after he completed his work there and headed for Dallas, Texas. There, in 1870, he opened his own business—and launched his successful career as an entrepreneur. His experience in Dallas allowed Butler to sharpen his innovative side. Consequently, by the time he opened his Austin business, he felt no qualms about experimenting to improve his brickmaking techniques.

MAKING BRICKS WITH A COFFEE MILL

Butler's Austin plant produced handmade bricks, a "soft mud" process in which clay is set in wooden molds. Even though he was new in the business,

Butler wasted no time introducing innovative brick-making techniques. He installed one of the first "Coffee Mill" brickmaking machines in Texas to improve production. Any machine would have been welcome to Butler's employees. For the first 18 years of the plant's existence, workers dug the clay by hand. In some cases, they used picks and shovels. More often,

Butler's Clay Bank, Austin Circa 1903

Courtesy Austin History Center, Austin Public Library
#CN 02149

they used scrapers (called fresnoes). They hauled the clay from the field in dump carts pulled by one mule. There was about a yard of clay per load. At the plant, the clay was mixed with water to make soft mud, then fed by augers into soft mud machines. The next step was to force the mixture into wooden molds. After a couple other operations, the molds were wheeled manually to 5 1/2-foot high racks and placed about 8" apart to dry. Finally, they were placed in the kilns. The procedure was tedious at best, so there is no doubt the employees welcomed additions like the "Coffee Mill."

The machine, patterned upon the same instrument used to grind coffee beans, forced softened mud into molds. The product was then covered with cloth and dried in the open. The cloth served two purposes: it could be dampened to prevent accelerated shrinkage and provided protection against inclement weather. The end product, which was called "sun-dried brick," caught on quickly in Dallas. Butler had to expand his capacity quickly.

The two rectangular, up-draft kilns he started with were not enough to keep up with the demand. He had to add two more. Each kiln had a capacity of 200,000 units. Despite his initial success, Butler still had an urge to move on. Michael Butler was not a man who ignored his urges, so on he went.

The peripatetic brickmaker had visited Austin and resolved to move there based on his initial love affair with the state capital's beauty and the business opportunities the city offered. Therefore, he invited his brother Patrick to emigrate to the United States and join him in the brickmaking business. Patrick did not pass up the chance. He arrived in Dallas in 1871. Two years later, Michael sold his company to Patrick and moved to Austin.

HE WHO LIVES BY THE SWORD, BUILDS BETTER BRICKS—AT LEAST IN AUSTIN

At first, people might question the wisdom of building a successful business and then leaving it behind to move to a new place, especially when that new place could already be the "Brick Capital of the World." There was no shortage of brickmakers in Austin. Many of the early houses there were showpieces that featured the beautiful pastel-colored bricks, called "Austin Sands" or "Austin Buff," which were made of the peculiar clay endemic to the area. Friends and relatives had to wonder, then, whether Michael Butler was a few bricks shy of a load himself. (The fact that the company is in business well over a century after it opened shows that he was not.)

Butler had shown in Dallas that he was a man who took advantage of timing and technology. In leaving the city in 1873, he was simply demonstrating his vision, and he would not allow anything, even his rocky start in Austin, to destroy it.

The flood that destroyed his first plant in Austin in 1875 did not deter Butler one bit. He viewed the disaster as a temporary setback, which was why he rebuilt so quickly. In doing so, he displayed his own tenacity and deep faith in Austin. Sales justified that faith.

Butler opened his new plant in South Austin in 1875. This time, he built his facility a bit away from the river banks. The plant featured five up-draft kilns, which contributed to a new age of brickmaking in the city.

Butler Brick Company, Austin, TX Circa 1903

Courtesy Austin History Center, Austin Public Library, # CN 02150

For example, Butler's brickmakers added a great range of colors to the buff-colored bricks so prevalent in the area simply by applying their knowledge about temperature's effects on brickmaking and the natural characteristics of the clay. Bricks stacked the farthest away from the kiln fireboxes would turn out red. Those closest turned out green to reflect the fact that they were partially melted from the heat. These bricks, called "mustard greens," were smaller than the regular bricks and clanked when tapped. Most bricks, however, ranged in color from a buff (yellow) to salmon.

Just as colors were important to Butler's business, so was quality. Consequently, just as he did in Dallas, he wasted no time in introducing the latest in brickmaking technology. Butler installed a "Sword Machine," which was actually an early version of a stiffmud machine, that continued the use of the soft-mud process, but greatly improved the quality of the units and increased production besides.

Although making bricks remained essentially a manual process, the introduction of machines improved the quality of the finished product. (It is one of the ironies of the brickmaking world that Butler installed the Sword and other modern machines in his plants over the years. The brickmaking industry has always been somewhat resistant to automation!) The Sword machine in particular made bricks more uniform in shape and size than soft-mud machines did.

Soft-mud bricks, which are manufactured by using molds, tended to have five good sides and one rough side, because the excess clay had to be cleared off by means of a hand-held wooden strike to make the brick conform to the top of the box mold. This created air pockets and drag marks as the strike was dragged across the semi-dry clay. Butler's Sword eliminated this problem and improved the quality of his products. The fact that he was willing to spend money to produce a better product earned him the respect of his customers and the people of Austin. That, more than anything, made his business a success, which, in turn, enhanced his personal life.

An announcement in the October 17, 1878, *Austin Statesman* indicated just how successful Butler was on both accounts. As it explained:

> Mr. M. Butler and Miss Mary J. Kelly were married last evening at 8 o'clock in the Catholic Church by the Rev. D. J. Spillard. The Church was hardly large enough to accommodate all who were present....We now have evidence that he has been as successful in love-making as in brick-making. Mr. Butler is deserving of the prize he has gained.

(It is worth mentioning here that the 19th-century definition of "love making" differed considerably from its modern counterpart. The reader is advised to substitute the words "courting," or "wooing," or "romancing.") For the next few years, his family and his plant grew rapidly.

Michael and Mary produced two sons and a daughter in the first few years of their marriage: John Francis, (August 21, 1879), Mary Margaret (August 25, 1881), and Thomas James (May 25, 1885). In the process, they established a peculiar trend in the Butler family. Most of the members who married had three children! As Michael's family grew, his company expanded apace.

Michael & Mary Butler and Children September 1898

Courtesy Austin History Center, Austin Public Library
PICB 01478

Butler became more active in commercial and social activities. Local papers noted in 1884 that he had a Captain McFall survey the lots on the street leading past Major Ryan's preparatory to the erection of eight "elegant brick residences." The lots later became known as the "Butler Flats." In July of that year, he appeared as chairman of the Committee on Bricks, which were to be displayed by the Travis County Exposition Society. He also performed a unique bit of public relations by donating 5,000 bricks as a prize for the winner of a boat race between Captain Lucy and Charles Cortissoz. (For the record, Cortissoz won by default.)

In November 1885, citizens laid the cornerstone of a New Fireman's Hall. The cornerstone contained a "score of items," including Butler's business card and a receipted bill against the city for pressed brick in the building—which he donated as a volunteer fireman! (He was a member of the Colorado Fire Company No. 2.) Butler was not only a purveyor of bricks, but he was also a cornerstone of Austin's society—and a prime mover in the community.

1886 was a banner year for Butler's brickmaking company. He installed a new (and ponderous) machine that turned out thousands of bricks daily. Once again his timing was good, as builders needed millions of bricks in order to complete the magnificent new state capitol being constructed in Austin.

A *Statesman* reporter wrote in the January 21, 1886, edition regarding progress on the Capitol, "Yesterday the masons were laying the brick lining for the vaults in the eastern wing of the building. The bricks are from Mr. Mike Butler's kilns, that gentleman having a contract to supply five millions of first class brick." Certainly business was booming for Butler, as tax records of 1887 showed.

Butler was listed as one of Travis County's principal taxpayers in the $20,000 to $100,000 range in 1887. This indicated that the company was growing. Business was so good that Butler branched out into real estate and railroading. Here was another oddity in Butler's life. Railroads brought the era of Victorian architecture to Austin, along with the threat of outside competition for local brickmakers. Actually, they had nothing to fear. Just to build a house of brick in Central Texas in 19th-century Central Texas using *local* brick was considered somewhat of a luxury. Imported bricks were so expensive ($45 - $50 per thousand, compared to $8.50 - $10 per thousand for local bricks) that they did not threaten the local brickmaking market. After all, only the *very* rich could afford imported bricks. In truth, Central Texas business operators saw the railroads as a way of expanding their local markets and bringing more prosperity to their towns. Their view proved correct.

Butler became a substantial land owner, holding farm lands all around Austin, as well as property in the city. In December 1887, he, along with several other people, filed a charter of a Railroad Corporation with the Secretary of State. The corporation, formed to build, operate, and maintain a railroad between Austin and McGregor in adjacent McLennan County, had a $1 million capitalization. That was merely one of Butler's many business ventures at the time.

CAN ANYONE MAKE ENOUGH BRICKS TO KEEP UP WITH BUTLER'S PROJECTS?

Not only did Butler furnish millions of bricks for the State Capitol,but he was busy in 1888 producing others for the International & Great Northern Railroad's new Union Passenger Depot in Austin. That same year, he proposed construction of a building for the Board of Trade which he offered to finance and construct. (The building opened in 1890.)

Another ongoing project in which Butler involved himself was the construction of a new St. Mary's Church, reputed to be one of the finest in the South. The church included the installation of two bells in the main tower. Butler donated the larger of the two, a 2,008-pound bell, cast by the McShane Foundry of Baltimore, Maryland. The bell carried the initials of Butler's three children. Obviously, Butler realized the value of good community relations, but his involvement went beyond donating a bell to a church.

Butler advertised his products in the 1891 Labor Day parade in Austin via a float bearing his company's banner on which riders made bricks as they rode. That same year he became a member of the local Elks lodge and an officer besides. He capped off the year by visiting England, Ireland, and Wales for three months. The vacation was a well-earned respite from his growing business—which continued to expand considerably. It was growing so fast, in fact, that Michael brought his nephew, John J. Butler, from Ireland in 1892 to learn the trade and act as foreman at the South Austin plant. Apparently, John learned the business well. He ran the plant until it burned in 1912. After that he oversaw the old Zilker plant north of the river until he died (more on that plant anon).

BRICKMAKING, RAILROADING—WHAT'S NEXT?

In 1893, community leaders organized the American National Bank in Austin, which listed Butler as a member of the Board of Directors. Not surprisingly, the bank quickly became one of the strongest financial institutions in the state. What timing! That was the same year Butler expanded his company into Houston, although the Austin plant remained the backbone of the company's operations.

Martin Kuno Sachs, a German immigrant who had come to America in 1881, remembered that "I came to Houston on January 16, 1893, and started the Butler Brick Works." He was a manager and part owner of the facility from then until August 16, 1915, when "a storm demolished [it] and we stopped operation for it did not justify us to rebuild on account of the clay be-

Butler Brick Works, Houston, TX

Courtesy Austin History Center, Austin Public Library
PICA 24443

ing too far distant from the plant." The plant may have suffered an ignominious end, but it had a promising beginning.

Butler competed on an equal footing with the established Houston brickmakers from the onset. No sooner had Butler opened his Houston establishment than he had a contract to pave with bricks the first street to be surfaced in Houston. He also built two buildings of renown in the city.

The first was the Bine Building (1893-94) on Main Street. This was not only the first "skyscraper" in Houston, but it was the first building with elevators. In 1900, he constructed the first apartment building in the city. This structure, known as the "Butler Flats," was located on the corner of Rusk and Fannin Streets.

According to the *Indian Wars and Pioneers of Texas*, Butler had quite an impact on both Austin and Houston. The book reported that both plants "are doing a large business, employ a large force of men, and annually distribute large sums of money broadcast in these communities." Moreover, the book said:

> His brick (sic) have so far taken the place of stone in building, that the public streets are now bordered with handsome brick blocks and beautiful architectural residences, a happy result that could have never been otherwise obtained.

(The book's write-up about Butler makes one wonder whether he ever visited Kansas and helped build a yellow brick road.)

Butler continued to produce bricks by the carload in Austin. He got a lucrative contract for the new Oil Mill in Austin which the *Statesman* said involved one million bricks. The number sounded impressive, but Butler's plant was capable of producing far more than that.

The *Industrial Advantages of Austin, Texas, or Austin Up To Date*, published in 1894, mistakenly reported that Butler's plant, which it described as "one of the most important brick manufacturing concerns in the South," had been in continuous operation for a "period of about twenty-eight years." The book may have had that part wrong, but it made no mistake concerning the actual work that went on at the plant.

The brief entry in the book described Butler's Austin complex as:

brick yards, factory, and property [that] cover an area of about eighty-six acres, and the works are especially well located in reference to shipping conveniences....The mechanical equipment and apparatus are of the best....There are four kilns in operation, and the motive power is obtained from a fifty horse power engine and a sixty horse power boiler.

The write-up also credited Butler on a personal note. "The enterprise has always been conducted upon liberal and fair principles, and we are pleased to accord it here that proper share of attention to which it is in every way entitled." The *Industrial Advantages* was not the only publication which spoke in glowing terms of Butler's operation.

A March 22, 1894, article in the *Statesman* provided some important information about "A Leading Industry...M. Butler Brick Factory."

The Mike Butler Brickyard has gained a Statewide reputation and is known for the excellency of the A-1 bricks manufactured. One hundred acres are owned by Mr. Butler, the plant alone covering two acres.

In 1894. the plant is turning out 30,000 bricks per day, although its capacity is three times that amount. The yards are supplied with their own water service.

Mike Butler has recently invented a machine for the purpose of handling bricks, which is a great labor-saving device and will cause a revolution in the handling of bricks. He has recently built one on his premises.

The invention demonstrated just how well-rounded Michael Butler was. He received a patent for his machine in 1895. That should not have come as a surprise. Butler had a knack for tinkering that could only prove beneficial to the company. He passed this knack on to his oldest son.

EDUCATION IS THE WAY TO SUCCESS

Butler had acquired most of his brickmaking knowledge through experimentation and practical application. He wanted his children to learn brickmaking through a formal education process. Consequently, he urged John Francis to attend Ohio State University, which featured an excellent program in Ceramics Engineering.

Michael recognized that if John Francis were to work in brickmaking, he would have to acquire as much knowledge as possible in ceramics. The science was crude at the time, but it would have to improve and he wanted his son to be in the forefront of whatever advancements occurred. John Francis had other ideas, though.

Young John's interests ran more toward architecture than brickmaking. Michael recognized that his children had dreams and ambitions that did not necessarily coincide with his own. He wanted to see the company stay in business after he passed on, but he also wanted to respect his son's wishes. Therefore, he and John Francis agreed that the young man would attend Ohio State for one year. After that, if he still preferred architecture, his father would send him to any school of his choice to pursue that profession. John Francis stayed with ceramics—and his choice may have made Michael wish he had not.

WHAT YOU ARE DOING IS GOOD, DAD, BUT WE HAVE TO MAKE SOME CHANGES

John Francis received a Certificate in Ceramics from Ohio State in 1899 (along with a red "O" for his prowess in baseball and football). As he explained in his biography, "I finished the course, but I didn't get a diploma, 'cause the ceramic course was young and it didn't include enough credits for an engineer's degree. But the year after I left there, they started to give the degree." Degree or not, he learned enough to return to Austin and inform Michael that the bricks he had been producing for 16 years were good—but they could be better. He suggested that his father search for a better grade of clay to improve his bricks. Michael accepted the suggestion at once. Michael Butler recognized that standing pat was a sure way of losing out to competitors. He had not earned his reputation as a leader in the brickmaking industry by refusing to make changes or take chances. He gave John Francis permission to seek the better clay. Like his father, John Francis was a man of action. He undertook the search at once.

Young John visited The University of Texas, A & M College (as it was called then), and the School of Mines in El Paso to gather information about clay deposits in Texas. He learned only that knowledge of Texas' geology was extremely limited, and that no information related to clay deposits in the state was available. That did not dissuade the Butlers. They simply built a laboratory in Austin for testing clays, along with a test kiln for determining their shrinkage, color and refractory characteristics. John Francis began scouting for desirable clay minerals. He found some suitable clay, but it was located in West Texas' Brewster County, which was hardly an ideal place as far as the Butlers were concerned.

The clay was in very rough country, several miles away from the nearest railroad. That made transportation problems difficult, if not impossible. However, the Butlers' lexicon did not include the word "impossible." As is often the case with successful businesses, luck entered the picture.

THE LUCK OF THE IRISH IS NOT ALL CONCENTRATED IN SOUTH BEND

The words Notre Dame and luck have long been synonymous. But, there are plenty of other Irish people who share the school's traditional luck. Michael and John Francis had plenty of it.

At the time John Francis searched for a better clay, the Austin plant burned wood for watersmoking the brick and lignite coal for the high temperature flashing. Back in the company's early years, it had cut some of its own wood on the plant site. The company procured "cedar" timber from up the Colorado River. (The cedar was actually juniper. It was called cedar only because of its red heart. The poor hill country folks who cut this wood for pay were known as "cedar choppers.") The wood was floated down river to a log boom near the plant.

As 1890 approached, the wood supply grew short. A Mr. Wilke in Elgin (about 30 miles east of Austin), from whom Butler had purchased wood many times, offered to sell him 1,000 cords. Butler learned that the wood came from a different location than anything Wilke sold him previously, so he dispatched John Francis to inspect the offering. When young Butler arrived, he learned of an additional 1,500 cords which had not been hauled to the railroad tracks for loading. Wilke offered him three options: purchase all 2,500 cords, the 1,000 cords with the remaining stumpage, or all 2,500 cords with the land from which they had been cut. The Butlers opted to pursue a combination: purchase the 2,500 cords, with the condition that they be given 90 days in which to inspect the stumpage.

John Francis Butler did the inspecting. As he did, he noticed several deposits of promising-looking clay in three different places on the banks of Sandy Creek. He analyzed samples from each of the three spots. All proved to be of consistent quality—and the best which his search to date had uncovered! Consequently, the Butlers received a 31-day extension to get ample time to determine the depth of the deposit and the quality available.

John Francis determined that the clay would suffice from both a quality and quantity standpoint. He sent samples to Ohio State for analysis, which confirmed John Francis' findings. As a result, the Butlers purchased the wood, the stumpage, and the land. More important, and no doubt unbeknownst to them at the time, they secured the company's future. Michael Butler built a new plant on the land. He moved the company's headquarters there in 1903. At about the same time, the company established distributorships in many cities in Texas, Louisiana, Arkansas, Oklahoma, and New Mexico. In keeping with the growth, the company used differnt names.

The Austin and Houston plants continued to operate under the name Butler Brick Works. (They changed once again on February 16, 1931, to the Butler Brick Company.) On October 9, 1903, a separate entity, the Elgin Butler Brick and Tile Company, was incorporated. This transpired in the company's 30th year of business, which Butler obviously did not intend to be his last. The term of incorporation was for 50 years!

INCORPORATED OR UNINCORPORATED: BUSINESS IS PROFITABLE EITHER WAY

On February 12, 1907, the Butlers announced the incorporation of another entity, the Elgin Pottery Company, to be located on the brickyard in Butler, six miles east of Elgin. The company would manufacture terra cotta, enameled brick, clay furnaces, flue thimbles, flower pots, fire clay slabs, and floor tile. This company never achieved the success the family hoped for.

The Butlers' reputation grew as the company aged. As the January 10, 1909, *Statesman* said, "The Company makes a superior quality of face brick. The Butler Brick has long demonstrated that it is useless to send off to other States to get brick, when just as good can be had at home." The paper ended the article on an ominous note, though: "Colonel Butler and his Son are in Battle Creek, Michigan, where Colonel Butler is a patient." The article did not say for what he was being treated, but it turned out to be serious.

Michael Butler died on February 25, 1909, at the age of 67. The paper reported that his death was not "entirely unexpected, as he had been in ill health for some time." The entire community mourned his death. Fortunately, he left the company in good hands.

LIKE FATHER, LIKE THE SONS, TOO

Michael Butler designated in his will that his estate remain whole and intact within the Chatelaincy of his wife, Mary Jane. (A chatelaine is the mistress of a castle or chateau.) She did not actively run the company, though. John Francis assumed the dual roles as the company's President and General Manager. His brother, Thomas James, resigned his job as a teller at the American National Bank and became Secretary-Treasurer. The two men wasted no time in making important business decisions.

One of their first moves was to return the company's headquarters from Elgin to Austin. In 1909, they relocated the South Austin plant office from the brickyard site to Room 8, First National Bank Building, in Austin. John Francis made a significant move of his own. He married Mary Camille Wood in Okla-

311

homa City in 1910. Like his parents' marriage, their union produced three children, Michael Wood (1911), Helen Elizabeth (1913), and Frances Camille (1917). The family's expansion kept pace with the company's.

By 1910, the Butlers' holdings included three plants (South Austin, Houston, and Butler), the sales offices in Dallas, a network of distributorships licensed by John Francis and Thomas James, and banking and real estate holdings. Michael's two sons traveled the length and breadth of Texas and began acquiring reputations as shrewd businessmen themselves. They were well known in social, fraternal, and business circles. The brothers erased any doubts anyone might have had about their ability to continue their father's success.

John Francis had acquired a reputation as the highest authority in Texas on the quality of all varieties of clays. That did not deter him from overseeing with his brother the steady expansion and improving the facilities to keep up with the ever-growing building program extant in Texas. The company broadened its sales and distribution network to handle the growing workload. Then, in 1912, disaster struck.

THE WHOLE PLANT BECOMES AN OVEN

Fire all but destroyed the Butlers' South Austin plant in 1912. Only two kilns survived the blaze, which caused $100,000 worth of damage. The disaster posed a serious problem for the Butlers.

The timing of the fire could not have been worse. The bricks the company produced from the high-quality clay available in the area were in demand throughout Texas. There existed at the time of the fire a building boom that demanded Butler products. Once again, luck was on the Butlers' side.

Their only serious competitor, Colonel Andrew J. Zilker, an ice merchant, operated a brickyard across the river from the Butler plant which he had built in 1902. Proving that imitation is indeed the sincerest form of flattery, Zilker had modeled his plant on Butler's facility, and used the same type of clay extensively. Brickmaking did not interest Zilker as much as he thought it would. He announced his intentions to dispose of his brickmaking business, which piqued John Francis' interest. After a series of negotiations, the Butlers leased the plant for 100 years, with Mr. Zilker to pay all taxes, then rebuilt it in its entirety to match their demanding criteria. That solved the problem of how the Butlers would meet the demands for their products in Texas. The timing of the deal was also extraordinary in light of events in Houston.

The Houston plant manufactured red-colored face and common brick to supplement the buff-colored products made in the Austin-Elgin area. In 1912, the plant became enmeshed in the Houston city limits, which meant an automatic increase in taxes. The Butlers decided this would be too much of a financial burden for them, so they sold the plant to the Dickson Car Wheel Company and sold the products remaining. They also decided to abandon the Elgin Pottery Company because it was not generating the profits they desired. There were also a few family changes around the early 1900s.

Thomas James married Josephine Robinson in 1913. They had five children: Mary Josephine (1913), Thomas James, Jr. (1914), Robinson Paul(1915), an unnamed child who did not survive (1916), and Martin (1917). Unfortunately, Josephine died in 1918 as a result of the virulent influenza epidemic which swept the country. Her death devastated Thomas James, but in the true tradition of the Butler family, he carried on despite the loss.

Elgin-Butler Clayfield, Circa 1920

Courtesy Austin History Center, Austin Public Library #PICA 24461

World War I had no significant impact on the Butlers' business. Whereas some industries suffered a loss of business during the conflict, the Butlers did not. They were subject to the restriction of materials imposed by the government and the dearth of workers who joined the armed forces, but they retained enough of both to work on military construction projects at Penn Field and Camp Mabry in Austin. The end of the war came as a relief nonetheless.

Following the war, there occurred a surge of public construction and an increase in private work. The Elgin-Butler Brick Company grew very busy in the first couple of years after the conflict ended. The company provided materials to a great number of customers in its trade territory. The boom continued relatively undisturbed until 1928, when the nationwide economic downturn restricted the number of construction projects in progress. There was one major administrative event in the period: Attorney Walter H. Walne, Mary Margaret's husband, joined the company as Vice-President.

THE BUTLER DID NOT DO IT

The depression years were so bad that it could hardly be said "The Butler did it," for neither the Butlers nor any other brickmakers did much of anything during the era. Business dropped off significantly between 1929 and 1939. (The nadir occurred in 1933-34.) The company conducted the bulk of its business in that period by furnishing products through the federal Public Works Administration's projects. The Butlers' estate was so well founded, however, that the company survived the "Great Depression" in reasonably good shape.

One event that took place on January 5, 1932, had a beneficial impact on the company's workforce. That was the introduction of the company's first Sick & Health Benefit plan.

The plan was by no means as complex—or expensive—as modern benefit programs. It did offer company employees some protection, though, and that was critical, especially in those trying times.

The plan was elegantly simple. According to its provisions:
- The signers below, with families, hereby agree to pay the sum of $1 per month. Single men pay $0.75 per month.
- This money will be paid to the treasurer of said benefit on the 5th day of the month.

315

- There will be a board consisting of 3 men. This board will be selected by Employees.
- This board will pass on all claims, and their decisions will be final.
- This benefit covers all Doctor bills, and Medicine, that this board recommends to be paid.
- All members must be paid up and in good standing to receive benefits.
- This will include all members of immediate family, consisting of Man, Wife, and Children.
- If dues per month prove to be too much or too little they will be increased or decreased by members of the board to cover expenses.
- You also agree that this board has power to make bylaws to govern said benefit.
- Any one wishing services of a Doctor will notify any one member of the board day or night.
- This board has secured the services of Dr. W. E. Campbell, who will come out. Day trips for $3.50 and night trips for $5.00. Drugs used by members of said benefit will be gotten from E. Roy Jones Drug Store, as we can get a discount from him.

That was the entire plan in its simplistic elegance. It may not compare in length or complexity to today's employee health packages, but it sufficed for the company's employees' needs. A total of 46 employees signed the original agreement!

The company amended the by-laws a bit after the plan went into effect. For example, the terms of coverage changed to:

- This benefit covers all Doctors bills, but no medicine, that this board recommends to be paid. This benefit will not pay for baby cases, but will lend members the money to pay the doctor and said money will be paid back by the member without interest. This benefit will not pay venereal cases. This takes the same ruling as the baby cases.
- The signers agree for the amount stated above to be held out each month of their pay.
- It is also understood that Dr. Campbell will be the doctor used and that if anyone calls another doctor, the charges will be paid by the one calling the doctor unless it is passed on by the board.
- Hospital and Surgery cases will be paid by the board and charged to the member and he will pay this money back into the treasury without interest.

Apparently, these revisions were acceptable to the company's workforce.

The plan demonstrated Elgin-Butler's concern for its employees, especially during the critical 1930s when jobs and money were at a premium. This concern for employees was a trademark of Elgin-Butler, as it was (and still is) of all the companies discussed in this book. The plan's introduction was by no means the only event of significant importance that occurred at Elgin-Butler during the 1930s.

First, in 1932, John Francis' son, Michael Wood Butler, became the third generation of Butlers to join the company. He had studied Business Administration at the University of Texas, which was a drastic departure from family practices. The company had survived 59 years without a business major at the helm. Michael's knowledge could only help strengthen the company's management. Then, in 1935, death struck the family again.

The company founder's wife, Mary Jane, died that year. Her death led to a rearrangement of the management structure. The Butlers formed a Board of Di-

Manufacturing, Elgin-Butler Circa 1930

Courtesy Austin History Center, AustinPublic Library
PICA 24460

rectors in which each adult in the family held membership. The chain of command included John Francis Butler as Chairman of the Board, and Thomas James Butler as the President. The hierarchy remained in place for several years.

In 1938, yet another third-generation family member joined the ranks. Thomas James Butler, Jr., equipped with a Bachelor of Ceramic Engineering degree from Ohio State University (shades of John Francis), came aboard. He and his cousin Michael Wood Butler had a positive impact on the company. In fact, they had collaborated prior to 1938 on an innovation that had a profound effect on the Elgin-Butler business!

COUSINS OF WHOM GRANDFATHER WOULD BE PROUD

The two young men realized that hollow clay-tile building units could be beneficial to the company's business. They certainly had not invented the process, but they saw no reason why the company could not manufacture them. They recognized that these hollow units could easily displace solid-wall units so prevalent in wall-bearing construction, particularly as backing in the walling of steel and reinforced-concrete framed structures. The pair also saw a future for the units as a finished interior material. So they began their quest to find the perfect hollow units.

Immediately after Thomas James, Jr., graduated, his father, then manager of the Elgin-Butler plant, set him to work trying to develop a high grade, refractory fire brick. (A number one class fire brick can withstand temperatures of 3,400 degrees Fahrenheit.) Developing such a brick would have improved Elgin-Butler's fire brick market considerably.

At the time, the clay at the EBBCO plant was being put to a variety of uses, including face brick, pressed brick, and medium duty fire brick.(EBBCO fire bricks are used in smokestacks, chimneys, and fireplaces. It fuses at about 2,800 degrees.) Thomas Sr. wanted his son to develop a fire brick that could withstand 3,100 degrees and be used in industrial settings.

Thomas Jr. roamed Texas with a homemade test drill hitched to the rear of his truck looking for clay samples that would raise the heat capacity of the Elgin clay. The search proved futile at first. The young man decided he would have to go out of the state to find an additive that would work. He found it in Missouri.

Thomas' research showed that a 40 percent mix of Missouri "flint clay" and EBBCO clay would bring the fire brick up to the 3,100 degree heat range. Unfortunately, transportation costs would have made the effort unprofitable, so young Thomas abandoned the search and turned his attention to other endeavors.

Toward the end of the search for the "perfect" clay, Thomas Jr. and plant co-workers embarked on perhaps the most successful product development project in the company's history up to that point. In another effort to create new market niches, he, his cousin Michael Wood Butler, who was working the sales end of the effort, and several other people worked to create an impervious glaze that could be used on face brick and structural hollow tile. They were not the first in the industry to develop this product. EBBCO, through its sales force, represented several East Coast and Midwest firms that manufactured different kinds of glazed ware. Nevertheless, the Butlers were leaders in the relatively new field of glazes, which was, in fact, the company's primary market.

The first efforts involved the use of salt, which, when thrown into the kiln fireboxes, would vaporize, leaving a clear glaze on the exposed surfaces of the ware. Later, they used a sand and lime mixture. However, they decided that the quality of the glaze was somewhat poorer than what they were aiming for.

The fact that the ceramic body and the glazes were made of different materials led to problems when the material was exposed to repeated freeze/thaw cycles. The heat coefficients of the two materials were so different they would heat up and cool down at different rates. The differences caused cracks to appear in the glaze. In some cases, the glaze would pop off at the edges. Also, the use of both salt and the sand/lime combination limited them to only a clear coat on the material, which also limited the range of colors.

The Butlers and their co-workers found it necessary to develop a ceramic glaze in which the coefficients of the glaze and the body would be much closer than in the other formulas used. Perfecting such a process necessitated a great deal of laboratory and production testing. The effort required a much more complicated process than the simple ingredients, basically water, clay, and color additives, suggest. Even today the process is by no means taken for granted. It *still* requires a great attention to detail.

Needless to say, the research proved successful. EBBCO developed a material that was impervious to water, easy to clean, and resistant to repeated freeze/thaw cycles. None of the company's competitors in the region even came close to EBBCO's glaze expertise or the range of colors that it developed to take advantage of the new process. The company considered the process a major step forward. Although Thomas Jr. is generally credited with the work, he pointed out that he could not have done it alone and insisted that his co-workers receive part of the credit. Regardless of who was responsible, the new process was a boon for the company, and is still a strong selling point.

After finalizing their process, the young Butlers secured a lucrative contract for glazed products. EBBCO quickly manufactured and delivered the first order received at the Elgin plant. The event may have seemed insignificant at the time, but its importance became more pronounced in later years.

Glazed structural hollow tile and face brick have grown in importance over the years vis a vis EBBCO's bottom line. Today, they provide a substantial portion of the company's income. In fact, the products are credited with pulling the company through the economic slump that affected Texas in the late 1980s. Now, EBBCO sells its glazed products throughout the United States and overseas. As company historian Jeffrey A. Twining says, "In a way, we have overcome transportation costs and competition through specialization." The people who developed the glaze six decades ago certainly would not argue the point.

WAR, WAR—THERE'S ALWAYS A WAR

Unfortunately, before the Elgin-Butler Company could capitalize on its hollow units, another war impacted business. World War II presented a serious challenge to Elgin-Butler's capabilities. Like it did with most other challenges in their history, though, the company responded with alacrity.

Kentric Stagner, who joined the company in 1935 as manager of the company store, remembers clearly the problems Elgin-Butler encountered during the war. (Stagner is *still* employed by the company in a part-time capacity.) He recalls that the company shipped as many as 25-30 railroad cars of bricks per week at the height of the war. Each car carried a minimum of 15,000 bricks. The total of between 375,000 to 450,000 bricks per week required a great deal of labor intensity, some of which German prisoners of war supplied.

According to Stagner, labor was so scarce during the war the prisoners housed at nearby Camp Swift were pressed into service at the company's plant. The prisoners were some of Rommel's troops who had been run out of Africa. They contributed mightily to Elgin-Butler's operations and enhanced the company's ability to meet the demands prompted by the war. As a result, Elgin-Butler provided prodigious amounts of material to the war effort. It even expanded outside of Texas' borders!

The company manufactured products for armed forces installations, an expanded list of cities in Texas, and four locations in Oklahoma. One of the biggest projects in which the company participated was construction of the United States Naval Hospital at Pierce Junction, near Houston. There, builders used 600 carloads of face brick, glazed tile, facing tile, and hollow building tile. The job was billed as the largest individual masonry job in the Southwest. It should have come as no surprise to people familiar with Elgin-Butler's history that the company would be involved in the project.

The family and the company incurred two major losses during the war. From a human standpoint, there was a moment of sadness. Lieutenant Robinson Paul Butler, Thomas James' younger son, and a U. S. Navy pilot, died towards the end of the war. Young Robinson took off from a carrier on May 10, 1944, and was never heard from again. He was listed as "Missing in Action." The loss of a family member is never easy to take. This one hit the close-knit Butler family hard.

In true family fashion, they picked up the pieces of their loss and continued to expand their business, although one of their old buildings fell into disuse. The

Austin plant which the Butlers had leased from Colonel Zilker fell victim to the Office of Price Administration's price freeze. The Butlers decided they could no longer operate the plant at a profit, so they placed it on a standby basis. Effectively, this meant the aged plant would never operate again. Sure enough, in 1958, the Butlers gave it to the S. B. Franks Company for demo-

Loading a Boxcar - Mid 1940s

Courtesy Austin History Center, Austin Public Library
PICA 24404

lition. That historic moment marked the end of Butler's production in Austin. From that point on, all the company's production took place in Butler.

Shortly after the war, the youngest of Thomas James' sons, Martin Butler, joined the company. Martin Butler added yet another area of expertise to the company. He graduated in 1940 from Texas Agricultural and Mechanical College with a Bachelor of Arts in Petroleum Engineering. He spent most of the war helping build Liberty ships. Martin did join the navy in 1945, but was discharged the next year. After that, he joined the company's staff. So did several other family members, albeit indirectly, between 1936 and 1945.

There was a spate of family weddings during the 1930s and 40s. Michael Wood Butler married Mary Wilson Russell in San Antonio on March 13, 1936. They had three children: John Russell Butler (1936), Meta Camille (1940), and Michael Limerick (1945). Six years later, on August 21, 1942, Thomas James Butler, Jr., and June Hughes were wed. They, too, had three children: Diana Barbara (1945), Helen (1948), and Thomas Kelly (1952). Finally, on August 2, 1945, Martin Butler married Margaret Walling and they had...you guessed it, three children: Robert Martin (1951), Elizabeth Ann (1953), and Catharine Cecelia (1956). The Butlers not only made good bricks, but they made sure there would be plenty of heirs to carry on the family business!

PROFITS ARE UP IN THE "HEIR" AT ELGIN-BUTLER

Indeed, there has never been a shortage of Butlers to run the company business. As of November 19, 1990, there were still seven Butlers working for the firm, which is into its fifth generation! They were:

Michael Wood Butler
Vice President & Chairman of the Board
Thomas James Butler, Jr.,President
John Russell (Russ) Butler
Vice President & Chief Executive Officer
Michael Limerick Butler ,Treasurer
Robert (Bob) Butler ,Plant I Supervisor
Helen (Butler) Young,Office Manager
Michael Richards (Dick) Butler
Salesman, Dallas Office

There are also several shareholders who manage the company's general affairs on an ad hoc basis. The family ties go beyond the Butlers, though.

The *Statesman*, which has been covering the company since its inception, reported in its September 10, 1990, edition that about a dozen Elgin-Butler employees grew up at the Elgin plant, "following parents and grandparents who also worked for the company." One, the aforementioned W. K. Stagner, has been there over 55 years. Another worker, Gary Owen, who grew up in company housing, is a fourth-generation employee.

Owen manages one of the company's two plants (aptly named Plant II), which makes 1.5 million bricks a week. Plant II specializes in commercial/residential brick and lists around 125 different product lines with an infinite number of blends. By contrast, Plant I manufactures mostly glazed brick and structural hollow tile for hospitals and similar buildings. Its output is around 800,000 bricks (or their equivalent) per week. The combined 2.3 million bricks per week is a lot of production, but it is only a fraction of what the company hopes to produce in the years to come.

Owen, who has a bachelor's degree in Biology and Agricultural Sciences from Texas A & M University, typifies the family atmosphere that surrounds Elgin-Butler's workforce. He became a plant manager in 1973, but he did not just fall into the position. Owen began working for the company at the age of 15 when he worked there during the summer. (One of the company's traditions is to hire relatives of employees during the summer.) Since Gary's father, grandfather, and great-grandfather had also worked for the company, it could almost be expected that he, too, would join Elgin-Butler Brick someday. After all, the company's three major traditions are their commitments to quality bricks, extended family, and history. These commitments have kept the company in business since 1873—and will keep it going well into the next century and beyond.

WE DON'T WANT TO WORK FOR NOTHING, BUT WE WILL IF WE HAVE TO

The company's commitment to people is no secret. Fortunately, commitment is not a one-way street. The people whose lives are entwined with Elgin-Butler's existence (and that is just about everyone who lives in or near the company's home base) have demonstrated their faith in the company, too.

Current CEO Russ Butler compares the residential brick market to a light bulb: it's off and on. As such, the company experiences periodic downturns. One of the most severe occurred in 1988, when it was forced to make drastic cuts in the workforce. The company cut production and operations companywide and asked employees to take an across-the-board pay cut. Management also reduced overtime earnings. The employees responded positively.

Butler told a reporter from the *Elgin Courier* that "We've tried to do what has to be done in the fairest manner." Apparently, employees agreed if Butler's comments are any indicator. "What is particularly heartening to me," he said, "is the number of people who have worked for years and years and are volunteering to work for nothing." Perhaps that should not have come as a surprise to Russ Butler, based on the close working relationship between management and workforce that has existed since 1873. The relationship has been one of the highlights in the company's history—and that history is extremely important to the Butlers.

LET'S NOT WORRY ABOUT THE 21ST CENTURY UNTIL WE STUDY WHAT WE DID IN THE 19TH AND 20TH CENTURIES

The Butlers have a healthy respect for the importance of history in a company's continued success. Russ Butler feared that much of the company's history (or company memory, as family members prefer to call it)was being lost during its periodic purges of files and equipment. He asked himself one simple question in that regard: "Are we throwing away something that may be of value to future generations?" The answer was YES. He took immediate action to ensure that Elgin-Butler's history *would* be preserved. That's when he hired Twining, the company historian. As he explained in the June 14, 1990, *Statesman*:

> We have third-generation people who are still alive and alert and working for the company. They have a tremendous amount of knowledge, and when it's gone, it can't be recaptured. So we've hired a historian to capture this information. Then whoever wishes to use it can.

This attitude concerning history is refreshing. It demonstrates Elgin-Butler's concern with where the company has been, and, more important, where it is going. Elgin-Butler does not plan to be out of business anytime soon—and its employment and sales figures are proof of that.

The company employs approximately 400 people today. Most of them work at Elgin-Butler's 2,000-acre site in the town of Butler, which is home to the bulk of the company's operations. There are a few who work in sales offices in Austin, San Antonio, and Dallas. Not everyone can be in Elgin, since somebody has to keep track of customers' preferences in brick, which has been a company trademark since 1873. Even today, homeowners in different locales have special tastes in colors.

Houston homeowners favor red or burgundy brick. Dallas residents are partial to gray shades, while Austin customers prefer beige and terra cotta colors with a "used" look. Regardless of preference or location, Elgin-Butler employees are able to produce whatever customers want. They have been doing so for well over a century, and practice can only make them better.

THE BRICKS ARE STILL PILING UP

Elgin-Butler continues to expand. The company bought out its chief competitor in Austin, Elgin Standard Brick Company, in 1965. The company generated $18 million in sales in 1990, which was down from its peak of $20 million in 1986, but still considerable nonetheless. EBBCO's bricks can be found in places ranging from homes in Japan to the U. S. Embassy in Mexico City to chemical vats in Malaysia, Canada, and South America. Nationally, it has extended its territory away from Austin. For example, Elgin-Butler had brick jobs going on in Chicago, North Carolina, and Florida in late 1990. Its bricks have beautified buildings like the Wyndham Hotel Greenspoint in Houston, the Oakbrook Center in Illinois, and the Galveston (Texas) County Jail. There's no telling where Elgin-Butler's presence will be felt next.

The company makes thousands of different bricks and structural glazed hollow tile in various shapes, sizes, and colors. All are made from clay mined on the company's site. No more than 2 acres per year are mined, so the lack of clay will not be a problem for some time to come—nor will the variety.

The variety can be attributed to the fact that Elgin-Butler continues to be innovative and aggressive in its search for new products and customers. For example, one of EBBCO's glazed brick and hollow tile products is attracting prison officials' attention because it can be easily cleaned, is strong, and can be threaded with reinforced steel bars. One of Elgin-Butler's brochures, headlined "Go directly to jail...," promotes modular ceramic system units that are ideal for "jails, schools, hospitals, or any other security, seismic, or institutional application." Elgin-Butler truly leaves no stone—or brick—unturned in its quest for perfection, sales—and perpetuity.

Chapter 13

1877

Homestake Mining Company

**THERE'S GOLD IN THEM THAR HILLS—AND WE'RE
GOING TO MINE IT**

If ever there was a company that profited from "mining" its own business, it is Homestake Mining Company, which is based in San Francisco. The company opened its first mine in Lead, Dakota Territory (now South Dakota), on April 9, 1876. It formed as a California corporation on November 5, 1877, became listed on the New York Stock Exchange in January, 1879, and has been going into a hole ever since—but with positive results.

A COMPANY MAY NOT WEAR EYEGLASSES—BUT HERE'S ONE WITH PERFECT VISION

Homestake provides an excellent example of a company whose management had—and continues to have—unlimited vision. The company faced a mid-life crossroads during the mid-20th century at which, if management chose the wrong direction, Homestake could have been consigned forever to a position as a second-rate corporation. Worse, it could have meant the company's demise. Fortunately, management had the vision to see the direction in which mining technology and the world's needs were headed. Management decided to concentrate on mining as the company's only business. But, to its mind, mining was mining. Whatever opportunities arose in the field, Homestake would be there to take advantage of them. Based on history, management made the right decision, as Homestake's present-day existence as one of the world's leading natural resources mining corporations attests.

Homestake remained a fairly "local" operation from the opening of the Lead mine until 1942. The war forced a halt in its operations until 1945, at which point the company resumed work on a small scale. There was no indication at that time that Homestake would ever be anything but a small mining operation in South Dakota, let alone expand throughout the world. Then came the atomic age, which changed Homestake's business outlook.

During the 1950s, astute company management realized that the United States—and the world—was entering a new technological era. It had two choices: continue extracting a few ounces of gold per year out of the South Dakota mine or expand into other mining operations. Management chose expansion—and Homestake has been growing ever since.

HOMESTAKE GETS THE SHAFT—AND ENJOYS IT

Homestake's first diversification was into uranium mining. From 1953 to 1957, it acquired properties in Utah, Wyoming, and New Mexico. The company's business prospered, which encouraged it to pursue other mining interests. Homestake plunged into several new research and development and acquisition ventures in the 1960s.

In September of 1962, Homestake joined American Metal Climax Inc. (AMAX) to develop lead/zinc properties in the Buick area of southeast Missouri. A year-and-a-half later, in May, 1964, Homestake went international when it joined a consortium developing the Allen potash project in Sasketchewan, Canada. A little less than two years from that point, Homestake Iron Ore Company of Australia, Ltd., as a partner, began production and shipping of iron ore at Koolanooka, Australia. The next move took place in October 1967, in South America, when Homestake, through its subsidiary, Compania Madrigal, began the development of copper, lead, and zinc deposits in Peru. From there, it was back to Canada, and a valuable return of investment in the company's research and development expenditures.

In April, 1968, the Allen potash mine in Sasketchewan began production. Nine months later, production began at the Buick lead/zinc complex in Missouri. Finally, to cap off the extremely busy decade, the company's first silver mine, the Bulldog, located in Creede, Colorado, began production. In only eight years,

Homestake grew from a tiny one-mine operation in western South Dakota to a large concern operating on three continents. Management's vision certainly paid off—and it continued to play a vital role in corporate decisions.

Just as management knew when to enter a deal, it also recognized when to pull out. In June, 1974, the Koolanooka iron ore reserves were depleted. That fact made Homestake's decision easy; it simply closed the mine and pulled out. The company did not leave Australia, however. About a year-and-a-half later, in December 1975, Homestake Gold Limited formed to participate with Kalgoorlie Lake View (Pty.) Ltd. in the KMA gold mining partnership in Western Australia. Four years later, this organization became listed on the Swiss Stock Exchanges in Basel, Geneva, and Zurich. That listing recognized Homestake as a true international corporation and positioned it for even more expansion. The company did not wait long to grow even more.

IS HOMESTAKE GOING BACKWARDS? THE COMPANY'S OVER 100—BUT THE 80S HAVE BEEN THEIR GOLDEN YEARS

In August 1980, Homestake announced the discovery of the open-pit McLaughlin gold mine, located 70 miles northeast of the company's San Francisco headquarters. (Company geologists actually discovered the mine in 1978.) For Homestake, the discovery was like finding gold in its own backyard! Five years later, Homestake poured the first gold from the mine, and applied an innovative new process in doing so.

Homestake's mining techniques had improved considerably since the 19th-century "pick and shovel" days in South Dakota. At McLaughlin, it extracted gold through the world's first successful use of acid pressure oxidation technology utilizing autoclaves (containers for sterilizing, cooking, etc., by super-heated steam under pressure) for treating gold ores. This process may not mean much to the lay person, but it had significant ramifications for Homestake.

Production at McLaughlin has grown at an amazing pace since 1985. As output increases, production costs decline (see the table below). Both production and costs promise to do so for quite a while, as reserves at the facility demonstrate.

Homestake Mining Company
McLaughlin Mine

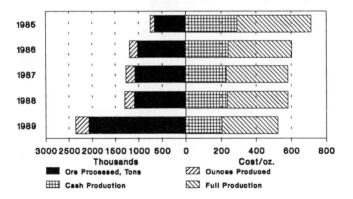

Proven and probable gold ore reserves at McLaughlin total 20,259,000 tons—and the mine is only the third largest of the company's four active gold mines in the United States. Both Homestake in South Dakota (28,859,000 tons) and Round Mountain, the company's largest (which is the world's largest open pit), in central Nevada (68,144,000 tons), are larger. (A

335

fifth mine, Wood Gulch, in northeast Nevada, closed operations in late 1989.) Only Mineral Hill, located north of Yellowstone Park in Montana (546,000 tons), is smaller. Homestake owns this in partnership with American Copper and Nickel, which manages the facility. The first gold from this mine was poured in July 1989. These domestic mines represent only a part of the company's overall gold mining operations.

Homestake still has interests in gold mines in Canada, Australia and Chile. In April 1988, it acquired a 73.3 percent ownership interest in North American Metals Corporation, of Vancouver, British Columbia, which is 50 percent owner of the Golden Bear mine in the northwestern part of the province. The company completed mine construction there in late 1989 and saw the first gold poured in January 1990. To date, results there have been less than spectacular, but Homestake has high hopes for the mine's future. The company is not used to seeing profits or expectations go "down under," unless they do so in Australia.

Homestake's Australian operations are significant and growing. The company owns 80 percent of Homestake Gold of Australia Limited (HGAL). In 1989, HGAL purchased a 50 percent interest in a portion of the Kalgoorlie gold district and a 2 percent additional interest in Kalgoorlie Mining Associates. The owners formed a separate company, Kalgoorlie Consolidated Gold Mines Pty Ltd., to manage the consolidated operations and oversee production from existing mines and mills and the construction of the new Finiston mill, which began operating at the end of 1989. Homestake is already planning a $65 million expansion of the plant, although it has been deferred temporarily pending further analysis.

Homestake also owns the new Fortnum gold mine, 90 miles north of Meekathara, in western Australia, from which the first gold was poured in October 1989. Based on its expansion and success in Australia, Homestake has never received a chilly reception there. Much the same can be said about their South American operations, where their "Chile" reception has given them a new lease on life on that continent.

Homestake operates the El Hueso mine high in the rugged Andes Mountains, about 600 miles north of Santiago, under a ten-year lease acquired in June 1988. The company has invested significantly in plant modifications and changes in operating practices there. It completed an extensive exploration program in 1989. Homestake's hopes for success at El Hueso are as high as the Andes—as are its expectations in its other mining interests.

OUR MINES MAY BE DEEP, BUT THEY SHOULD NOT PLACE US IN A HOLE

Although Homestake's core interest is gold, it remains active in its other operations. However, management does not hesitate to divest company holdings in operations that do not prove profitable or are unpredictable. For example, in February 1981, the company augmented its uranium holdings by acquiring United Nuclear Corporation's 70 percent partnership interest in the New Mexico operations. The operations resulted in severe losses in the late 1980s ($500,000 in 1987, $5.7 million in 1988, and $7.2 million in 1989). Consequently, in November 1989, the company ceased conventional uranium mining at its

Grants, New Mexico facility. Two months later, it suspended milling operations there. It has also adjusted other mining interests.

In September of 1983, Homestake sold its interests in the Madrigal copper, lead, and zinc operations in Peru. The company did not abandon such mining altogether, though. In fact, it increased its activity.

In May of 1986, Homestake acquired AMAX' 50 percent interest in the jointly owned Buick lead and zinc operations in Missouri. Two years later, in November, it combined those operations with those of St. Joe Minerals Corporation to form the Doe Run Company. (Homestake owns 42.5percent of the operation.)

The Doe Run Company is North America's largest fully integrated primary lead producer. Homestake exercised a propitious use of timing to involve itself more heavily in this type of operation. Homestake maximized by-product production in order to take advantage of continuing high copper and zinc prices. Although 1989 operating earnings decreased by twelve percent from 1988 ($26.3 million versus $29.8 million respectively), Homestake was satisfied with the results—especially in light of the 1987 earnings, which were only $12.5 million! What is really telling about the Doe Run operations is the company's attitude about safety and the well being of its employees.

Doe Run comprises 6 mines, 4 mills, and 2 smelters, all of which feature alternating operating schedules to meet existing market conditions. The company has recommended that a secondary lead production facility be constructed there, which would increase the total lead output. What the company emphasizes in its 1989 annual report, however, is the facility's safety record!

According to company statistics, the Herculaneum smelter at Doe Run set a refined lead production record of 238,935 tons and improved productivity to an all-time high of 1.82 hours per manshift. Despite these records, the mine finished 14 consecutive months, over one million man-hours, without a lost-time incident. That the company boasts of this record is not surprising. Homestake prides itself on being a good corporate citizen. It is extremely active in special projects, which the public recognizes and appreciates.

For example, Homestake has donated approximately $1 million in cash and property to the Mt. Rushmore Society to assist in the renovation efforts for Mt. Rushmore. (Homestake has a vested interest in the area, since Lead is only a few miles away.) The company received kudos from Bat Conservation International, which wrote in the Spring 1989 issue of its publication, BATS, "What distinguishes the McLaughlin mine is their firm commitment to wildlife conservation and their sincere efforts to provide enduring protection for their resident bats." Even the United States Department of Interior, Bureau of Land Management, has praised the company.

The BLM awarded a certificate of appreciation to Homestake in recognition of "Your sensitivity and dedication to the protection of the flora and fauna in a mining environment on public lands." Indeed, the company demonstrates its commitment to environmental responsibility by treating reclamation as part of the mining process. It also takes into account people's concerns in company operations by providing for families and businesses affected by Homestake's expansion. Such commitment makes Homestead a well-respected corporate citizen, facilitates doing business, and enhances its prospects of a profitable future—which, it is fairly safe to say, is what lies ahead for the company.

The company continues to reorganize and seek new opportunities. After all, there may be no more volatile industry than mining. Gold and silver prices fluctuate wildly, conditions in the major oil-producing countries have drastic effects on the costs of petroleum, and new technology creates demands for different minerals. All of these factors influence Homestake's business operations.

For instance, the company reorganized in May 1984 under a Delaware corporation and formed Homestake Mining of California. Homestake Gold Limited re-incorporated in June 1987 as HGAL, which became listed on the Australian Stock Exchange four months later, and 20 percent of its capital stock was sold. That was one more major step for the company in the 1980s as far as the stock exchange aspect was concerned. In November 1982, the parent company's (Homestake Mining Company) stock had been listed on the Frankfurt and London Stock Exchanges. Four years later, in October 1986, it was listed on the Paris Bourse. The company had become a major player in the international market as it continued to adjust to changing world conditions.

Within the space of six months in 1984-85, the company got out of silver mining and entered the oil business. In June 1984 Homestake acquired Felmont Oil Corporation in order to extend its energy interests. The transaction included Felmont's 25 percent interest in the Round Mountain gold mine. A few months later, in January 1985, Homestake stopped production of silver at the Bulldog silver mine in Creede, Colorado, in response to depressed silver prices. The acquisition of Round Mountain proved fortuitous.

In March 1987, partners in the Round Mountain operation announced a $131 million expansion plan to increase gold production to 320,000 ounces per year. Homestake's share was fixed at $33 million of costs and 80,000 ounces of production. Two years later, in February 1989, participants agreed to further expansion by contributing separate property holdings to the operation, including the modernized Manhattan gold mine and mill. Homestake is still heavily involved in the Round Mountain project, and expects to be for some time to come. Meanwhile, Homestake disposed of the company from which it acquired its 25 percent interest.

OF ALL THE PETS IN THE WORLD, THE HARDEST TO MANAGE IS A "PET"ROLEUM

Homestake divested itself of its Felmont Oil interests in two separate transactions. First, in April 1989, it sold two of the company's blocks for $23.6 million. A few months later, it announced plans to sell the gas and oil business to a subsidiary of Torch Energy Advisors for approximately $97.5 million. It completed the transaction successfully in Houston, Texas, on December 28, 1989. Once again, Homestake was in a position to concentrate more on other mining interests.

As Homestake heads for the 20th century (and deep into its second century of business), the company continues to solidify its position as a leader in the industry. It remains heavily committed to domestic and international exploration of precious metals, particularly in the western United States, Canada, and in the vicinity of its operating mines.

Domestic exploration expenditures in 1989 alone were $11.8 million, one-third of which was dedicated to operations in South Dakota. The company also acquired the majority of the Canadian mineral exploration properties of Esso Minerals Canada for $3.3 million. It is interesting to note the magnitude of the $3.8 million exploration expenditures in South Dakota. After all, it was in that state that Homestake got its beginning back in 1876. Certainly, the company is not spending the money there out of a sense of sentimentality. No corporation can survive very long doing that. Rather, companies, especially the survivors included in this book, succeed based on a number of factors that do not include sentimentality. Homestake is spending money in South Dakota because it makes good business sense to do so. Make no mistake, it is good business sense that has gotten Homestake to this stage in its history—and will no doubt carry it a lot farther.

Chapter 14

1888

The Baton Rouge Water Company

A WATERED DOWN HISTORY

There are some companies that stay in business for a century or more based on the quality of their goods and service, and their ability to beat the competition. There are other companies that are in business because they have to be, e.g., public utilities and water companies. Whether their existence is guaranteed or not is moot. Regardless of their perpetuity, they still must offer good service and quality products. One such company is the Baton Rouge Water Company.

The company has been in "business" since 1888. Its sole purpose is to supply the city of Baton Rouge with water. It does its job well—with the help of nature.

WATER SO GOOD YOU WOULD THINK IT CAME FROM HEAVEN

On November 8, 1887, Baton Rouge's Common Council contracted with E. Smedley and John H. Wood of Dubuque, Iowa, to "construct, build, maintain, operate and own a system of water in the city of Baton Rouge and to supply said city and its inhabitants with water." The plant was to pump 2 million gallons of water in a 24-hour period. The company obtained water from the Mississippi River and filtered it prior to delivery. It was an efficient system. There was only one thing lacking: customers. Most people in the area had their own cisterns and they were not about to buy water from someone else when they could produce their own for no cost. That did not faze Smedley and Wood.

The two men began construction of the company's facilities in 1888. They did not skimp on quality. With an eye to durability, physical attraction, and the future, they erected on leased ground adjoining the Water Works a 100-foot high, 15-foot diameter standpipe of riveted wrought-iron plates that could hold 132,000 gallons of water. This ornate structure stood unchanged until 1937, when the company extended its height to 110 feet.

The following year, the company replaced the standpipe's original wooden cover with a metal umbrella roof and increased its capacity to 146,000 gallons. The standpipe served the company for another 25 years. That 75-year service span stood as a tribute to quality workmanship and set a standard for company service that has endured since 1888. The fact that the standpipe is unique is evidenced by the fact that in 1975 it was placed on the National Register of Historic Places as an example of engineering skill.

The Historic Standpipe

Courtesy Baton Rouge Water Company

Originally, the city's water supply came directly from the Mississippi River (which may account for the dearth of customers in the company's early years). Of course, the company treated the water before delivering it, but most local people still preferred the water they got from their own cisterns. Management felt that it could improve on the quality of the water taken from the river, so the company drilled its own wells. It drilled the first local well at a depth of 190 feet in 1889 and a second, deeper one in 1896. As a result, the company provided water of a much higher quality.

THERE'S NO WATER LIKE HOME WATER

On April 5, 1910, the Iowa firm that managed the city's water supply turned it over to the Baton Rouge Water Company. Mr. C. C. Bird, a partner in the Louisiana Fire Insurance Company's Bird & Ross Agency (see next chapter) became the company's first president. The company grew slowly—but steadily—from that point until World War II. Midway through the war, it ran into its first formidable problem. Conceivably, if management had not acted quickly to resolve the problem *before* it got out of hand, the situation could have resulted in the premature demise of the Baton Rouge Water Company.

There were 75,000 people living in the Baton Rouge area around 1943. The entire population's water supply came from deep wells via centrifugal pumps taking direct suction from wells at or near the ground surface. That method had served the company well for years. Suddenly, due to increased competition for water, the company faced a crisis.

Many of the industries in the area, e.g., Standard Oil of Louisiana, Firestone Tire and Rubber, DuPont, and Aluminum Company of America, stepped up their wartime production *and* their use of water. The rapid recession of water levels alerted company management to a possible crisis which could affect service to its customers. Management had an answer to the problem: install deep-well turbine pumps. That was easier said than done, since the company had to get permission from the Office of War Utilities, War Production Board, in Washington D. C., to do so.

346

Despite the fact that dealing with government agencies was harrowing in peacetime, let alone during the most extensive war in the world's history, Company President H. P. Connell and Engineer L. C. Eldridge acted *at once* to forestall problems. They submitted a priority application to the board for permission to install the pumps and build a 2.5 million gallon reinforced concrete reservoir besides.

Connell and Eldridge pointed out quite truthfully that without the pumps the company could not survive. They added that the pumps only met the minimum requirements to keep the company in business. Baton Rouge Water still needed water storage facilities to serve its customers. At the time, the company drew its water from only three stations, Lafayette Street, Lula Avenue, and Government Street. The company desperately needed to preserve the continuity of supply and the reserve storage necessary during a fire. (Based on the Louisiana Fire Insurance Company's experiences on Government Street, the reserve was absolutely necessary.) The board granted both requests. The company's immediate response to averting a crisis assured its existence—and survival.

THE COMPANY RECEIVES HIGH WATERMARKS

After World War II ended, the company entered an era of unprecedented expansion. In 1961, it moved into new headquarters designed to serve its customers more efficiently. The facility included an expanded parking area and the "latest modern conveniences," i.e., a drive-up window and a night depository. Then, in 1985, it opened another office building to better accommodate its operations and customers. Expansion was by no means restricted to company buildings;

management took steps to guarantee the supply and quality of its water, too. The company may never run out of it, but it does want to make sure that the quality of what is available is high. Nature gives the company a boost in this regard.

Some of the water the company provides may be as old as 2,000 years! It is rainfall that lands near Vicksburg, Mississippi, where the company's water originates. The water enters the ground near Vicksburg, about 140 miles north of Baton Rouge, and travels south through rock and sand formations in which it is purified so effectively that the company has to provide little treatment of its own. That trip takes nearly 20 centuries! The water has never been treated as well as Baton Rouge Water takes care of it, though.

The company maintains several storage sites for the water. There are two concrete low-level reservoirs under a former office building in the city which are available for emergency purposes. These have a capacity of 1,325,000 gallons of water. There is also the Lula Reservoir, the result of the World War II petition to the War Production Board.

The Lula Reservoir is 111 feet by 150 feet, 8 inches, with an inside depth of 20 feet. Like the company's original standpipe, it is a solidly constructed structure that is designed to serve for a long time. In fact, the reservoir was drained recently, inspected, and found to be in excellent condition. The company washed, refilled, and chlorinated it—then put it back in service! It also took advantage of state-of-the-art technology to upgrade the facility.

Baton Rouge Water installed two automatic valve actuators and a modified altitude valve, all of which are remotely controlled. These will allow the reservoir to be filled with one of two wells at night when the system demand is down. All the actuators, altitude valves and centrifugal pumps at stations are automatically controlled and monitored from a central Supervisory Control room at the company's main office. Of utmost importance to customers, the company runs an extensive testing program to guarantee water quality.

The pure water that travels south from Vicksburg is withdrawn through 53 deep wells strategically drilled to depths of 600 to 2,700 feet. That water is monitored continually. Water is not pumped to customers until it is chlorinated to exacting tolerances. Once it is, then the water is safe to drink—and that is a lot of water.

According to recent company statistics, it pumps an average daily rate of 43,000,000 gallons of water through its 1,300 miles of distribution lines. (As a measure of growth, the average daily rate is 21 times that of 1888.) Baton Rouge Water serves some 84,000 accounts (its average household customer consumes 205,000 gallons of water annually) and 6,000 water hydrants, a far cry from the early days when the company had trouble attracting customers.

Obviously, Baton Rouge Water takes its mission seriously. It is not about to let its reputation for quality service and product slip one bit, even though the company has no competition and its continued existence is practically guaranteed. This is one company that is a survivor because of its positive approach to business—and the fact that it will not provide watered-down service or product to its customers.

Chapter 15

LOUISIANA COMPANIES

1890

The Louisiana Companies

100 YEARS OLD—AND STILL THE YOUNGEST KID ON THE BLOCK

Can you imagine being 100 years old and having others laughing at you because you're nothing but a kid? That may not happen too often in human life, but it does in corporate years. Consider the case of the Louisiana Companies.

THERE'S NO INSURANCE AGAINST SUCCESS—BUT THERE IS SUCCESS IN INSURANCE

The Louisiana Companies began in Baton Rouge as the Louisiana Fire Insurance Company in 1890 (or 1899 or 1898, depending on whose version of the company's history is to be believed). The time was right for the formation of such a company.

Baton Rouge, like the rest of Louisiana and the South, was still in the process of recovering from the devastating effects of the Civil War. The city had a new railroad, water works, gas works, electric light company, and a street railway. In addition, there was a majestic new state capitol building that symbolized Louisiana's hopes for a prosperous future. As the Baton Rouge *Weekly Advocate*, itself one of the oldest businesses in the city, editorialized, "Baton Rouge is steadily growing in importance, in size, in population, wealth, in trade and social refinement." Several of the city's most prominent citizens agreed, which is why they banded together to form their own local fire insurance company.

Fire was a serious problem in Baton Rouge around 1890. People did a lot of cooking on wood stoves and heated rooms from grates. It did not take too much for a flame to grow into a full-fledged fire which was not extinguished until it consumed entire blocks. Thus, residents relished the idea of a local fire insurance company to help them offset their losses. In response, a group of businessmen taking advantage of one of the leading contributors to business survival, i.e., timing, formed the Louisiana Fire Insurance Company.

The company's founders were extremely practical men. They made it a practice to cover only one, or sometimes two, dwellings or businesses on a single block. This minimized their risks considerably. They also decided that concentrating solely on fire insurance was not in their best interests. Since one of their founders was a steamship agent, and Baton Rouge was a busy transportation terminus located on the Mississippi River,it was only natural that they would offer marine and river insurance too.

The company opened officially for business on January 1, 1891. The office was open 9 a.m. to 5 p.m., six days a week. Within four months, it opened its first field office in Jackson, Louisiana. Perhaps some of the people concerned with the company wondered why they operated any offices at all. After all, there was no one collecting on policies. The company did not sustain its first loss for nine months!

NO GOVERNMENT HANDLES MORE BURNING ISSUES THAN GOVERNMENT STREET

Perhaps the biggest mistake the Louisiana Fire Insurance Company made was to insure buildings on Baton Rouge's Government Street. A building on that street owned and insured for $500 by Dr. Thomas J. Buffington burned on September 14, 1891. That led to the first claim against the company, which it paid the next day. In the process, it established a reputation for fairness and honesty in expediting claims that exists to this day.

A little over a year later, another fire destroyed a church and several houses on Government Street. According to the December 30, 1892, *Daily Advocate,* "The Louisiana Fire Insurance Company, notwith-

standing its heavy losses in the fire Wednesday—
which by the way was the largest one we have had
since the war—will still be able to pay an annual dividend to its stockholders of about 25 percent." The paper added that the company had paid its loss before
the sun went down and that "this is prompt, this is
business, and speaks in golden words of the strong
and well managed company." No doubt such words
are high praise to a company's owners, management,
employees, and shareholders, especially in its formative years. The trick is to attract similar praise a hundred or more years later. That the Louisiana Companies has been able to do.

A VENERABLE INSTITUTION AT THE AGE OF TWELVE

The Louisiana Fire Insurance Company hardly
rated a full-fledged president in its first few years of existence. It seemed like the principals played "President for a Day." Its first president, Andrew Jackson
(no relation to the ex-United States President of the
same name), served only one year. He declined to
serve a second. Richard H. Burke took over and died
before his term ended. That brought in Charles J.
Reddy, who served until 1900. Next came O. B.
Steele, who began a trend toward management longevity—and stability.

A lack of presidential longevity notwithstanding,
the company prospered, primarily due to the efforts of
secretary Thompson Bird.Shortly before his death in
1902, the *Advocate* wrote:

> Among the fixed and successful institutions of Baton Rouge is the Louisiana Fire Insurance Company, of which Captain O. B. Steele is president and Major T. J. Bird secretary. It has done a safe and splendid business for a number of years and has the backing of the substantial men of the city.

That was high praise indeed for a young company on the way up.

AN INSURANCE COMPANY INSURES ITSELF

The company made a significant move in 1907 when it signed a reinsurance agreement with the German American Insurance Company of New York (later known as the Great American Insurance Company). The contract provided that German American would reinsure at 100 percent the business written by Louisiana Fire. This reduced Louisiana Fire's risk and stamped it as a viable insurance institution. A few years later, two more important events in the area of management occurred to help Louisiana Fire take its place as a respectable insurance company.

The company's growth between 1891 and the mid-1920s was easy to follow through the history of its physical expansions. At its inception, the company occupied quarters in the Doherty Hardware building. In 1901, it moved into a two-story brick building housing the First National Bank. Seven years later, the company moved into the new Masonic Temple. There, it shared offices with the Bird & Ross Insurance Company, which it operated.

Louisiana Fire stayed put until 1925, when it moved into the new Louisiana National Bank building. During the early 1920s, the company organized the Louisiana Underwriters Agency, which succeeded Bird & Ross. The last move occurred just one year before Joseph Warren Berwick, Jr., (who preferred to be called by his middle name) arrived, and four before Shreveport insurance man Justin R. Querbes, Sr., assumed a controlling interest in the company. These two combined to initiate a management growth that had a significant impact on the company's future.

Querbes became company president on April 29, 1929. One of his first acts was to place Berwick in charge of the business. The two led the company through a steady growth through the 1930s. Despite the fact the depression gripped the country, Louisiana Fire paid a dividend every year to its stockholders. That led to a further expansion in 1941, when the company entered the mortgage banking field. It negotiated a servicing contract with the Prudential Insurance Company of America and closed the first year of business with $1,250,000 in mortgage loans.

World War II put a crimp in the company's growth. It also placed Berwick's management career on hold. He went into the army in 1942. Harold Knox, who replaced Berwick and now serves on the company's board of directors, describes the wartime years as "more or less a holding operation." Berwick returned in 1946 and became president of Louisiana Underwriters. Simultaneously, he served as the parent company's secretary. No doubt the employees of the company were pleased to see him return. Berwick believed that the strength of any company lay in the dedication of its workforce. He did more than believe it, though. He acted to make sure the employees were well taken care of.

THE GOLDEN YEARS: THE 1950s

The 1950s were good years for the company in most respects. The mortgage loan business increased dramatically. Its original $1,250,000 mortgage loan portfolio increased to $75 million in loans to home-owners and commercial borrowers throughout Louisiana. (The company has since dropped the mortgage loan business.) In 1955, the company formed Louisiana Mortgage & Realty, Inc., to adapt to changing business conditions. This led to successful real estate operations.

Another significant change was the switch from manual to automated operations. Frank J. Clesi, current vice president and treasurer of Louisiana Companies, automated the agency and laid the groundwork for the company's later expansion into computer services. There was also an unexpected—and tragic— change in leadership.

Justin Querbes, Sr., died in a plane crash on January 10, 1954. His son, Justin, Jr., who had served on the board of directors since 1937, replaced him. Although the company felt the loss of the senior Querbes on a personal basis, it proceeded on a business level without losing a beat.

Berwick made sure that the company's loyal workforce would remain dedicated. He established a vacation spot in Florida to which key employees could retire for a week to replenish their energy. Berwick owned a trailer which he had purchased in Lake Charles to use as a duck hunting camp. He had it moved to a beach near Panama City for employee use. The company replaced it with a larger mobile home and added a second. It made the trailer available to key employees one week a year and even added what Berwick called "fun money" for their use. That gave some employees a temporary vacation home. Meanwhile, the company looked for a new permanent home of its own.

Louisiana Fire Insurance Company acquired a new site in the 1950s. Construction for a new home office began in 1958. Early the next year, the company opened its new headquarters. More significantly, it adopted a new name. In 1959, the business became the Louisiana Companies. That did not become the company's official name for another twelve years, though.

In the 1960s, the company positioned itself for further growth without backing off from its commitment as an insurance company by opening several branch offices throughout the state. First, in 1965, it purchased the Parkerson-Dupuis Agency of Lafayette. The following year it acquired the Wurzlow Insurance Agency in Houma. Then, in 1969, it purchased the John L. Wasey Agency in Lake Charles. The expansion necessitated a new name—and a new game.

NEW NAME, NEW GAME

Originally, Louisiana Companies was the amended name for Louisiana Mortgage & Realty. In 1971, the parent company amended its charter to change from an insurance operation to a general business corporation. At that point, the Louisiana Fire Insurance Company became Louisiana Companies and the subsidiary company reverted to Louisiana Mortgage & Realty. At about the same time, it allowed the reinsurance contract with Great American to expire. That marked the demise of Louisiana Fire—and the birth of a "new, improved" diversified corporation.

Growth continued in the 1970s. The company purchased the Litton Agency in Opelousas, which became an agency. It expanded its headquarters in 1979-80 and added a separate data processing building. That move proved wise, as the company dropped its mortgage lending business in favor of providing data processing services for the mortgage banking industry. The service is based on the company's forty years of experience in originating, processing, and servicing loans. This experience led to the development of a multi-company company system called LOANSERV, which is designed specifically for financial institutions in processing its lending operations.

Computer services play an important role in today's Louisiana Companies' operations. As times change, so does the company. It has replaced its combined insurance, mortgage loan, and real estate operations with insurance and computer services. No doubt there will be more changes in the future as the company seeks profitable niches in the business world—and improves its formula for survival.

Warren Berwick, who died in 1983 after 57 years with the company, once said that when there were customers waiting on the moon, the company would be there in space ships. That day may not be far off. If it happens soon, it will be a coup for new president Justin Querbes III, who took over the presidency in

1989. His election made him the third generation of the family to serve in that capacity over a span of 62 years. Such longevity is a sign of a stable company, and one that promises to be around for a long time to come. That is the case with the Louisiana Companies, a young survivor—but a survivor nonetheless.

Chapter 16

How Did We Get So Old?

**THEY MAY NOT BE IN THE SEWING BUSINESS, BUT
THEY SHARE SOME COMMON THREADS**

We have seen that there are a lot of companies in the country that have survived a century or more. We've looked at brief histories of newspapers, public utility companies, financial institutions, breweries, and companies in other industries. (The profiles included here are by necessity concise and focus on individual companies' strongpoints.) Each company profiled has experienced its own unique problems and confronted them in its own way. Each has different corporate cultures, goals, product lines, values...in short, the companies profiled in this book are decidedly distinct entities.

The companies may be distinct from one another, but they share some common threads. There are the classic textbook factors that jump immediately to mind (and which smack of the Boy Scout creed), e.g., flexibility, dependability, adaptability, diligence, and prudence. However, they tell only part of the story. There are far deeper reasons than those for a company's success. It is these threads that we will examine here.

The factors covered in this chapter do not cover the gamut completely, but they are the most significant threads. Certainly, readers who delve more deeply into each company's history will most likely find a few more. It is the sixteen major common threads below that are the focus of this chapter. Bear in mind that they are listed in no particular order of importance, since they are all equally important as far as the survivors are concerned.

THE LIST OF COMMON THREADS

- [ ] LUCK
- [ ] CLOSE RELATIONSHIPS WITH EDUCATIONAL INSTITUTIONS
- [ ] ACCEPTANCE OF SETBACKS AS INEVITABLE
- [ ] LEARNING FROM MISTAKES
- [ ] PAYING ATTENTION TO ROOTS
- [ ] FILLING NICHES
- [ ] ADAPTATION TO UPDATED TECHNOLOGY
- [ ] ATTENTION TO DETAIL
- [ ] CONTINUOUS DEVELOPMENT OF SAGACIOUS, COMPETENT LEADERSHIP <u>FROM WITHIN</u>

☐ ADHERENCE TO THE THREE "I'S"
☐ VISION
☐ UNMITIGATED CONSUMER LOYALTY
☐ STRONG EMPLOYER-EMPLOYEE RELATIONSHIPS
☐ GOOD CORPORATE CITIZENS
☐ SELF SUFFICIENCY
☐ WISE DIVERSIFICATION

Let's examine them one at a time, but in the form of tips for today's managers. They can be valuable learning lessons for contemporary business operators or people contemplating going into business who want to survive.

DO NOT DISCOUNT LUCK

There are some people who scoff at the idea of luck as a contributing factor to longevity. Yet, luck has a great impact on how successful companies are in their business dealings. It even changes their directions at times.

Perhaps First Pennsylvania Bank would never have had the chance to survive for more than 200 years if the King of France had been in a bad mood the day John Laurens asked him to guarantee a $470,000 loan from the Dutch. And certainly Procter & Gamble would not have produced a soap that floats as quickly as it did—indeed, if it would have at all—if it were not for luck. No one there set out purposefully to invent a soap that floats or soap flakes as a substitute for bars. Both products came about strictly by accident. And with what product do most people identify Procter & Gamble today? It's Ivory Soap, the soap that floats. If it were not for luck, Procter & Gamble would not have become a household name as quickly as it did. We can rest assured that P&G will never discount luck as a factor in its longevity, and neither will most of the other companies that are survivors.

In the final analysis, luck can present opportunities which clever managers take advantage of to improve their products and services. Turning luck into opportunity is a valuable management technique—and one which is a prime contributor to a company's success.

DEVELOP CLOSE RELATIONSHIPS WITH EDUCATIONAL INSTITUTIONS

Successful companies never overlook the need for constant employee training. They:

- take advantage of every opportunity available to ensure themselves a well-trained workforce
- utilize in-house and external training programs to ensure the availability of effective, up-to-date training
- measure *very* carefully training costs vs. needs

The third step is crucial. Some companies eliminate or postpone training for employees as a cost-cutting mechanism during lean times. Doing so retards employees' progress and weakens management's abilities. Successful companies do not follow this practice. Rather, they recognize a constant need for training as a hedge against failure. This certainly has been the case with the companies in this book.

Following the three steps above allows successful companies to keep up with the latest technology, management techniques, etc.—and apply what they learn to everyday operations. Increasingly, this search for training has led companies into business-education partnerships that benefit both sides. These partnerships have never been more critical than they are today. Each company profiled in this book has paid close attention to training and education, and has spent many years cultivating symbiotic relationships with external educational institutions.

The companies included here are located near major educational facilities. (It is not mandatory that successful companies locate next to prestigious universities. They should, however, establish close ties with educational institutions.) That is more by design than accident. Many of Atlanta Gas Light's employees are graduates of Georgia Tech, for example. Coors is located only a few blocks away from the Colorado School of Mines. The two have a symbiotic relationship that is mutually beneficial. Procter & Gamble has a close working relationship with the University of Cincinnati, which has one of the best cooperative education programs in the country. ("Co-op" traces its beginnings to the school, which began its program in 1910.) Simply put, businesses cannot survive without well-educated workers whose training never ends.

The partnership is a two-way street. Colleges may supply a steady stream of qualified graduates to meet businesses' needs, but the companies must do something for the schools, too. They can provide funds and equipment for research and development purposes, support schools through corporate grants, etc. And, it is worth remembering that the business-education partnership does not have to be at the college and university level. It can be at the high school, elementary, or even kindergarten levels, for that matter. The essential thing to realize is that it is in both businesses' and schools' best interests to work closely together. Such a partnership is not only in individual entities' interests, but it can enhance the complete economic structure of the country as well.

ACCEPT SETBACKS GRACEFULLY; THEY ARE INEVITABLE

Every company receives business setbacks at some time or another. Companies like Aetna are especially susceptible to cyclical economic downturns, for example. Atlanta Gas Light almost went out of business because of the unavailability of gas during the Civil War. Likewise, Homestake Mining, which had a limited business to begin with, almost collapsed when the government shut down its mining operation from 1942-1945. Coors ran into unanticipated problems during prohibition. It is not the setbacks that are important, though; it is how companies respond to them that counts.

Every company profiled in this book has had its share of setbacks. Obviously, they have all overcome them and survived. Certainly, companies should not sit back and do nothing about them. Management has to take action to overcome setbacks. Astute managers do so, and well. The subjects of this book have proved that obstacles can be surmounted—and have to be if a business is to survive.

LEARN FROM MISTAKES

Just as companies can anticipate setbacks, they must also recognize that they will make mistakes. These can be as simple as overproducing a product to as serious as branching out into business areas about which they know nothing. Consider Aetna's expansion into non-insurance functions in the 1970s. Management realized quickly that the company was not ready for such diversification, at least not at that particular time, so it withdrew quickly from the non-insurance business and concentrated on what had made the company successful.

The Laclede near-fiasco in its first foray into oil and gas exploration is another example of how a company can learn from mistakes. No one in the company's management knew much—if anything—about oil and gas leases. This cost the company dearly for a while, but the managers learned quickly about the necessity for leases. They acted rapidly to hire experts in the subject who carried them through the initial stages of the leasing process. Management was not afraid to admit they were novices in this area and compensated wisely for their lack of knowledge. This ability to learn from mistakes—and apply what has been learned—separates successful companies from failures. That is a lesson that can come in handy for any business.

PAY ATTENTION TO ROOTS

Successful companies pay attention to their pasts and apply their accumulated knowledge and experience to the future. That survivors are proud of their histories is evident in this book. Every company in the book jumped at the chance to be included. In most cases, they provided enough documentation to keep UPS in business for several months. Certainly, they are not shy about sharing their histories with the world. And why not?

There is nothing wrong with businesses flaunting their success, especially if their stories give other business operators insights into success that they can apply to their own companies. After all, successful corporations are willing to learn from their competitors' experiences. They do not ignore history, whether it be their own or someone else's. There is always something to be learned from history.

Newer companies should not ignore history, either. Based on their success and longevity, the survivors have become role models for contemporary businesses, which would be well advised to study their own histories in hopes of becoming survivors themselves.

FIND A NICHE AND FILL IT

The most successful companies in the world are those which fill niches left vacant by competitors. Look at Dexter's development of the teabag, for example.

Dexter put a great deal of time, effort, and money into developing the paper that gave the company superiority in the realm of teabags. The company backed Faye Osborne 100 percent and accepted his setbacks as its own. When Osborne finally succeeded in developing the exact porous paper he set out to find, the company benefited tremendously. Dexter has been the "King of Teabags" for over half a century now, and it has no serious challengers. The company found a niche and exploited it. That is one of the best ways to success for businesses large and small.

ADAPT TO TECHNOLOGY

There was a time when managers in some industries did not have to worry too much about technological advances. Improvements in machines and technology did not occur often in the United States—at least not in the 1700s and early 1800s. The Industrial Revolution changed all that.

The industrial revolution arrived late in the U.S. Historians generally date its start in this country to sometime around 1840, whereas the British industrial revolution took place between 1760-1830. (Remember, several of the companies included in this book were already in business prior to the arrival of the revolution. They had to scramble to adapt, but they did so—and survived.) It may have been slow arriving here, but when it hit, it did so with a bang.

Many of the companies in this book were on the so-called "leading edge" of the revolution. Dexter and Procter & Gamble incorporated the latest technology in the machinery they used to manufacture products. The *Hartford Courant* utilized the most advanced printing presses available to stay ahead of its competitors. Even the companies such as Elgin-Butler and Kenyon Corn Meal, whose product lines sometimes defied technological advances, used what they could to improve production.

Remember Michael Butler's Sword machine and Paul Drumm's firefighter's boot? They might not have resulted in dramatic leaps forward for Elgin-Butler or Kenyon Corn Meal, but they did represent progress— which goes hand-in-hand with technology.

There can be no doubt that progress and technology are inseparable. Perspicacious managers at the companies profiled in this book certainly recognized the relationship and applied technological advances *as they occurred!* That accounts in great part for why they are still in business—and will no doubt keep them on the leading edges of their respective industries.

PAY ATTENTION TO DETAIL

Most companies pay attention to detail some of the time. The most successful ones pay attention *all of the time!*

Paying attention to detail includes every aspect of the business: control over finances, production, and personnel, careful planning, sufficient expenditure for research and development, all of which the companies in this book have recognized. Make no mistake, it is awareness of—and attention to—the little details that lead to ongoing success. Each succeeding generation of leadership applies the lesson about attention to detail—and breeds even more success. If they don't, they have failed as executives, and no company can afford to compete without a succession of competent leaders.

CONTINUALLY DEVELOP SAGACIOUS, COMPETENT LEADERSHIP FROM WITHIN

One of the most salient characteristics contributing to the success of the companies in this book is their in-house developed management. There is no doubt that companies that develop a steady succession of able leaders with copious amounts of business acumen have an edge on their competitors who prefer to hire outsiders to manage.

Look at Coors, for example. The corporation is almost 120 years old, yet each of its companies is run by a Coors family member. Leadership has been passed down from generation to generation, and each family member who joins the company is well versed in Coors operations. They do not simply step in and assume a top management role, though. Each serves an apprenticeship *before* rising to a significant leadership position. The same holds true for other companies.

Elgin-Butler presents another example of a family-run company that has survived and grown under different generations. Today, the company is run by a fifth-generation family member. Yet, the company has not suffered at all as far as growth and stability go. This is attributable to in-house development of management, which is not a monopoly of family-run businesses.

Some of the other companies mentioned here have experienced similar success with internal development of their top-ranking executives. Both Laclede and Atlanta Gas Light have had a series of presidents who practically spent their lifetimes with their companies.

By the time men like Lee Liberman and Joe LaBoon became presidents of their respective companies, they had been with them for years. When Liberman became president of Laclede in 1970, he had been with the company almost a quarter of a century. Similarly, LaBoon had joined Atlanta Gas Light in 1939 and did not become president until February of 1976. That gave him ample time to learn about the company— and to train successors. Obviously, these companies fared well by "growing" their own leaders who had ample time to learn the business from the ground up.[1] Any other company that follows a similar pattern will do the same.

IMPLEMENT THE THREE "I'S"

Of course, management's longevity will be of little use if they do not apply the three I's of leadership: imagination, innovation, and ingenuity. Managers, and, by extension, their companies, who do not follow these principles simply will not succeed.

Consider this classic case of ingenuity. In 1933, William Preston Barnes, president of the Louisiana National Bank (now Premier Bank), exercised his ingenuity to save his business. (Louisiana National, Baton Rouge's oldest bank, opened in 1882.) Many of the nation's banks, including Louisiana National, were forced to close that year. Louisiana National was the only bank in Baton Rouge, and one of the first in the country, to reopen.

---

1 For a detailed explanation on how to do this, see Arthur G. Sharp, *The Profesional's Guide to In-House Recruiting.* International Information Associates, 1990.

During the four-day national banking holiday in March, 1933, Barnes secured $400,000 in cash to meet depositors' requests for withdrawals. On re-opening day, he made sure huge stacks of the money were visible behind each teller's window. The money bolstered customers' confidence in the bank, which was exactly what Barnes had hoped for. By the end of that day, the bank had taken in more deposits than were withdrawn. That is the type of ingenuity that management must display in order to stay ahead of its competitors. Unfortunately, it is not all that common—except among the survivors!

Robert Morris showed a great deal of ingenuity in fetching $470,000 that landed in the wrong city during the Revolutionary War. He was lucky the money arrived in the right country, but he still had a problem getting it the 300 miles from Boston to Philadelphia. Morris did not view the situation as a problem, though. He simply exercised his ingenuity and dispatched a few wagons. That may sound simple today, but he had to do more than call the AAA, get a Trip-Tik, and send a fleet of armored trucks up an interstate highway through the British army. Complications aside, he applied common sense and ended up with the money in his bank. That's ingenuity at its finest.

And imagination? Michael Butler had plenty of that! How many business leaders would think of donating bricks as a prize for a boat race? Butler did, and scored a public relations coup in the process. The machines he invented to facilitate brickmaking in an industry which has traditionally eschewed automation is another tribute to his imagination. Certainly he did not hold a patent on that commodity.

Innovation is another principle of sound management that abounds among the leaders of the companies profiled here. Sometimes it is as simple as the use of a fireman's boot to direct ground corn or wheat into a collection bin. Certainly, a firefighter's boot may not be of use to many people after it is retired, but the Drumms saw the practicality of the object. It may not be a high-tech piece of equipment, but it gets the job done! That certainly falls under the heading of innovation—and ingenuity, too.

Innovation can be somewhat more sophisticated. A prime example is Dexter's introduction of *rolls* of toilet paper. Putting toilet paper on rolls may sound like a simple concept today, akin to slicing bread, but it was not just a few decades ago. Whoever first conceived of *rolls* of toilet paper applied an innovative idea that propelled Dexter to a leadership position in toilet paper sales. Similarly, Aetna became innovative in introducing new lines of insurance to attract customers who were almost sure to buy other types from the company. There is no doubt, then, that liberal doses of the three "I's," along with a modicum of vision, can be a healthy recipe for a company's well being.

APPLY VISION

Vision is one of management's greatest assets. Unfortunately, too many executives do not utilize it.

There are managers who conceptualize extremely well, but who fail to provide details. Ideas, no matter how innovative, are of no use if they cannot be developed practically. The managers who have led the companies in this book to success have all had the vision necessary to keep themselves ahead of their competitors—and survive for a century or more.

Remember Osborne's work with long fiber paper? Not only did Dexter capitalize on Osborne's development of a suitable teabag paper, but it had the foresight to apply for domestic *and* foreign patents as soon as possible. Dexter's ability to protect its products through foresight had as much to do with the company's staying in business as did the development of the long fiber paper itself. Its sale of the English patent to the Crompton Paper Company resulted in a cash infusion that practically saved the company from going out of business! This type of farsightedness is typical of successful companies, and goes hand-in-hand with paying attention to detail.

Coors demonstrates farsightedness in the extreme. Its management decisions in the early 1900s demonstrated that even the most crucial decisions can be made with the future in mind. When prohibition was in vogue, Coors could not be sure it even had a future. Management's immediate concern was to develop alternative products that would get the company through the crisis at hand. Management had survival in mind, however, and it made the correct decisions at the time.

Homestake Mining had to make similar decisions in World War II when its operations were suspended. Management not only surmounted the possible loss of the Homestake's livelihood, but it created a stronger company. The end of the war, rather than bringing about the demise of Homestake, meant a new beginning for the company.

Another aspect of vision is the ability to anticipate problems. That talent is what prompted the Baton Rouge Water Company to wade through red tape to upgrade the city's supply system prior to World War II.

The ability to anticipate problems—and to act to resolve them—is extremely important if a company is to survive.

In retrospect, the Coors, Butlers, Bulkeleys, Ottos et al mentioned in this book made major decisions with an eye to how they would affect their companies in the future, as well as the present. They developed and used foresight that escapes too many managers who think only of the immediate impact of a decision. For them, their companies' futures hinged on the decisions they made at the time they made them; consequently, *they considered more than the needs of the moment.* In short, they applied vision, which is one of the most significant factors that separates successful companies from failures. In fact, without astute management vision, no company can succeed or survive.

PROMOTE CONSUMER LOYALTY

A company's success is based on customer loyalty. The axiom is clear: no customers, no business.

Customer loyalty falls into two categories: listening to customers' comments, suggestions, and complaints, and providing them with the products they want. There is a direct correlation between the two.

There exist companies that pay little attention to customers' views. They do not respond to consumer letters or adopt customers' suggestions when feasible. Then, if they have problems, they cannot understand why. Successful companies, on the other hand, *and that includes every one in this book,* listen to consumers. Why else would Paul Drumm of Kenyon Corn Meal spend an entire weekend following up on—and resolving—a customer's complaint?

376

Why would Debbie Baker of Coors follow up customer contacts with a brief questionnaire inviting a critique of the company's service? It is simply because these companies care and rely on customer feedback to give them an indication of how the public perceives them.

Successful companies *actively* cultivate customer loyalty. They consistently take advantage of technological advancements and solid market research to introduce new products or update their old ones in response to customers' preferences and market conditions. For instance, Procter & Gamble followed an industry trend in the late 1980s of introducing less-expensive and less-risky line extensions instead of major new products. It did not simply place them on shelves and wait for consumers to respond. Rather, Procter & Gamble advertised extensively, regardless of whether the products were "new and improved" or just plain new. Most successful companies advertise heavily—and judiciously—to keep their names and products visible.

In 1988, for example, Procter & Gamble spent $1,506.9 *billion* on advertising, a 15.4 percent increase over 1987. Coors spent $200.8 million, a 28 percent increase over the previous year. (Procter & Gamble was the second leading national advertiser in 1988; Coors was 53rd.) Neither company has ever been shy about dropping unsuccessful products, either. Witness some of the products Procter & Gamble has discontinued over the years, e.g., Teem toothpaste and Oxydol detergent. Likewise, Coors dropped Herman Joseph's when consumers indicated through flagging sales their dislike for the product. Thus, knowing when to quit is a part of customer loyalty—and a trait that most successful executives possess.

There are companies that hang on to unsuccessful or outdated products too long. The key is to achieve a favorable balance between new and improved and breakthrough products. Managers must remember that they are putting the company's reputation squarely on the line with *every* item, so they cannot afford to get lax and allow inferior products or services to reach consumers.

The products they do manufacture must be uniform and consistent. If they are not, the products should be withdrawn from the market. After all, knowing when to quit is as important as entering a new market—and is a hallmark of all the successful survivors profiled in this book. About the only thing managers should not quit on, though, is their attempts to build strong, lasting relationships with their staff members. Every company mentioned in this book boasts of smooth management-employee workforces, which is a critical key to a corporation's success and longevity.

FOSTER A STRONG EMPLOYER-EMPLOYEE RELATIONSHIP

How many companies can claim long-term employees like Barney Kreiger at Procter & Gamble (47 years), Kentric Stagner (55 years) at Elgin-Butler, Warren Berger at Louisiana Companies (57 years), or the Walmsleys at Kenyon Corn Meal (a combined 115 years)? The reason people stay with companies so long is because they are satisfied. They are satisfied because their employers go out of their way to make their work lives as pleasant as possible. Certainly, the subjects in this book have done that.

Consider William Cooper Procter's concern for the welfare of Procter & Gamble's employees. Look at Elgin-Butler's introduction of an employee health program during the "Great Depression." Think about Atlanta Gas Light's guarantee of employment for all its employees who joined the military during World War II. These companies shared a concern for their employees that surpassed simply providing them with the amenities required by law. Rather, these companies dedicated themselves to retaining their workers for the long-term. In that, they succeeded.

One of the most important results of developing strong management-worker relationships is the company's ability to attract even more talented people. Employees who are satisfied with their work environments will tell other people. These others, in turn, will seek employment with companies recommended by their friends. This can result in one company establishing a monopoly of talent. The monopoly, combined with clever recruiting, can give one company a decided competitive edge over the rest of its industry. This state of affairs is common among the companies in this book. It is a definite plus to have talented employees seek them out. It makes recruiting top-flight employees simple—and ensures a steady supply of talent in all departments. Employing them is one thing: retaining them is another. None of the subjects in this book have had any trouble doing so.

The companies have exercised a variety of programs to foster strong working relationships and retain employees. One of the simplest devices is intensive communications programs. Managers recognized that the interests of the organization and their employees are inseparable. That being the case, they attempted to involve employees in the decision making process whenever they could. They communicated often and openly with employees. Managers listened to staff members and implemented their advice when it was practical. Their efforts paid off. How else can the generations of family members employed at Procter & Gamble, Elgin-Butler, Coors, et al be explained? It is simply because successful companies have developed long-term, close-knit relationships with their employees, and with the communities in which they reside as well.

BE A GOOD CORPORATE CITIZEN

Any business that wishes to succeed in today's competitive corporate world must be a good "corporate citizen." No company can exist anymore without returning something to the community in which it has facilities. This nebulous "something" can be taxes, contributions to civic programs or the arts, tutoring programs for students, or any of a host of other activities. The company must participate willingly—and happily.

A perfect example of a well-known company that functions well in a community is the Heroman enterprises in Baton Rouge. Several Heroman businesses are among the oldest in the city. Every local company that supplied information for this book said "ask Billy Heroman" for information about the oldest businesses in the city. Apparently, Heroman has such a good relationship with city officials, residents, and business people that his name is used as a verbal "landmark" in Baton Rouge. (Ironically, he did not supply any information about the Heroman enterprises for this book!) It is the ability to become a local landmark with a reputation for cooperation that establishes a business as a good "corporate citizen."

The companies in this book have all developed strong reputations within their communities as solid citizens. When a community appreciates a company, it will do whatever it can to retain it. The fact that the companies included in this book have stayed put throughout their existences speaks well for the importance of being a good corporate citizen. It also serves as a reminder to today's up-and-coming businesses to work on strengthening their own company-community relationships.

BE AS SELF SUFFICIENT AS POSSIBLE

Here is one of the most significant common denominators among these companies. Examples abound:

- Coors started making its own cans and bottles—and implemented a recycling company to ensure the return of those it produced
- Procter & Gamble began growing its own trees to make sure it had enough to meet the growing demands for its paper products
- Laclede began developing its own fuel sources—and went so far as to explore geographical regions in which geologists were sure no oil or gas existed
- Louisiana Companies opted to expand insurance lines to make sure that it did not put all its proverbial eggs in one basket

These companies simply could not rely on other sources for critical supplies or services. By developing their own resources, they stayed a step or two ahead of the competition. They did not simply go off in a hel-ter-skelter fashion, though. They considered carefully how they would develop products that would make them self sufficient. They did the same in the area of diversification.

DON'T HESITATE TO DIVERSIFY—BUT DO IT WISELY

Every one of the companies in this book has grown considerably since their inceptions. Their growth is due to the usual factors: changing market conditions, international expansion, population increases, etc. There are other reasons, though, e.g., optimism, good timing, and patience. Let's look at some of these reasons.

The management of all the companies anticipated expansion at some point in their companies' exist-ences. Yet, none tried to grow too soon or too rapidly. Their growth has been slow and steady, which allowed them to escape being swallowed up or going into bankruptcy.

Business history is replete with companies that ex-panded too rapidly and ended up as footnotes in li-braries and archives—or as subsidiaries of Coors, Procter & Gamble, and the rest!

Procter & Gamble presents an excellent example of a company that has expanded wisely over the years. At first, the company stayed strictly with soap prod-ucts and candles. Gradually, it expanded its product lines to include food products, paper goods, baby dia-pers...the list goes on. The company never entered a new arena without intensive research and adequate funding, though.

On the other hand, Procter & Gamble was never complacent to the point where it eschewed expansion. Neither did the company ever compromise its principles nor let its competitors force it into making moves for which it was not prepared. The company *always* initiated change before being forced into it. Generally, Procter & Gamble set the pace for its competitors, rather than the other way around. Today, it sells as diverse a line of products as one can imagine—but its growth, be it domestic or foreign, is still controlled carefully.

Procter & Gamble achieved its current status through a combination of controlled growth, careful planning, and wise acquisitions. When it wanted to get into the coffee business, rather than start from the ground up, it acquired a company that already had a good reputation in the field. Management subscribed to the maxim that says "In the absence of knowledge, acquisitions may be best." It did the same with orange juice and snacks. Procter & Gamble simply combined these acquisitions with the knowledge its own employees had gained over the years to expand when the time was right. Like the management of most successful companies, it was cautious in its risk taking—but successful!

Cautious risk taking may sound like an oxymoron, but it is not. Rather, it is an advisable approach to expansion, which is why it is one of the more evident common denominators in this book. It took Coors almost 100 years to leave behind its status as a regional brewer and expand nationally. It is only in recent years that Coors has entered markets outside the United States. Its cautious approach is paying off handsomely, which is further evidence of the value of cautious expansion.

Like most companies which wish to succeed and survive, Coors cannot sit still. Let's face it: the company that sits still is the company that will eventually fail—and failure is neither the goal nor the fate of a survivor! There is no better evidence of this than the companies profiled in this book.

Chapter 17

There Aren't Enough Birthday Candles In The World

The preceding chapters have presented the brief histories of only a few companies in this country that are over 100 years old. The truth is that there are a large number of such companies, all of which can teach lessons about survival. They range in size from small to massive and somewhere in between. Space does not permit the inclusion of all of them in this book, although all of them deserve some recognition for surviving so long. The following pages list a few of these companies.

To all companies which consider themselves survivors, whether they are included on the list or not, congratulations on your longevity—and may you be around when the volume celebrating your 200th, or, in some cases, 300th, anniversary is written.

1711

Kenyon Mill , Usequepaugh RI

1752

Caswell-Massey, New York NY

1764

Hartford Courant, **Hartford CT**

1767

Dexter Manufacturing, Windsor Locks CT

1768

Encyclopedia Britannica, Chicago IL

1784

Bank of Boston, Boston MA

1789

**United Methodist Publishing House
Nashville TN**

1797

The Georgetown Times, **Georgetown SC**

1801

Daily Post, New York NY

Revere Copper & Brass, Inc., New York NY

1802

DuPont, Wilmington DE

1803

E.I. Du Pont De NeMours & Co., Seneca SC

Guignard Brick Works, Lexington SC

Philadelphia National Bank, Philadelphia PA

1805

Newstedt-Loring Andrews,Cincinnati OH

1806

Colgate-Palmolive Company, New York NY

1807

The Western Star, Lebanon IN

1810

Lukens, Incorporated, Coatesville PA

D. B. Sutherland & Sons, Inc., Bloomfield KY

1813

J. P. Stevens & Co., Inc., New York NY

1816

Baltimore Gas & Electric Company, Baltimore MD

1817

The Atkins & Pearce Manufacturing Company
Covington KY

1819

Bardstown Mills, Bardstown KY

The Bromwell Company, Cincinnati OH

Stiglitz Corp., Inc., Louisville KY

1820

Cokesbury Book Store, Cincinnati OH

Comstock, Ferre & Company, Wethersfield CT

1821

Charleston Office Supply Company, Charleston SC

1822

Henry Vogt Machine Co., Louisville KY

1823

Consolidated Edison Co. of New York, New York NY

1824

January & Wood Co., Maysville KY

1826

Cincinnati Equitable Insurance, Cincinnati OH

1828

Lemon & Son Jewelers, Louisville KY

**Merrell Dow Pharmaceuticals U. S. A.
Cincinnati OH1830**

**Del Industries (nee James A. Wulteck, Inc.)
Cincinnati OH**

Graniteville Co-Vaucluse Division, Graniteville SC

Lazarus, Cincinnati OH

Smith, Kline Beckman Corp., Philadelphia PA

Teasdale-Fenton Cleaners, Cincinnati OH

1831

Catholic Telegraph , Cincinnati OH

1832

Houghton Mifflin Company, Boston MA

Merkeley-Kendrick Jewelers, Louisville KY

Rogers Corporation, Rogers CT

Zellerbach, Cincinnati OH

1833

**Brown & Sharpe Manufacturing Company
North Kingston RI**

Cooper Industries, Houston TX

McKesson Corp., San Francisco CA

VBM Corp., Louisville KY

1834

Stedman Machine Company, Aurora IN

Bourbon Stock Yards , Louisville KY

1835

Huntington's Book Store, Hartford CT

Osborne Coinage Company, Cincinnati OH

1836

***The Edgefield Advertiser*, Edgefield SC**

**Mount Vernon Mills-LaFrance Industries
LaFrance SC**

**Schaefer & Busby Funeral Home Inc.,
Cincinnati OH**

1837

**Cincinnati Gas & Electric Company
Cincinnati OH**

Deere & Co., Moline IL

Max Wocher & Sons, Cincinnati OH

Procter & Gamble, Cincinnati OH

1838

Louisville Gas & Electric Co., Louisville KY

Riordan Stained Glass Studio

Covington KY

1839

Brinly-Hardy, Louisville KY

Todd Corporation, Cincinnati OH

The Knoxville Journal
Knoxville TN

1840

Emery Chemicals, Cincinnati OH

Tufts Funeral Home Inc., Loveland KY

1841

The Cincinnati Enquirer
Cincinnati OH

1842

The Fechheimer Brothers Uniform Co.
Cincinnati OH

The L. T. Verdin Company
Cincinnati OH

1843

Eagle-Picher Industries, Inc.
Cincinnati OH

Nelson Printing Corporation
Charleston SC

Spartanburg Herald-Journal
Spartanburg SC

Stanley Works, New Britain CT

1844

Banner Corporation, Abbeville SC

R. L. Bryan Company, Columbia SC

Rotex, Inc., Cincinnati OH

West Point-Pepperell, Inc., West Point GA

1845

J. Bacon & Sons, Louisville KY

Brunswick Corporation, Skokie IL

Bybee Pottery, Waco KY

1846

Church & Dwight Co., Inc., Princeton NJ

The Marion Star, Marion SC

Mead Corporation, Dayton OH

The Stearns & Foster Co., Cincinnati OH

The William Powell Company
Cincinnati OH

1847

Hummel Industries, Cincinnati OH

L. Vaughan Company, Providence RI

Vehr Printing Company, Cincinnati OH

Western Union, Louisville KY

1848

Cave Hill Cemetery Co. Louisville KY

Morton-Thiokol, Inc., Chicago IL

Mosler Inc., Cincinnati OH

Pearson Funeral Home, Louisville KY

The C. W. Zumbiel Co., Cincinnati OH

1849

Brooklyn Union Gas Company, Brooklyn NY

Burlington Northern Railroad, Fort Worth TX

Coolidge Hotel, White River Junction VT

Hubbard-Hall, Inc., Inman SC

Keowee Courier, Keowee SC

Old Fitzgerald Distillery, Louisville KY

Pfizer, Inc., New York NY

Pratt & Lambert, Buffalo NY

Vine Street Hill Cemetery, Cincinnati OH

1850

American Express, New York NY

Danbury Mutual Fire Insurance Company
Danbury CT

Dun & Bradstreet, Louisville KY

Gibson Greetings, Inc., Cincinnati OH

1850 (cont'd)

Levi Strauss, Inc., San Francisco CA

Matthews International Corp., Kershaw SC

E. K. Morris & Co., Inc., Cincinnati OH

Nanz & Kraft Florist, Inc., Louisville KY

The Henry Nurre Co., Cincinnati OH

Union Times Co., Union SC

**Adam Wuest Inc. - Serta of OH
Cincinnati OH**

1851

Corning Glass Works, Oneonta NY

New York Times Company, New York NY

The Stacey Manufacturing Co., Cincinnati OH

Western Union, Upper Saddle River NJ

1852

Anheuser-Busch, St. Louis MO

The Earle-Blain Co., Cincinnati OH

Good Samaritan Hospital, Cincinnati OH

**The McAlpin Department Store Co.
Cincinnati OH**

The Sorg Paper Company, Middletown OH

Tri County Publishing Co., Lancaster SC

1853

Aetna Insurance Companies, Hartford CT

**W. Mack Johnson Funeral Home, Inc.
Cincinnati OH**

Marcus Paint Company, Louisville KY

Murdock, Inc., Cincinnati OH

1854

G. Bittner's Sons, Louisville KY

W. R. Grace & Company, New York NY

Hillerich & Bradsby, Louisville KY

Hilliard-Lyons, Louisville KY

**Liberty National Bank & Trust Co.
Louisville KY**

Muldoon Memorials, Louisville KY

**Northwestern Mutual Life Insurance
Louisville KY**

News Publishing Co., Bowling Green KY

1855

Carolina Newspapers, York SC

**Rumford Chemical Works
(nee Wilson, Duggan & Co.), Providence RI**

1856

Atlanta Gas Light Company, Atlanta GA

Blum Ornamental Glass Co., Louisville KY

Louisville Water Company, Louisville KY

Southern Standard Cartons, Louisville KY

1857

Laclede Gas Light Company, St. Louis MO

1858

American Printing House for the Blind
Louisville KY

Biemis Company, Inc., Minneapolis MN

Buecker Machine Iron Works, Inc.
Newport KY

Citizen's Fidelity Bank & Trust Co.
Louisville KY

Diebold, Incorporated, Canton OH

Dolfingers, Inc., Louisville KY

General Box Co., Louisville KY

R. H. Macy & Co., Inc., New York NY

Manville Corporation, Denver CO

1859

American Standard, Louisville KY

1860

Equitable Life Assurance Society, Louisville KY

Kentucky Paper Box Co., Louisville KY

Pullman Company, Princeton NJ

Struck Construction Co., Louisville KY

1861

Kentucky Wood Products, Bowling Green KY

Yellow Cab Co., Louisville KY

1862

Duncan Wallcoverings, Inc., Louisville KY

Heimerdinger Cutlery, Louisville KY

1863

Auburn Leather, Auburn KY

Matt Corcoran Co., Louisville KY

First National Bank , Louisville KY

Harbison & Gathright, Inc., Louisville KY

William Stockhoff & Son, Louisville KY

The Travelers Insurance Companies, Hartford CT

1864

Albers Inc., Knoxville TN

P. H. Glatfelter Company, Spring Grove PA

J. B. Ratterman & Sons, Louisville KY

1865

Bosse Funeral Home, Louisville KY

Buschmeyer's, Louisville KY

John Cruze Co., Inc., Knoxville TN

***Newberry Observer*, Newberry SC**

Weisenberger Mills, Inc., Midway KY

Lewis Seed Co., Louisville KY

Louisville Bridge & Iron Co., Louisville KY

Milliken & Company, Spartanburg SC

The National Horseman, Louisville KY

Vulcan Hart Corp., Louisville KY

1866

Bensinger's, Louisville KY

Louisville Cement Co., Louisville KY

A. N. Roth Co., Louisville KY

Publisher's Printing Co., Louisville KY

Reynolds & Reynolds Company, Dayton OH

Sherwin-Williams Company, Cleveland OH

1867

Acme United, Fairfield CT

J. Edinger & Son, Louisville KY

1868

Courier-Journal , Louisville KY

Dixie Clay Co., Bath SC

Gatchel's, Louisville KY

General Electric Co., Louisville KY

George W. Park Seed Co., Greenwood SC

McIlhenny Company, New Iberia LA

Strawbridge & Clothier, Philadelphia PA

1869

Campbell Soup Company, Camden NJ

Chester News & Reporter, Chester SC

Gould, Incorporated, Rolling Meadows IL

Henry Freuchtenicht Co., Louisville KY

H. J. Heinz Company, Pittsburgh PA

Jacob's Inc., Greenville SC

Keys Printing Co., Greenville SC

Kingley Walker Flowers, Louisville KY

George Pfau's Sons, Louisville KY

Torbitt & Castleman Co., Buckner KY

Wetteran, Inc., St. Louis MO

1870

**Atlantic Richfield Co. (nee Atlantic Refining)
Los Angeles CA**

Bauer's Since 1870, Louisville KY

Blatz Paint Co., Louisville KY

Brown-Forman, Louisville KY

**Dalton Brothers Brick Co.
Hopkinsville KY**

Oscar Ewing Inc., Louisville KY

Louisville Title Insurance Co., Louisville KY

Michaels Architectural, Inc., Florence KY

Penn Mutual Life Insurance, Louisville KY

Peter-Burghard Stone Fab., Louisville KY

Standard Oil Co., Ohio, Cleveland OH

1871

R. R. Donnelley & Sons, Chicago IL

Glenmore Distilleries, Louisville KY

Grand Union Company, Wayne NJ

Hiott Printing Co., Pickens SC

Ingersoll-Rand Co., Inc., Woodcliff Lake NJ

***Pickens Sentinel*, Pickens SC**

1872

Kentucky Stone Co., Princeton KY

Kimberly-Clark Corporation, Dallas TX

F. S. Schardein & Sons, Louisville KY

1873

Elgin Butler Brick, Austin TX

Adolph Coors Brewing & Manufacturing Co.
Golden CO

Hubbuch in Kentucky, Louisville KY

Kohler Company, Kohler WI

Moore's Home Improvement Center
Fort Thomas KY

Schulz's Florist, Louisville KY

Times-Mirror Company, Los Angeles CA

1874

Greenville News-Piedmont
Greenville SC

Hopkinsville Milling Co., Hopkinsville KY

News & Press, Inc., Darlington SC

A. O. Smith Corp., Milwaukee WI

J. F. Wagner's Sons, Louisville KY

1875

Armour Food Company, Louisville KY

Bridges, Smith & Co., Louisville KY

Bruns Monumental Co., Inc., Columbia SC

Community Communications, Inc., Barnwell SC

Container Corporation of America, Louisville KY

J. V. Reed & Co., Louisville KY

1876

Bommer Industries, Inc., Landrum SC

Bradford Soap Works, Providence RI

Eli Lilly & Company, Indianapolis IN

Logan Company, Louisville KY

Marlboro Herald-Advocate, **Bennettsville SC**

Oldham Era, Louisville KY

Union Carbide, Danbury CT

1877

Homestake Mining Company, San Francisco CA

Tatum-Embry Co., Louisville KY

1878

The American Baptist, Louisville KY

Conner Manufacturing Co., Louisville KY

Newman National, Knoxville TN

1878 (cont'd)

Press & Standard, Walterboro SC

Rapid City Journal, Rapid City SD

The Record, Louisville KY

1879

Chevron Corporation, San Francisco CA

South Central Bell Telephone Co., Louisville KY

Stride-Rite Corp., Cambridge MA

Taylor Drugs, Louisville KY

F. W. Woolworth Company, New York NY

1880

Eastman Kodak Company, Rochester NY

1881

Dumochel Paper Company, Waterbury CT

Kansas City Power & Light Company
Kansas City MO

1882

Exxon Corporation, New York NY

International Multifoods Corporation
Minneapolis MN

Premier Bank (nee Louisiana National Bank)
Baton Rouge LA

Universal Foods Corp., Milwaukee WI

1883

Kroger Company, Cincinnati OH

PPG Industries, Inc., Pittsburgh PA

State Publishing Company, Pierre SD

Swan Baking Company, Knoxville TN

The White Lily Foods Co., Knoxville TN

1884

Cincinnati Milacron, Inc., Cincinnati OH

Peter Kilwit Sons, Inc., Omaha NE

NCR Corp., Dayton OH

1885

AT&T, New York NY

Baton Rouge Lumber Company, Baton Rouge LA

Consolidated Natural Gas Company
Pittsburgh PA

M. A. Hanna Company, Cleveland OH

Huttig Sash & Door Co., Knoxville TN

Johnson Controls, Inc., Milwaukee WI

Lamme's Candies, Austin TX

Norton Company, Worcester MA

W. J. Savage, Inc., Knoxville TN

Stauffer Chemical Company, Westport CT

Sunshine Mining Company, Dallas TX

1886

**Atlantic City Electric Company
Pleasantville NJ**

Boston Edison, Boston MA

**Coca-Cola Company
Atlanta GA**

Johnson Wax, Racine WI

**Johnson & Johnson
New Brunswick NJ**

Pacific Enterprises, Los Angeles CA

**Sears, Roebuck & Company
Chicago IL**

Upjohn Company, Kalamazoo MI

1887

**Baton Rouge Water Works
Baton Rouge LA**

**Commonwealth Edison Company
Chicago IL**

Spring Industries, Inc., Fort Mill SC

1888

Austin White Lime, Austin TX

**Liquid Carbonic Industries Corp.
Chicago IL**

Multimedia, Inc., Greenville SC

1889

Adams Extract, Austin TX

M. Licht & Son, Inc., Knoxville TN

McCormick & Co., Inc, Hunt Valley MO

Stone & Webster, Inc., New York NY

1890

Louisiana Companies
Baton Rouge LA

Pacific Gamble Robinson Company
Kirkland WA

Bibliography

Austin Board of Trade, *The Industrial Advantages of Austin, Texas*, The Akehurst Publishing Co., Austin, Texas, 1894.

Coffin, David Linwood, *The History of the Dexter Corporation, 1767-1967*, The Newcomen Society in North America, New York, 1967.

East, Charles, *Louisiana Companies: The Vision Continues*, No Publisher Listed, 1990.

Fries, Michael T., *History of Austin "Sands Common" Brick*, Unpublished Thesis, The University of Texas, 1984.

Galbraith, John Kenneth, *The Great Crash*, Houghton Mifflin Company, Boston, 1961.

Hooker, Richard, *Aetna Life Insurance Company: Its First Hundred Years*, Aetna Life Insurance Company, Hartford, CT, 1956.

Lang, Joel, "From Thomas Green to Times Mirror," *Hartford Courant*, November 4, 1990.

Osborne, Fay, *The History of Dexter's Long Fiber Paper Development*, Unpublished history.

Schisgall, Oscar, *Eyes on Tomorrow*, J. G. Ferguson Publishing, Chicago, IL, 1981.

Sharp. Arthur G., *Corporate Downsizing: An Employee's Diary*, International Information Associates, Yardley, Pennsylvania, 1988.

Sharp. Arthur G., *The Professional's Guide To In-House Recruiting*, International Information Associates, Yardley, Pennsylvania, 1989.

Stedman, Oliver H., *Usquepaugh, Biography of A New England Mill Community*, Queen's River Press, Usquepaugh, Rhode Island, 1976.

Stern, Madeleine B., "Hartford's Oldest Surviving Bookstore," *American Bookseller*, November 8, 1982.

Stiles, Henry R., *The History of Ancient Windsor*, New Hampshire Publishing Company, Somersworth, New Hampshire, 1976.

Tate, James H., *Keeper of the Flame: The Story of Atlanta Gas Light Company*, Atlanta Gas Light Company, Atlanta GA, 1985.

THE AUTHOR:

☐ Arthur Sharp is a prolific freelance writer. The author of *Corporate Downsizing* and *The Professional's Guide to In-House Recruiting*, he has written hundreds of articles on business and history topics.

He is a member of the business faculty at Central Connecticut State University at New Britain, and is a resident of the town of Rocky Hill, CT.

Index

A

B

C

D

F

G

H

I

J

K

L

M

N

Q

R

U

V

W